IN SEARCH OF GOD'S IDEAL WOMAN

DOROTHY R. PAPE

*A Personal Examination
of the New Testament*

*InterVarsity Press
Downers Grove, Illinois 60515*

InterVarsity Press is the book
publishing division of
Inter-Varsity Christian Fellowship.

ISBN 0-87784-854-8
Library of Congress Catalog
Card Number: 75-21453

Printed in the United States of America

Acknowledgment is made to the
following for permission to
reprint copyrighted material:
From New Testament
Commentary, I—II, Timothy
and Titus *by William Hendriksen.*
Copyright 1957 by William
Hendriksen and published by
Baker Book House and
used by permission. From The
Christian Family *by Larry Christenson,*
published and copyright 1970,
Bethany Fellowship, Inc.,
Minneapolis, Minnesota 55438 and
reprinted by permission. From
Are Women Human? *by Dorothy*
Sayers, published and copyright 1971,
William B. Eerdmans Publishing Co. and used
by permission. From The Ministry
of Women in the Early Church *by*
Jean Daniélou, published and copyright 1961,
The Faith Press Ltd., Bedfordshire, England
and used by permission.
From The Awakening *by Marie Monsen,*
published by A. S. Lunde & Co.,
Oslo, Norway and used by permission.
From Daktar/Diplomat in Bangladesh *by*
Viggo Olsen. Copyright 1973.
Moody Press, Moody Bible Institute of Chicago.
Used by permission.
From Pastoral Problems in First
Corinthians, *by J. Stanley Glen.*
Copyright © *MCMLXIV, W. L. Jenkins.*
Used by permission of
The Westminster Press.

To my husband Bill, who,
in a beautiful spot in the French Alps before we were married,
taught me to think through
Bible passages myself with the help of the Spirit
before turning to the human experts

CONTENTS

WHO IS GOD'S IDEAL WOMAN?

In our small apartment in Tokyo one Saturday morning my hands were still wet in the dishpan as the 8 A.M. English newscast, courtesy of the U.S. Military Far East Network, came to an end. Thus it was inconvenient to switch the radio off immediately, and I found myself listening to the Message of Israel program.

Since it was Mother's Day weekend, the Jewish chaplain had chosen as his subject the famous verses on the "virtuous woman" found in Proverbs 31. As I listened above the clatter of breakfast dishes, the words suddenly formed a new image in my mind. Here was a bulging-muscled Amazon type—"She girdeth her loins with strength, and strengthened her arms"—which I had not noticed before in most Protestant preachers' "spiritualized" versions. Here was obviously no demure Japanese "inside" wife nor Western woman of the place-is-in-the-home, chained-to-the-sink-and-ironing-board stereotype.

In fact, she appeared a busy executive, not only efficiently organizing her domestic staff but dealing in real estate and import and export trade, with a girdle business on the side. She was probably also a wine manufacturer. Indeed, her husband, merely sitting among the elders at the gate, would seem an idle, colorless man if one did not know from the story of Absalom that that was the place of civil justice and administration. She seemed to be the actual breadwinner of the family, and her husband trusted in her because he had no lack of material comfort.

The passage further informs us that she had a costly and luxurious wardrobe and a home tastefully furnished with expensive materials. She is also attributed with absolute confidence in her own ability to meet any future emergency.

I began to wonder if this was as appropriate a model for the woman missionary, or indeed any mother, as many ministers would have us think as each year they expound this favorite Mother's Day text. I felt an urge to study this passage for myself, to see what it was really all about and what it had to say to help or inspire me in this present day.

Looking first in the *Amplified Old Testament,* I found that the footnotes referred to this woman as "God's ideal woman," and could not help wondering if this stalwart, affluent matron was necessarily God's final blueprint of what he wants of my sex, any more than the all-powerful king of Proverbs must be his ideal form of government.

With feminine docility I had always accepted this passage uncritically as a description of the ideal wife and mother—which most ministers claimed it to be—though secretly thankful I lived in a day when I did not have to wrestle with spindles and distaffs! Never having had much contact with church women's groups except as a missionary speaker on furlough, since most of my work was with college students, I had never taught this passage nor studied it thoroughly. Now I felt a strong desire to know what this woman was really like. Is she indeed "God's ideal woman"?

Some Surprises   As I studied seven commentaries and the *Amplified Old Testament,* I discovered some surprises.

First, I found that this passage is an acrostic poem, or alphabetic ode, each line beginning with a different Hebrew letter in consecutive order. This would naturally limit what could be said about this woman, just as we would always find some differences between a poem and a blueprint of an identical subject.

Then I had always thought of this passage as an account of the actual wife of the writer, perhaps because of his words in verse 29, "Many daughters have done virtuously, but thou excellest them all." Yet I found the beginning of the chapter tells us the writer is King Lemuel, and the activities of this woman hardly seem to fit a queen. Some commentators think it is a theoretical description of Lemuel's ideal wife, possibly a projection of his mother (who sounds the dominant type) or else the kind of wife she had counseled him to look for.

Perhaps that is why the busy, night-and-day schedule attributed to this woman seems to allow no time for romance or companionship with her husband; though no doubt, according to the custom of that day, he found this with his newer wives or concubines. We do not read of her spending any time with the children either, these probably being left much of the time in the care of some of the many maids. Yet Lemuel feels confident that both the children and their father will have nothing but praise for this human dynamo, who in spite of her great efficiency never gets impatient with others, for "in her tongue is the law of kindness" (v. 26).

It was a surprise to find that no one really knows now who Lemuel was, although rabbinic tradition believed *Lemuel* was a name signifying an attribute of Solomon. Certain differences in construction and vocabulary (for example, a few Aramaic words) have caused some men to suggest the poem is a later addition to Solomon's proverbs.

I could not help wondering why God had caused it to be included in the canon of Scripture. Accordingly, I read through the whole book of Proverbs again, noting all it has to say about woman. Since she generally appears in a very unfavorable light, such as in the constant references to the "wiles of the whore," "strange women," "contentious women" and even "the odious woman," I could only conclude that God in his merciful kindness wanted to show that these things were at least not true of every woman.

Proverbs contains a wealth of spiritual truth, as well as worldly wisdom, and quotations in the New Testament verify its inspiration; yet one cannot help marveling that, given so much wisdom by God, Solomon failed so obviously to apply it to his own later life. Was his advice to his son to "rejoice with the wife of thy youth ... let her breasts satisfy thee at all times" (5:18-19) written early in his life, or after he had married his 700th wife or obtained his 300th concubine? In these circumstances, would his advice carry much weight? Solomon is constantly denouncing "the strange woman," yet 1 Kings 11:1 tells us he "loved many strange women." Like most of us, he found it much easier to put all the blame on others, the women in this case, and none on his own weakness. So perhaps God wanted to restore some balance to the picture of woman whom he in love had created as a helpmeet for man.

A Male Monopoly No doubt because few women have had the necessary Hebrew, Greek and theological qualifications, the writing of Bible commentaries has been a male monopoly, and I was amused to note the various slants with which this passage in Proverbs 31 is viewed. Some commentators are very prosaic, making terse statements to the effect that what the writer valued in a wife is domestic efficiency or summarily dismissing her as "a good woman, a good wife, a good mother and a good shopper." Others evidence a touch of masculine superiority by telling us that her "wisdom" is limited, of course, to good judgment in domestic affairs or even that her "strength and honor" are merely derived from her husband's firm financial and social position. One man goes so far as to claim that God's ideal woman must be a wife—a view not shared by Paul in the New Testament.

On the other hand, there are the romantic or idealistic types who describe this passage as "the most inimitable portraiture of female character" or as an "exquisite picture of a truly lovely wife." One states in over-flowery language a truth with which most women would be inclined to agree: "The sweetest, daintiest, purest blossoms of a woman's heart will flourish only when she is praised by him she loves best." Another rather wistfully expresses the thought that it may not necessarily be bad to have a beautiful wife, even though verse 30 does say, "Favour is deceitful, and beauty is vain."

One commentator with insight and humility thought that before writing his piece he would consult one of the current secular women's magazines to find out more about women's needs and problems. In a now long defunct periodical (a little different in tone from our modern slicks) he found two quotations he felt appropriate: "Nothing so dampens the ardour and joy of a man or his children as an incompetent woman at the head of the household; and nothing can be a greater source of strength than the woman who gives an impulse to all that is good and right, and checks evil by a significant look, or softly spoken word." And, "In every case, loveliness, loving-kindness, and wisdom, and the making of the beautiful and the adornment of life, should be by woman combined with their work." This latter could certainly be true of the single woman too.

While that Jewish chaplain, along with most commentators, considered this passage just a description of a good homemaker, the editors of the first edition of the *Amplified Old Testament* go to the opposite extreme. They appear to do more amplifying in this section than any other in an attempt to make every activity of this woman represent a spiritual quality. It is a refreshing change to have these characteristics attributed to a woman, but one wonders if it is wholly justified here. For a man to get personal inspiration from these verses he would understandably need to spiritualize the woman's chores, and in a sermon or his private devotions this may be acceptable. It does seem questionable, however, to do this not only in footnotes but in the actual text of Scripture. The first edition read:

"She seeks out *the* wool and flax (of which righteous character is made?) and works with willing hands *to develop it*" (v. 13).

"She rises while it is yet night and gets (through communication with her God?) *spiritual* food for her household" (v. 15).

"Her lamp (of faith and dependence upon God) goes not

out" (v. 18).

There is something a little unsatisfying about this. Household chores cannot be spiritualized away. While there may still be a few men who delude themselves that housework "does itself," it is in the actual doing of some of these mundane tasks that we women feel the need for divine grace. When the baby has diarrhea, the cat vomits on the carpet or the saucepan boils over, it seems better to clear up the mess as quickly and cheerfully as possible than to stand around trying to figure out some spiritual truth to be seen in it.

I have since read that some older theologians (evidently thinking that God would hardly bother with such detail about a woman) regarded the whole passage as allegorical. Rudolph Stier took the women to represent the Holy Ghost; Ambrosius, Augustine and others, the church. This mind-boggling view seems to me very farfetched.

A Conclusion and a Quest   What is the real purpose of this passage for us? Certainly it may help a woman understand what a future or present husband is likely to look for in a wife. But is it possible that *God's* ideal woman might be more than is here portrayed? Can we find any clue to the answer to such a question as (given the absence of a bevy of maids and other differences in our present economy) just how God would prefer the precious hours of a woman's day to be spent? I did not feel convinced that all the data was included in this poem, though certainly many of this lady's characteristics are of permanent value.

It is abundantly clear that she was not lazy and was an excellent organizer. We are also told she was sensible and wise, although apparently burning the candle at both ends. This perhaps was due to her great physical strength. She was unselfish and probably charitable—not a snob. One commentator says that "holding out her hand to the poor" did not necessarily mean giving charity, but was rather a friendly, encouraging gesture. She was a cheerful, positive-thinking, kindly spoken person, and did good and not evil to her husband all his days. Most important of all, she "feared the Lord," and this may have been the secret of all her other wonderful accomplishments. It is interesting, however, that one-half of one verse is given to her relationship to God and thirty and one-half verses to her physical qualities, activities and material possessions.

So once again I asked myself, Is this a final blueprint of "God's ideal woman"? Is there in reality any such person? What does God really think about woman?

Obviously these questions could only be answered after a consideration of what the New Testament has to say. Thus I began an exciting odyssey through each New Testament book, searching for every reference to *woman* or *women* in its inspired pages. It was an enlightening, sometimes puzzling and shocking, yet very rewarding experience which I was glad to share with my fellow missionaries through a series of brief articles for the Ladies Page of the quarterly, *Japan Harvest.*

Since coming home from Japan, I have encountered the clarion claims of the Women's Liberation Movement, with charges and countercharges about the effect of Christianity on the position of women. I completed this manuscript several years later in Germany where my husband and I have been working. Home for summer vacation I have just read *All We're Meant to Be* by Letha Scanzoni and Nancy Hardesty. The subject of that book is closely related to this, but their aim is a little different. Their book is directed only to women while this is to all who are concerned about God's plan and purpose for Christian women today. Some of the Scripture passages and other sources cited are the same in both books, though I examine the biblical text in greater detail. I am certainly thankful for God's leading me to many of the same relevant extra-biblical sources in the difficult circumstance of having to research and write this book in four countries.

In two or three areas those authors go further than I since I honestly am not always certain what God has in mind. Still I am glad that Christians other than myself are wrestling with issues and examining the Scriptures afresh. I hope that many more will enjoy taking a new look, through the eyes of one who has spent twenty years in non-Christian countries and cultures, at how Christ himself and the early Christian writers really portray woman.

I

WOMAN IN THE GOSPELS

1
IN CONTRAST TO OTHER RELIGIONS

To read through the four Gospels to see what they reveal about woman and, in particular, Christ's dealings with women, is rewarding and thrilling—at least for a woman. To me it brought new insights.

In general, both by word and action, the Lord portrays the fact, stated by Paul, that in Christ "there is neither male nor female" (Gal. 3:28). Occasionally, he almost seems to favor women by demonstrating special compassion, giving great praise or revealing some of the greatest New Testament truths to them; and never does he utter to them the strong rebukes he addresses to both his own disciples and the national religious leaders. Nowhere is there any statement of the inferiority of woman, nor are there any lists of do's and don'ts applying to her in particular. Indeed, the harmonious balance of the references to the two sexes in the Gospels is so permeating that few who have grown up in a Christian culture are consciously aware of it.

"Women, Dogs, and Other Impure Animals"   One of the first things that should strike us is the considerable number of contacts and conversations that Christ had with women. We are so familiar with these that we probably do not even notice them as remarkable, especially if we have no first-hand knowledge of other religions. For example, Gautama, later known as the Buddha, from the time he deserted his young wife and baby to begin his great search for Enlightenment, constantly shunned women. Although today he is credited with a great universal compassion and love for all living creatures, his attitude to women is somewhat reminiscent of Solomon's judged by the sayings attributed to him: "Women are evil, jealous and stupid." "Avoid the sight of them." "Do not speak to them."

Gautama believed that only a celibate monastic life would enable a man to tread the difficult path to Enlightenment. He assumed that a woman's innate desire for a family would be too strong for her to endure such monasticism for long, and also that she would prove a temptation to the men who sought to follow that path. It was only after constant pleadings from the aunt who had brought him up that Gautama allowed the formation of a monastic order of nuns. This order had very restrictive rules, which included a humiliating subordination to men; for example, a nun, however old, must always stand in the presence of a monk, however young. He also prophesied, very mistakenly, that since women had come into his religion it would not last five hundred years.

In Hinduism, to be born a woman was regarded as evidence of some failure in the previous life, and, although it was an improvement on being born an insect or non-sacred animal, she still had not merited the highest state of being born a male. She was therefore merely a body for the sexual pleasure of a husband, condemned to burn on the funeral pyre if he should die first, which itself would be attributable to some omission on her part. Even when this practice of *suttee* was made illegal by the British rulers of India, at the instigation of the great evangelical social reformer Lord Shaftesbury, for a long time a widow was little more than a household drudge, perpetually disgraced.

Confucius had little to say about women except to lay down rules governing their duty to father, husband and eldest son. His disciples were men, and his teaching was mainly concerned with the state and with the character of the ruler. Women in China were treated with a little more respect than in most other Asian countries, however, and a first wife never lost her status even when others were taken to produce sons.

I have read that outside many Moslem mosques there used to be a sign, "Women, Dogs, and Other Impure Animals not Permitted." Although Mohammed seems to have respected his first wife, a wealthy widow who had originally employed him in her caravan business, in later life he obviously regarded women as existing merely for the sexual use of men. One of his own wives was a six-year-old with whom he began intercourse when she was nine. Early travelers and missionaries in Moslem lands told horrible tales of the conditions in which the women there lived. Women in these countries have rarely been accorded legal rights until recently. Just months ago women were finally allowed to enter the mosques for worship, but they may only stand at the back, behind the kneeling men.

The influence of Greek culture was still strong in Christ's

day, and although Plato had advocated equal education for women, few agreed with him. Aristotle admitted that "moral goodness is possible in every type of personage, even a woman or slave," but the general feeling of the time was that a woman's highest praise consisted in not being mentioned at all. In the light of such sentiments, Christ's frequent contacts with and references to women are all the more remarkable.

Even an orthodox Jewish man was taught to thank God daily that he was not born a woman. An American preacher once mentioned that he had recently attended an Orthodox Jewish wedding in Israel. The bride said she would introduce her grandfather, a rabbi, to him and his wife, but warned that the wife must not try to shake hands with the rabbi. In fact, when the introduction was made, the rabbi ignored her completely, speaking only to the husband. How revolutionary, then, the attitude of the Master as he moved about and taught in the Israel of his day, full of grace and truth, of courtesy and compassion, and with comprehension of the needs and capacity for spiritual insight of the women of that day and of all time.

Two Favored Women We do have one picture of woman at her worst in the Gospels, although it is not in any association with Christ. No, I am not thinking of the woman "taken in adultery," but of Herodias and her daughter; the one out of pique demanding the head of John the Baptist, the other callously displaying it on a dish before the assembled guests. This cruel murder was more than matched, however, by Herod the Great's slaughter of the infants in Bethlehem, as well, incidentally, of his own wife and several sons—thus causing Augustus Caesar to say in a witty pun that he would rather be Herod's hog than his son.

In happy contrast to the murderous Herodias, the first women we encounter in the Gospels are the two specially favored by God with miraculous conceptions: Elizabeth, the wife of the priest Zacharias, and her young relative, Mary of Nazareth.

Some of the words used to describe Elizabeth reveal much about the feeling toward women in that day. That sad word *barren,* with its connotation of "useless, unprofitable, empty," is used to denote her (Lk. 1:7). Elizabeth herself, when sure that she was pregnant, praised God, saying, "Thus hath the Lord dealt with me . . . to take away my reproach among men" (Lk. 1:25).

Until very recently, in most parts of the world, a woman has been seen mainly as a baby-producing machine, as someone to perpetuate the family line of the father and also to carry on the worship of the ancestors. Even Martin Luther, great Christian that he was, stated, "If a woman becomes weary, or at last dead from child-bearing, that matters not; she is there to do it." For a woman not to become pregnant has usually been taken as a sign that she is displeasing to the gods and has been regarded as just grounds for divorce or the taking of a concubine. Even in modern Japan some husbands do not register their wife on the family record at the ward office until she has produced a son.

Yet Elizabeth had not been displeasing to God, for the Scripture states specifically that she and her husband "were both righteous before God, walking in all the commandments and ordinances of the Lord blameless" (Lk. 1:6). In fact, God had chosen her for the high honor of bearing a son who, "in the spirit and power of Elijah" (Lk. 1:17), was to prepare the way for the Messiah. Furthermore, he was to be "filled with the Holy Ghost, even from his mother's

27

womb" (Lk. 1:15), so that in a very special sense Elizabeth enjoyed the presence and power of God within her.

God first gave the news of Elizabeth's pregnancy to the father, who found it hard to believe even though he had long prayed for it. Concerning Jesus' birth it was to Mary, the mother, that the announcement initially came. Surely here, in this girl chosen above every other one in all the generations of the Jewish race, we would expect to find "God's ideal woman," if there is such a thing. Yet in contrast to the bustling, brawny matron of Proverbs, we have no clue as to the kind of figure Mary had, what kind of housekeeper she was, how late or early she worked, what kind of clothes she wore. We know that she was of the royal house of David, as was Joseph, but there appears to have been no wealth left in their branches of the family, judging by the temple offering of two turtle doves after Jesus' birth.

There are a few other facts we can discover about Mary. She was a thoughtful person, as evidenced in her question to the angel, "How shall this be?" (Lk. 1:34). Then she "cast in her mind what manner of salutation" the angel had given (Lk. 1:29), and later "she kept all these things, and pondered them in her heart" (Lk. 2:19). She also had an extensive knowledge of the Scriptures, and possibly some poetic gift, for there are at least twelve Old Testament references in her famous outburst of praise known as the *Magnificat.*

At the marriage in Cana, she gave the best advice any person has ever given to another when she told the servants, "Whatsoever he saith unto you, do it" (Jn. 2:5). Perhaps it was this trait which made God see her as the best human vehicle he could find for the incredible purpose he had in mind. At any rate, the angel Gabriel was sent to her with the message, "Thou art highly favoured, the Lord is with thee! Blessed art thou among women!" (Lk. 1:28).

Mary was frankly puzzled and alarmed at this supernatural greeting. The angel hastened to tell her she had no need to fear, assuring her again she had found favor with God. Then he revealed the way in which God was going to demonstrate his approval: She was to conceive and bear a son who was to be called *Jesus.* "He shall be great, and shall be called the Son of the Highest: and the Lord God shall give unto him the throne of his father David: and he shall reign over the house of Jacob for ever, and of his kingdom there shall be no end" (Lk. 1:32-33).

Mary's response was not immediate, ecstatic joy at this news, which some authorities tell us every Jewish maiden hoped for. "How shall this be, seeing I know not a man?" she asked (Lk. 1:34). This seems rather strange since Mary was already betrothed to Joseph. However, the footnotes to Luke's Gospel in the *Cambridge Greek Testament* series quote one view that "an *immediate* conception is the idea conveyed by the Hebrew source underlying Luke's Greek, and Mary's question is natural, and not incredulity but surprise," since she was not yet married.

At any rate, Mary was not reproved for scepticism, as was Zacharias when he doubted the ability of his wife to conceive in old age. Instead, with inimitable delicacy of description Mary was given details of how she was to become the mother of this Holy Son of the eternal God Almighty: "The Holy Ghost shall come upon thee, and the power of the Highest shall overshadow thee: therefore also that which shall be born of thee shall be called the Son of God" (Lk. 1:35).

The Buddha, Princess Blooming-Tree-Blossom and the Sky-Kami The annotator of the above-mentioned Greek version of Luke's Gospel dismisses this whole narrative as having "little historical foundation . . . entirely character-istic of the naive supernaturalism of primitive and popular thought, completely uncritical towards wonders." Surely he must see that neither Zacharias nor Mary was naively cre-dulous and that there is something in the wording of the explanation given Mary which is of a far different quality than the birth legends of other great religious figures.

Of the Buddha, legends not written until several cen-turies after his death variously claim that in a previous existence he was a bird and an animal and that his mother dreamed that a small white elephant entered her side. When the time of the birth arrived, she stood upright, sup-porting herself with the branch of a fig tree while, accord-ing to one account, a god gathered up in a sheet the child of her womb. Another version has some of the gods re-ceiving him in a golden net and worshiping him—where-upon the baby surveyed the ten quarters of the world, took seven steps across it and cried in the voice of a lion: "I am the chief in the world. This is my last birth. There is now no existence again."

The *Kojiki* and *Nihonji,* translated together as *The Sacred Scriptures of the Japanese,* carry the story of how a sky deity, grandson of the supreme Sun Goddess, mated with a human:

"Prince Sky-Plenty-Earth-Plenty-High-as-Sky's-Sun-Fire-Ruddy-Plenty meeting her [Princess Blooming-Tree-Blossom] as he walked on the seashore asked her, "Whose daughter are you?" . . . Then said he, "I am desirous of co-habiting with you. How do you regard this?" She answered, "Your handmaid is unable to say. My father, Great-Mountain-Possessor, will answer." . . . So the august grandchild [of the Sun Goddess] said to him, "I have seen your daughter, and desire her." The Great-Mountain-Possessor, greatly pleased, sent her [to him] whom he wedded for one night. . . .

Princess Blooming-Tree-Blossom became pregnant and at length gave birth to three boys. She took them in her arms and respectfully approaching Prince Sky-Plenty-Earth-Plenty-etc. said, "Your handmaid has given birth to these. It is not fitting that children of the Sky be privately brought up; therefore I bring them to you for your information."

But the Sky-Grandchild was slow to believe, and looked upon the children in mockery saying, "What! These are Princes of mine? How delightful is the news of their birth!" Angered, Princess Blooming-Tree said, "Why do you mock your handmaid?" Said he: "Surely there is doubt of this. . . . How can I, Sky-Kami [deity] though I be, cause one to become pregnant in one night? I suspect the children cannot be mine. They must be children of a Kami of the land."

At that, she was still angrier, and building a doorless hall . . . she entered it with her children, plastered it up with earth, and made a vow, saying, "If these children which I have conceived are not the offspring of the Sky-Grandchild, let them surely perish! But if they are his offspring, let them suffer no hurt." So saying, she set fire to the hall. But when the fire was first burning one child sprang out, announcing: "Here am I, a child of the Sky-Kami, and my name is Fire-Glow. Where is my father?"

Subsequently the other children came out unharmed. Then the mother took them to the Sky-Kami again. This time when he saw them he said,

"From the first I knew them to be my children. Yet as they were conceived in one night, I supposed suspicion would arise, and I desired to demonstrate to all that they are my children, and that the Sky-Kami can cause pregnancy in one night. Moreover I desired to demonstrate your own wonderous dignity and the surpassing spirit of our children!" . . . In spite of this, Princess Blooming-Tree was incensed and would not speak to him.

These interesting writings were compiled at the command of a Japanese ruler who, it is thought, wanted to connect his own ancestry with the Sun Goddess in order to secure the permanent supremacy of his dynasty, to which the emperors have belonged to this day. While purporting to be about events thousands of years ago, these writings were recorded no earlier than A.D. 700. I have quoted them in some detail so that they can be more knowledgeably contrasted with Luke's account, written from firsthand reports, of the incarnation of the Son of God within the body of Mary. Is it really only those who accept the divine inspiration of the Scriptures who can discern any difference in the nature of these two accounts and who can contrast the holy, omniscient, omnipotent God about whom the Bible consistently speaks with the sky deities of Japan or, for that matter, the more familiar gods of Greek mythology?

A Comforting Visit   Let us return now to Mary's meeting with the angel. After revealing how she was to become the mother of the Son of God, he gave her an added assurance of God's power by telling her that her elderly relative Elizabeth was already six months pregnant; "for with God nothing shall be impossible" (Lk. 1:37).

Following this encouraging declaration, Mary's response, I think we can assume, is typical of one whom God looks upon with favor, "Behold the handmaid of the Lord; be it unto me according to thy word" (Lk. 1:38). The full force of this is wonderfully expressed in J. B. Phillips' version: 'I belong to the Lord, body and soul,' replied Mary, 'let it happen as you say.' "

What a practical comfort and strengthening of faith it must have been to Mary to be able to confer with another woman who had also had a remarkable visitation from God and a miraculous conception. Without delay, Mary hurried off and traveled, apparently alone, the nearly one hundred miles to see Elizabeth.

The greeting she received must have been full of sweet assurance that it was no fanciful vision she had seen, but a true messenger of God. Elizabeth felt the child within her stir excitedly as Mary entered. Filled with the Holy Spirit, the older woman cried out,

Blessed are you among women, and blessed is your child! What an honor it is to have the mother of my Lord come to see me! Why, as soon as your greeting reached my ears, the child within me jumped for joy! Oh, how happy is the woman who believes in God, for He does make His promises to her come true. (Lk. 1:42-45, Phillips)

Then comes that famous song which some commentators consider so brilliant it must have been composed by Luke—obviously too good for a woman! Another commentator suggests it was a messianic psalm that might have been used by any Jew of the period. Three Old Latin manuscripts have the song coming from Elizabeth's lips. For the most part it is equally appropriate for both women, but the promise to "Abraham and his seed for ever" seems to refer to the coming of the Messiah and therefore would be more fitting coming from Mary.

Mary stayed with Elizabeth three months, possibly through the trials of morning sickness, then returned for the inevitable revelation of her pregnancy to her family and fiancé. But once again God smoothed the way by appearing to Joseph, while he was planning for a separation, and telling him that it was the Holy Spirit who had made Mary the mother of a son who was to be the Savior from sin (Mt. 1: 19-23). The angel added that this was to be the fulfillment of a prophecy of Isaiah: "Behold, a virgin shall be with child, and shall bring forth a son."

So we find angel messengers from God appearing to

both Zacharias and Elizabeth, to both Mary and Joseph. When the infant Jesus was taken to Jerusalem for the purification rite, he was publicly recognized and blessed both by the old man Simeon and the old prophetess Anna. From then on the harmonious balancing of the references to both men and women throughout the Gospel records continues to be impressive.

2
IN THE CONTENT OF CHRIST'S TEACHINGS

The complementary references to the sexes noted in the previous chapter, and particularly evident in the details of Christ's birth, are observable also in the content and pattern of Christ's teaching. For example, after performing some miracles in Galilee, he returned home to begin his public ministry in Nazareth; and in his first discourse he used as illustrations the Gentile widow who had cared for Elijah and the Gentile general, Naaman, who was healed of leprosy by Elisha (Lk. 4:25-27).

We read of a certain woman, crippled for eighteen years, whom Christ healed on the Sabbath in a synagogue. He evidently noted her in the women's gallery, called her down beside him and actually touched her, bringing immediate healing. In response, she "glorified God," presumably in an audible voice. When the ruler of the synagogue remonstrated at this double breach of law and custom, Christ answered, "You hypocrites; every single one of you unties his ox or his ass . . . on the Sabbath and leads him away to water. This woman, a *daughter of Abraham* . . . should be released from her bonds on the Sabbath" (Lk. 13:10-17, Phillips). Christ gave the woman a title of honor, not merely indicating that she was of more value than an animal but also emphasizing her spiritual status and privilege as a daughter of Abraham, the father of the Jewish race.

On another Sabbath, when he healed a man with dropsy and was again criticized, he merely answered, "Which of you shall have an ass or ox fallen into a pit, and will not straightway pull him out on the sabbath day?" (Lk. 14:5). Yet on the previous occasion he had taken the trouble to emphasize the woman's worth and spiritual status.

Christ raised from the dead young people of each sex, largely, it seems, out of compassion for the parents. These were the only son of the widow of Nain (Lk. 7:12-16) and the only daughter of Jairus, the ruler of a synagogue (Lk. 8:41-42, 49-56).

When some unbelieving Jews came demanding a sign from heaven, the Lord used both a male and a female illustration to drive home his point. He rebuked these Jews for not believing the evidence of what he had done already by saying that the men of Nineveh, who had believed Jonah's message and repented, would judge them for their unbelief. He added that the Queen of the South would rise up in judgment against them, for she had gone on a long journey to hear the wisdom of Solomon, while they had a greater than Solomon in their very midst (Lk. 11:29-32).

In his teaching about the kingdom of God, Christ used illustrations referring to both sexes. To explain the nature of the kingdom, he said it is like a man planting mustard seed in his garden and like a woman mixing yeast in her flour to make bread (Lk. 13:19-21). He also included what he knew they would regard as the worst of both sexes when he told the religious leaders that publicans and harlots would enter the kingdom of God before them (Mt. 21:31). To reveal his great concern for each individual member of lost humanity, Christ told the stories of a shepherd looking in dangerous places for his one lòst sheep and a woman searching and sweeping every nook and corner of her house for her one lost coin (Lk. 15:3-10).

Among the parables illustrating different aspects of prayer is one about a woman who finally got an unjust judge to act on her behalf simply because she persisted in asking him until he was sick of the sight of her. This is followed by the story of two men who went into the temple to pray. One, a Pharisee, prayed only "with himself "; the other, a publican, prayed a penitential prayer to God (Lk. 18:1-14).

In warning people to be ready for his second coming, Jesus used a parable about men to whom various amounts of money were given to use until their master's return and a parable about ten virgins, half of whom were not prepared for the coming of the bridegroom (Mt. 25). When explaining the suddenness of his coming, he stated that two men would be working in a field and one would be taken, the other left; two women would be grinding at a mill, with the same result (Mt. 24:40-41).

The Male and Female Principle in the Godhead   In contrast to this wealth of material touching on women in Christ's teaching, I have recently read a book on a certain Hindu sect which has only three references to women in its 191 pages—and these are only incidental to the teachings. One, for example, is about a young disciple who had been sent for training to a famous guru. When he arrived and was invited into the house, he saw the guru place his hand on his wife's shoulder in an affectionate way. It was considered very improper in India to perform such an action before others, and the young man was shaken, wondering how he could learn anything of an advanced spiritual nature from such a person. But just as he was about to leave in disgust, the guru removed his hand from his wife's shoulder and put it in the blazing fire! From this the disciple was said to have learned the truth of "nonpreferential discrimination," or that there is no distinction between Brahman's various manifestations.

While many religions have had both male and female deities, the latter have often been in the role of consorts to the gods; and all the gods are usually portrayed with various human failings such as jealousy, pride, lust. In the holy character of the creator God of the Bible there is a wonderful blend of the ideal characteristics of both father and mother. In the Old Testament Isaiah gives us a picture of the latter: "Can a woman forget her sucking child, that she should not have compassion on the son of her womb? Yea, they may forget, yet will I not forget thee" (Is. 49:15). A nursing mother may manage to forget a child for three or four hours or during a night's sleep before the discomfort of the unused milk supply brings remembrance, if not compassion. But God in his love does not forget his own for a moment; he neither slumbers nor sleeps. We also have a simile of motherhood in Isaiah 66:13: "As one whom his mother comforteth, so will I comfort you."

On the other hand, Christ often stressed the father nature of God and taught the disciples to use that name in prayer. He usually referred to himself as Son of Man. He once stated, though, that "the hairs of your head are all numbered" in God's sight, and, to me at least, this conjures up a picture of a mother lovingly brushing her child's hair each day, knowing so well each differing glint in color, each wayward curl or awkward cowlick. The co-creator of the universe also once attributed a mother's instinct to himself when he said, "O Jerusalem, Jerusalem ... how often would I have gathered thy children together, even as a hen gathereth her chickens under her wings" (Mt. 23:37).

It is true that we see both the male and female principles attributed to the powerful forces of nature by most animist religions. This is perhaps most evident in the well-known Chinese Taoist teaching of the *Yin* and the *Yang*. In the China section of *Religions in a Changing World* we read, *There is the* Yin, *which stands for earth, the moon, darkness, evil, and the female sex. On the other hand is the* Yang, *which includes Heaven, the sun, light, fire, goodness, and the male sex. The gods (Shen) are also associated with the* Yang *and therefore are in opposition to the evil spirits (Kuei) which are* Yin.

How different are these characteristics from Christ's teaching of a loving, personal God where the father/mother qualities are not opposed or in conflict but complementary and harmonious!

The Sexless Element in Christ's Teachings Christ teachings also contain an element which we might call *sexless*. Nowhere do we find Christ giving instructions to women as women, that is, nowhere does he give commands applicable to women only. He did not tell Martha and Mary they ought to be married. He did not rebuke the mothers present at the feeding of the four thousand for being away from home three days listening to theology. He did not give any directions about housekeeping or about women's place in the synagogue.

Even in his instructions to the disciples, there are few which obviously apply to men alone. The only ones I noticed were "Whosoever looketh on a woman to lust after her hath committed adultery with her already in his heart" (Mt. 5:28); "Whosoever shall put away his wife, saving for the cause of fornication, causeth her to commit adultery" (Mt. 5:32); and "Be not ye called Rabbi, for one is your Master, even Christ; and all ye are brethren" (Mt. 23:8).

It is noteworthy, too, that the things on which Christ said those who claim him as Lord will finally be judged—feeding the hungry, clothing the naked, visiting the sick and prisoners—are things which mostly can and should be done equally by men and women (Mt. 25:31-46).

When the Sadducees came with their story of a woman given to seven brothers in succession and asked whose wife she would be in the resurrection, Christ explained that in heaven there will be no marriage, but we shall be as "the angels of God" (Mt. 22:30), who presumably are unisex. Thus it seems our sexuality will be forgotten, or rather non-sexed, our chief delight being to see Christ's face and to serve him.

Finally, we cannot help noticing that in a few instances Christ seems to have taken special care to include women in his teaching. In Mark 7:10-11, when speaking about honoring parents, he repeats *father* and *mother* four times in two verses. At first I wondered if there was no word for "parents" in Greek, but later found a number of statements in the Gospels which include that word. So he seems to be emphasizing that both father and mother are to be honored equally.

When speaking of the cost of discipleship, he also included the female members of families as being affected. "Suppose ye that I am come to give peace on earth? I tell you, Nay; but rather division. ... The father shall be divided against the son, and the son against the father; the mother against the daughter, and the daughter against the mother; the mother-in-law against her daughter-in-law" (Lk. 12:51, 53). Again, "There is no man that hath left house, or brethren, or sisters, or father, or mother, or wife, or children ... for my sake, and the gospel's, but he shall receive an hundredfold ... houses, and brethren, and sisters, and mothers, and children" (Mk. 10:29-30).

Another memorable occasion when Christ deliberately added the female element is recorded by both Matthew and Mark. He was speaking to a large crowd, evidently in a house, when his mother and brothers came looking for him. "Then one said unto him, Behold, thy mother and thy brethren stand without, desiring to speak with thee. But he answered, and said unto him, Who is my mother? and who are my brethren? And he stretched forth his hand toward his disciples, and said, Behold my mother and my brethren! For whosoever shall do the will of my Father ... the same is my brother, *and sister* and mother" (Mt. 12:46-50; Mk. 3:31-35).

We do not know why he took the trouble to add that *sister,* but surely we have here part of the blueprint for God's ideal person—woman or man, young or old, married or single. They are the ones who do his will.

3
WOMEN IN CHRIST'S COMPANY

Christ did not call a woman to be among the twelve apostles chosen at the beginning of his public ministry to forsake their work and go with him everywhere. To have called a single woman would obviously have led to unsavory suspicions, while most married women were presumably busy taking care of their families. It is remarkable, therefore, that we later do find women traveling in his company.

The majority of us would agree, I think, that men are generally more qualified for such responsibilities. From a physical point of view alone, their voices are stronger and so more suited for preaching, particularly before the days of amplifiers. They are also free from the time-demanding work of bearing and rearing children. Further, many have objective, analytical minds, able to isolate the principles of theology or whatever. Perhaps the majority of women tend to be more interested in people than concepts, and, while this can be a real advantage in Christian work, it may sometimes degenerate into personality conflicts intensified by gossip, although these are certainly not limited to one sex.

It is noteworthy, however, that the Gospels record two occasions where Christ defended women's intuition against the reasoning of the Twelve. When some women brought their children to Jesus to be blessed, the disciples rebuked them and tried to shoo them away. At that, Jesus was "much displeased, and said unto them, Suffer the little children to come unto me, and forbid them not: for of such is the kingdom of God" (Mk. 10:14). When Mary of Bethany poured costly ointment on Jesus' head, the disciples were indignant at this "waste." The Lord said then that this woman's act would be told as a memorial to her wherever the gospel would be preached—as indeed it has. In contrast, there are a few of the Twelve, whom we generally suppose to be the most important church leaders, about whom the Scripture gives no detail and to whom it gives no commendation.

Female Volunteers   Considering the cultural context and the practical problems, it is all the more surprising to read that women were added to his company for an unspecified length of time:

It came to pass afterward, that he went throughout every city and village, preaching and shewing the glad tidings of the kingdom of God: and the twelve were with him. And certain women, which had been healed of evil spirits and infirmities, Mary called Magdalene, out of whom went seven devils, and Joanna the wife of Chuza, Herod's steward, and Susanna, and many others, which ministered unto him of their substance. (Lk. 8:1-3)

Some of these women, at least, were married, and one cannot help wondering how they were free to leave home and how they had money to contribute, when legally they were not independent persons. At any rate, it is good to know that there were some women willing to endure the discomfort of travel and uncertain lodging places in their efforts to minister to Christ and his disciples. Their liberality and gratitude seem a little different from the attitude of the Twelve, who, although they had initially left all to follow the Master, were very interested in what they would gain in return. Even when he had just told them of his imminent crucifixion, they were only concerned, apparently, with the most important seats in the kingdom.

It may well be justifiable to assume, as many have, that because Christ did not choose any women among the Twelve, there should be no women leaders in the Christian church. This book is certainly not meant as a brief for women ministers. However, it could be pointed out that he did not choose a Gentile either. In fact, he did not institute anything resembling most churches today, with one pastor trained in an academic seminary, Sunday schools and other things we now consider good and useful.

Furthermore, after the apostles replaced Judas by drawing lots (Acts 1:15-26), there seems to have been no later effort to perpetuate a ruling hierarchy of twelve men. Actually, Christ had promised the original apostles that "in the regeneration when the Son of man shall sit in the throne of his glory, ye also shall sit upon twelve thrones, judging the twelve tribes of Israel" (Mt. 19:28). Thus he seems to have ignored the whole future structure of the Christian church, only telling his disciples they were not to be like the Gentiles, lording it over others.

Whether Christ did not call a woman to be one of the Twelve out of consideration for the difficulties it might raise or out of a feeling that it would be wrong to have a

45

woman in such a position, we are not told. But he certainly did not object to their voluntarily joining themselves to his company.

Ever since these first women traveled with Christ, women have usually comprised the majority of any Christian congregation. No one who is not a woman can appreciate the sense of hope, comfort, understanding and inspiration a woman receives from studying Christ in the Gospels. And for those who were able to meet him on earth the effect must have been doubled. Nowhere does Christ use the words *subordinate* or *subject* in connection with women. He does not compare them on a superior/inferior basis with men. His words, "Take my yoke upon you, and learn of me; for I am meek and lowly in heart" (Mt. 11:29), seem so eminently right, an invitation we want to respond to in our best moments; and this invitation was apparently offered to all who were listening, men and women alike.

Shocking Words from Uninspired Commentators   When we turn from the inspired words of the Gospels to those of some commentators, we receive an unpleasant shock. I made my original study of the Gospels in Japan without consulting any commentaries and found it a tremendous inspiration and encouragement. Since being home, however, I have read other views, some which follow odd tangents from the base of the scriptural record.

Walter F. Adeney, for example, in *Women of the New Testament* states, "Our Lord's relations with the women who attended Him are distinct from His relations with men disciples in one very remarkable particular. He ministered to men; but women ministered to Him. In their case Jesus consented to receive gifts and service."

This idea is hard to substantiate from Scripture. Christ

did not minister only to men. He healed both men and women. He provided wine for all the wedding guests at Cana and fed the five-thousand and the four-thousand men plus many women and children. Nor do we find only women ministering to Christ. After a boy provided the loaves and fishes to feed the multitude, the disciples served everyone. A man with a pitcher donated the use of his upper room where Peter and John, not women, prepared the Passover Feast. Both Matthew and Zaccheus ministered to Christ by providing hospitality.

It does not appear that Christ did not *want* men to do any ministering, but rather that some of them were often too proud and thoughtless to serve. "One of the Pharisees" also held a feast for him, where the "woman who was a sinner" came with expensive ointment (Lk. 7:36-50). Jesus pointed out how the host, a man, had failed to show common courtesy, providing no water for his feet, no kiss of greeting, no anointing oil. At the Last Supper none of the Twelve offered to do the slave or housewife's job of washing feet. The fact that Christ "took a towel and girded himself " (Jn. 13:4) has surely been an encouragement to countless women as they have donned aprons to perform menial and unpleasant tasks. But it was given as an example to the *male* leaders of what they should be doing.

Charles C. Ryrie, in *The Place of Women in the Church*, also enlarges on the idea of women ministering to Christ: *In the life of our Lord, women had a special place as ministers to Him. This ministry consisted in caring for His physical wants by hospitality, by giving of money, and preparing spices for His dead body.* In response to this *Jesus allowed women to follow Him, He taught them, and He honored them with the first announcement of His resurrection. But equally important, He limited their activity by not choosing one of them for official work. Thus we may say that, while Jesus granted great freedom to women, and placed importance on their ministrations, He limited the sphere of their activity by glorifying the domestic responsibilities with which they ministered to Him. (emphasis added)*

Yet Luke 8 does not say that Christ let the women follow him *in response* to being ministered to by them. Evidently, it was he who made the first move. "Certain women, which had been healed of evil spirits and infirmities, ... ministered unto him of their substance." It seems that they loved and served him because he first graciously met their great needs. Peter's mother-in-law, too, was first healed by Christ, then ministered to him and the disciples. The idea of Christ only teaching women or allowing them to follow him after they fed him or gave him money seems utterly foreign to his character and reminds one more of the Buddha. When women continually pestered him to be allowed to follow him, he grudgingly gave in and allowed them to join his religion and to fill the monks' begging bowls with food every day.

The last part of Ryrie's statement also is questionable: "[Christ] limited their activity by not choosing one of them for official work. . . . He limited the sphere of their activity by glorifying the domestic responsibilities with which they ministered to Him." We agree, of course, that Christ did not call a woman to be one of the Twelve. But what exactly is "official work"? One preacher I heard suggested that Christ chose the Twelve for two purposes only, "that they might be with him, and that he might send them forth to preach" (Mk. 3:14). If so, Luke 8 states that the women were with Christ and the Twelve. And other passages mention women whom Christ sent with important messages, though granted these were not sermons. The woman of Samaria went to tell her village about Jesus, with the result that many believed in him. Mary and others were told to relay the glorious news of the resurrection. The woman with the issue of blood was required to make a public testimony to the crowd. At Christ's birth the prophetess Anna did quite a bit of speaking to those looking for the coming of the Messiah. We are also told she spent all her time at the temple, fasting and praying, instead of being occupied with housework (Lk. 2:36-38). While the activities of these women may not be considered "official work," they can hardly be classed as "domestic responsibilities" either.

And where in the Gospels does Christ especially "glorify" domestic work? The woman mixing bread does not seem any more "glorified" than the farmer sowing seed or dressing vines. During his visit to Bethany, when Martha was fretting about Mary's not helping her serve, Jesus said Mary's listening to him was the "good part" (Lk. 10:42). Also, he said we should not spend much thought on food and clothes, things usually regarded as domestic concerns.

I have no objection to saying that Christ glorified work, but there is no conclusive evidence in the Gospels that he only glorified *women's* work and limited their responsibilities to domestic affairs. To me, he glorified domestic chores by his own gracious interest and participation in them, providing wine for the awkward predicament at the Cana marriage feast, feeding the hungry multitudes, girding himself with a towel to wash the disciples' feet.

As we women face routine, sometimes dirty, household tasks, or when our family is at its most demanding stage, leaving us not a moment to ourselves, what a help it is to be reminded of his invitation to "Take my yoke upon you." If we do so, we will often find that much of the burden is eased from our shoulders onto his.

Finally, we have that priceless example of his "domestic"

concern and provision at the end of John's Gospel. The discouraged disciples had returned to fishing and after a fruitless night of toil wearily pulled to shore. There they found that the Lord, with the tender concern of a wife or mother, had a cheerful fire burning, breakfast cooking and an invitation to "Come and eat!" Who had fixed the fire of dirty charcoal and gutted the slippery fish? The risen Lord of Lords, with hands so brutally torn with hammer and nails, who to the very end proved that he came "not to be ministered unto, but to minister."

To such a Lord women have always been drawn, and later we shall find them bravely continuing in his company right through the long hours of the crucifixion, and beyond.

4
CHRIST'S COURTESY TO WOMEN

Having looked at women in general both in Christ's teaching and in his company, we come now to some of the most inspiring parts of the Gospels: Christ's contacts and conversations with individual women during his ministry on earth. Here again, I found some of my own discoveries and conclusions differed from some of the commentators'.

What is unique and revolutionary about Christ's attitude to women is his obvious concern and appreciation for them as *individuals*; not only did he deign to speak to them, but he actually revealed to them new spiritual truths. This is usually the most striking aspect for a woman, and also a cause of surprise for most men brought up in pagan lands. These contacts of the Lord with individual women we will try to look at with an unprejudiced mind, although granted, with a feminine eye.

Was Jesus Ever Discourteous to Women? One characteristic of Christ which amazes people from non-Christian cultures is his almost invariable courtesy to women. There are
a few possible exceptions to this, the first two, surprisingly
enough, involving his mother.

At the age of twelve, Jesus was taken to the Passover Feast
at Jerusalem. At the end of the first day of the return journey Joseph and Mary could not find him with any of their
party, so they returned to the city and finally discovered
him with religious leaders in the temple. His mother began
to rebuke him, saying, "Son, why hast thou thus dealt with
us? Behold, thy father and I have sought thee sorrowing"
(Lk. 2:48).

In any one else of that age his answer would seem pre-
cocious or even impudent: "How is it that ye sought me?
Know ye not that I must be about my Father's business?" It
was in fact a gentle rebuke to Mary, who had referred to
Joseph as his father, indicating she may have lost the sense
of Jesus' divine origin. Perhaps, as quite often happens, the
daily care of a home and several small children had blunted
her spiritual appetite and perception. She and Joseph seem
to have been remiss in not checking earlier in the day to be
sure that Jesus was with the party; however, this may just
indicate their complete confidence in him.

Some commentators take the view that any special worth
or greatness in Mary was merely due to her relationship as
mother of Christ, emphasizing "the blessing of motherhood." Ryrie states that the lessons learned from her are
"mostly related to the home," which leads one to the conclusion that Mary is significant as "a model of ideal Christian womanhood." He admits there is a dearth of material
about her, but quotes James Hastings as giving the true explanation of this: "This slightness of texture is itself a note

of genuine portraiture, for the reason that Mary was of a retiring nature, unobtrusive, reticent, perhaps even shrinking from observation, so that the impress of her personality was confined to the sweet sanctities of the home circle. . . . We see in the little that is told of her what a true woman ought to be."

Mary may well have been retiring and home-loving, but, with the possible exception of the angel's announcement of the coming conception, the scriptural record never shows us Mary at home. She is hurrying off to Elizabeth, then going to Bethlehem for the census, then to Jerusalem for purification rites, down to Egypt, back to Nazareth, then to Jerusalem again for the Passover, to Cana for the wedding, to Capernaum, to a city near the Sea of Galilee with her other sons to persuade Jesus to come home, and finally to Jerusalem again. It therefore requires an exercise of imagination to learn from her lessons "mostly related to the home."

While some see Mary as obtaining status and being a model of Christian womanhood only in her role of mother, I cannot help wondering if she may not have been of greater spiritual stature as a young single woman since God chose her at that time for the highest honor of nurturing within her body the very Son of God.

The second occasion when Jesus appeared to speak with a lack of courtesy to his mother was at the wedding at Cana, when she told him the bridegroom had run out of wine. His reply was, "Woman, what have I to do with thee? Mine hour is not yet come" (Jn. 2:4).

This is certainly a puzzling statement. A teacher, the head of the English department of the Chinese high school in Tokyo, once showed me this verse, which he had recently found in an English New Testament, and asked me how

Christ could possibly say such a thing to his mother. Both this teacher's Confucian background, with its strong emphasis on respect for parents, and his Roman Catholic faith, with its veneration of Mary, made the words repugnant to him.

There seems to be general agreement that (contrary to modern English usage) the term *Woman* was not disrespectful. And the fact that Christ used it again from the cross, instead of addressing Mary as *Mother,* suggests that his main purpose was to demonstrate that Mary could no longer hold a special relationship to him. Thus he removed any legitimate ground for Mariolatry, for adoring Mary as "Mother of God."

It is the remainder of Christ's reply which is more puzzling: "What have I to do with thee? Mine hour is not yet come." One man thinks this shows that the actions of the Son of God, after he had begun his divine work, were no longer dependent on the suggestion of a woman. (But might we not equally well add, of a man either?) Since he soon did what Mary was hoping for, it is still hard to know why he said his hour had not come. Mary, however, did not seem in the least offended, or silenced, for she turned to the servants and uttered the wisest advice ever given to any man or woman: "Whatsoever he saith unto you, do it" (Jn. 2:5).

The other possible exception to Christ's invariable courtesy to women was his conversation with the Gentile woman who begged for her daughter to be healed (Mt. 15:21-28). But the language experts tell us this was probably a witty play on words in which the woman joined. If he were only "Son of David," then she must remain a Gentile "dog"; but the latter word could also refer to a domestic pet who already had a place within the "Lord's" house. The exchange ended with Christ's high commendation, "O woman, great is thy faith."

Even when the mother of James and John, right after Christ had told them of his coming crucifixion, came with the selfish and presumptuous request that her two sons be allowed to sit on his right and left hands in his kingdom, he did not rebuke her. It was a natural ambition for a mother, and she did have a real belief that Christ was the Son of God, as far as we can judge. He merely replied, "Ye know not what ye ask. . . . To sit on my right hand, and on my left, is not mine to give, but it shall be given to them for whom it is prepared of my Father" (Mt. 20:20-23).

Three Adulteresses   To many people, men and women, the most surprising instances of Christ's courtesy are his interviews with adulteresses. Let us look first at the story in John 8:2-11. Many consider that this account is "poorly attested," in that it is omitted from a number of early manuscripts. But the incident is so superbly characteristic of Christ that it is hard to imagine any human mind concocting it. It would seem far more plausible, knowing how sex came to be regarded as evil in the Roman church, to assume that some over-prudish early Fathers feared it might encourage people in adultery and therefore omitted it from the record.

Jesus was teaching in the temple courtyard when some of the scribes and Pharisees came along dragging a woman. John tells us plainly what their motive was: to have something of which they might legitimately accuse Jesus. They set the woman in the midst of the circle of those listening to Christ and said, "Master, this woman was taken in adultery, in the very act. Now Moses in the law commanded us, that such should be stoned: but what sayest thou?"

Then came that tantalizing moment which it is hard to believe any human mind fabricated: "Jesus stooped down, and with his finger wrote on the ground." What did he write? I think an ordinary author would have told us. I have wondered if he wrote the words of Leviticus 20:10: "The man that committeth adultery with another man's wife, even he . . . the adulterer and the adulteress shall surely be put to death."

The woman's accusers continued to press him for an answer. So he stood up and uttered that amazing sentence which only the sinless Christ could have thought of saying, "He that is without sin among you, let him first cast a stone at her."

Then he continued writing. Did he write, "Whosoever looketh on a woman to lust after her hath committed adultery already in his heart?" Perhaps he merely wrote, "Where is the man?" These religious leaders claimed they had caught this woman "in the very act" of adultery, so obviously there had been a man present. Yet they in their injustice and hypocrisy had merely brought the woman, although the law of Moses had specified both the man and woman were to be killed. (This law, by the way, appears not to have been enforced in Israel for many centuries.)

In Ryrie's opinion, Christ "used this woman to teach some religious leaders the grace of forgiveness in mixing mercy with law." Surely this was not a matter of merely "using" her—a rather unpleasant term these days. Rather, he used the *occasion*, engineered by the evil intention of the religious leaders, to turn the tables on them and reveal their own injustice and hypocrisy.

John states that they "being convicted by their own conscience, went out one by one, beginning at the eldest, even unto the least." What a crestfallen procession! If they had merely been learning a lesson in mercy, this action would have been quite uncalled for.

Then Jesus stood up and spoke to the woman. If he had just wanted to "use" her as an object lesson, there would have been no need for further conversation after the religious leaders left. But he was concerned for her as a person. Instead of ignoring her now, as any rabbi would have done, he spoke those inimitable words of comfort and uplift, yet words which did not overlook her failure. "Woman, where are those thine accusers? Hath no man condemned thee?" Jesus asked. And when she replied, "No man, Lord," Jesus said, "Neither do I condemn thee: go, and sin no more."

These words, which so often stick in the gullets of the self-righteous, are like healing balm to anyone who has become conscious of sin in any form in his or her life.

Another woman, this one a locally recognized "sinner" so probably a prostitute, came to Jesus at a feast, carrying an alabaster box of very expensive ointment:

[She] stood at his feet behind him weeping, and began to wash his feet with tears, and did wipe them with the hairs of her head, and kissed his feet, and anointed them with the ointment. Now when the Pharisee which had bidden him saw it, he spake within himself, saying, This man, if he were a prophet, would have known who and what manner of woman this is that toucheth him: for she is a sinner. (Lk. 7:38-39)

Jesus knew what this man was thinking, and, after telling the story of the creditor who forgave two debtors, the one owing five hundred denarii, the other fifty, he asked his host which of the two debtors would be most grateful. Simon said he supposed it would be the one who was forgiven most. Then Jesus turned toward the woman and spoke a truth which has been evident down through the centuries in the Christian church: "Her sins, which are many, are forgiven; for she loved much: but to whom little is forgiven, the same loveth little." He concluded with a word for the woman herself, again one of comfort, renewal and hope: "Thy faith hath saved thee; go in peace."

The last of this trio of stories concerns the woman at the well (Jn. 4: 5-30). Some have dubbed her "the Samaritan harlot," yet Christ said distinctly that she had had five husbands and was now evidently living in an adulterous common-law situation—which is rather different from being a professional prostitute. It would probably have been easy to guess the life of a prostitute, but both the woman and the townspeople considered it remarkable that Jesus could know this woman's unusual and colorful, though probably very sad, past. (Incidentally, I find the word *harlot* comes very easy to the commentators, whereas Christ never used this word to refer to a particular woman. His only references to such were when he told the religious leaders that the publicans and harlots who believed John's message would enter the kingdom of heaven before them.)

Alfred Edersheim, in his *Life and Times of Jesus the Messiah*, grinds this woman into the dust from a different direction, with equally little justification, it seems to me. He refers to her as the "poor, ignorant Samaritan woman," "ignorant Samaritaness of the lower order," "humble, ignorant Samaritaness," and "the ignorant woman of Sychar." He further states, "Those who know how difficult it is to lodge any new idea in the mind of uneducated rustics in this country will understand how utterly at a loss this Samaritan countrywoman must have been to grasp the meaning of Jesus."

(By "this country" Edersheim is referring to England in the 1880s, and one cannot help sympathizing with its "rustics' " difficulty in understanding Edersheim, in view of his sometimes painfully tedious erudition. One of his sentences describing the situation at Sychar's well contains 118 words, and another 129!)

But to continue:

Verse 15 [of John 4] marked the utmost limit of the woman's comprehension. We can scarcely form an adequate notion of the narrowness of such a mental horizon as her's. This accounts for His speaking to her about His own Messiahship and the worship of the future in words far more plain than He used to His own disciples. None but the plainest statements could she grasp. . . . It is not unnatural to suppose that having reached the utmost limits of which she was capable, the Saviour now asked for her husband in order that . . . the horizon might be enlarged. This is also substantially the view of some of the Fathers.

How did the early Fathers come to this view? It is hard to think of any other than a bias toward masculine superiority.

I might have thought my own view was similarly biased had I not obtained it, I believe, from a male Bible teacher. Also, I have found that Paul Little in *How to Give Away Your Faith* has the same view, namely, that Christ's conversation with the Samaritan is a superb example of how to witness graciously to *anyone* about his or her need of a Savior. Certainly Little does not regard it as geared to the limitations of a grossly ignorant countrywoman.

In fact, there is little evidence in Scripture of stupidity on this woman's part. She at once recognized Jesus as a Jew, either by his dress or by the few words of his first short request, and she was surprised that he was not putting up the usual racial and sexual barriers. Neither was she ignorant of her country's history and religion.

Her question, "Sir, thou hast nothing to draw with, and the well is deep; from whence then hast thou that living water?" seems on a par with the learned Nicodemus' question: "How can a man be born when he is old? Can he enter the second time into his mother's womb?" (Jn. 3:4). Both failed to grasp the spiritual while concerned about the material aspect of what Christ had said. There seems to be an equal mixture of plain speaking and spiritual symbolism in Christ's discourses with both these individuals. But while the woman was gradually enlightened and ended up witnessing so that many in her village believed in Christ, Nicodemus evidently had to think things through a long time, to weigh whether the praises of men and a place in the Sanhedrin were worth more than a spiritual rebirth.

Unlike Edersheim, who believed that Christ told the woman to call her husband because she was too stupid to understand Christ's words by herself, Paul Little thinks his purpose was to cause her to face the fact of her own sin without being condemned by him. "Most of us," Little states, "are quick to condemn. Often we have the mistaken idea that if we do not condemn a certain attitude or deed, we will be condoning it. But this was not our Lord's opinion."

Edersheim rejected this view on the ground that the woman does not *say* she feels convicted, but rather goes on to talk about where worship of God should take place. Yet surely most of us have experienced within ourselves, or in dealing with other people, the tendency to turn to generalizations or questions to which there is no obvious answer, rather than face up to some personal sin or shortcoming. It is a common defense mechanism.

Christ gently brought the woman back to the main issue of not *where* but *how* God is to be worshiped. It is in spirit and in truth, by men and women, whether Jew, Gentile or half-breed Samaritan, who have drunk of that water of life which only the Messiah himself can impart. In this instruction his supreme courtesy to women again shone through.

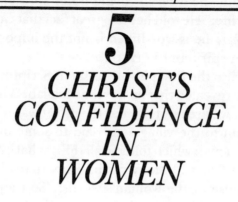

5
CHRIST'S CONFIDENCE IN WOMEN

The woman at the well provides a good example, on two scores, of the confidence Christ displayed in women. The first needs no elaborating. It was his completely unembarrassed assumption that women would not misconstrue his approach to or friendship with them. Otherwise he would never have spoken to this woman in the first place. The second was his confidence in the *ability* of women, even such an unlikely one as she, to comprehend spiritual truth. Ryrie notes that some of Jesus' most profound revelations about himself and his Father were given in private teaching to women and concludes, "That He even did such a thing indicates His appreciation not only of the intellectual capacity in woman, but also their spiritual capabilities."

Let us look at his revelations to this "low, ignorant Samaritaness." To such a seemingly unlikely candidate for theological insights he offered "living water springing up into everlasting life." He told her the great fact that God is spirit, and that *where* he is worshiped is not the important point but *how*, "in spirit and in truth."

She was also the first person (as far as Scripture records) to whom he revealed that he was the Messiah. Why he chose this woman we are not told, but the effect was widespread. First she ran to the village and said to some of the men, "Come, see a man which told me all things that ever I did. Is not this the Christ?" Many of the Samaritans believed in Christ because of the woman's words: "So they besought him that he would tarry with them: and he abode there two days. And many more believed because of his own word" (Jn. 4:29, 40-42).

Martha and Mary To see another example of Christ's confidence in women we will look at that famous scene in the home of Martha, Mary and Lazarus (Lk. 10:38-42). This incident probably occurred during the Feast of Tabernacles, and, being near Jerusalem, this household may have been expecting a number of visitors. Possibly Martha had heard about the Master when the Seventy were sent out, as recorded by Luke at the beginning of chapter 10. At any rate, Martha "received him into her house," and possibly some of the disciples, too. So quite naturally she was very busy with "much serving," perhaps including footwashing as well as the preparation of food.

Mary, as the younger sister, had possibly done the footwashing, but then had been captivated as the Lord began to speak to her about food for the soul. At any rate, she sat at his feet, listening, while Martha hurried back and forth and finally in exasperation came and said, "Lord, dost thou not care that my sister hath left me to serve alone? Bid her therefore that she help me."

Every woman who has ever been responsible for extensive hospitality can sympathize with Martha, and nearly every man, it seems, prefers to have a Martha around rather than a Mary. Yet what did Jesus say? With his usual courtesy and the gentlest of rebukes, he answered, "Martha, Martha, thou art careful and troubled about many things. But . . . Mary hath chosen that good part, which shall not be taken away from her."

Recently I was given the witty little book *Are Women Human?* by Dorothy Sayers, well-known British scholar and novelist. In one essay she wryly states,

I think I have never heard a sermon preached on the story of Martha and Mary that did not attempt, somehow, somewhere, to explain away its text. Mary's, of course, was the better part—the Lord said so, and we must not precisely contradict Him. But we will be careful not to despise Martha. No doubt, he approved of her too. We could not get on without her, and indeed . . . we greatly prefer her. For Martha was doing a really feminine job, whereas Mary was just behaving like any other disciple.

The Bible tells us Christ loved both Martha and Mary, however, and Martha's turn came for a great spiritual revelation. It was to her that Jesus spoke the astounding words which have brought comfort and hope to millions of people at Christian funerals: "I am the resurrection, and the life: he that believeth on me, though he were dead, yet shall he live: and whosoever liveth and believeth in me shall never die" (Jn. 11:25-26).

Easter Revelations Perhaps the most remarkable instance of Christ's confidence in women was when he gave the first revelation of his risen life to one or more women. As I read these Easter passages through in my first look at women in the Gospels, I wondered why Christ had given them this privilege of delivering the most startling piece of news the world has ever heard. Why not to Peter and John, the leading apostles, who apparently had been at that very spot just a few minutes before? I could only think that, being women, they would not be able to keep their mouths shut, whereas the men might keep it to themselves, thinking it too incredible to pass on without further evidence. Indeed, Christ later rebuked the eleven apostles "with their unbelief and hardness of heart, because they believed not them which had seen him after he was risen" (Mk. 16:14).

It was a surprise, therefore, to see Charles Ryrie's answer to this rather puzzling question:

The correct answer to the question of why God chose women to receive the news first has often been missed because it is so obvious. Women were honored with the news of the resurrection first simply because they were being faithful to womanly duties. . . . They were at the tomb . . . because they were bringing spices for the body. This was a woman's work. God so honored them because of their faithful performance of the responsibilities of their sex.

I had not heard of this womanly duty before, and Ryrie gives no source for his information. Certainly there is no indication of it in the Bible. Nicodemus and Joseph of Arimathea had already brought and applied nearly one hundred pounds of spices. John 19:40 tells us they wound the body in linen clothes "with the spices, as the manner of the Jews is to bury." In Acts 5:6 we are told that young men wound up the body of Ananias and buried it (without even waiting to inform the widow, apparently!).

Even if spicing dead bodies was a woman's duty, the reward seems out of all proportion to the duty. Why not give the privilege to Nicodemus and Joseph, who had already provided vast supplies of spices—and the tomb? Or to

John? He had had the courage to stay with Jesus during part of the trial and also to stand beside the cross, as well as to receive Mary into his home, something that could well have made his own mother jealous or made trouble with Mary's other children.

In any case, the women, like the apostles, seem to have completely ignored or forgotten Christ's teaching that he would be killed and rise the third day. If they had believed it, they would have realized there was no need for any spices. Actually, it was to the Twelve that the Lord had said he would rise again, and they may not even have told the women since it seems to have made so little impression on them. But even if the women had not heard from Christ or the disciples that he would rise again, they had heard the message of the angels (Lk. 24:4-6). Either they did not believe it or else the disciples talked them out of it, for the next time they went to the tomb the angel said to Mary, "Why weepest thou?" and she answered, "Because they have taken away my Lord, and I know not where they have laid him" (Jn. 20:13). Soon after that Christ revealed himself to Mary Magdalene.

Ryrie states that such instances as these "are ample proof of His revolutionary recognition of women, His confidence in their capabilities, and His concern for their education and welfare," but cautions us to remember that most of the Lord's teaching was given to men, and especially to the Twelve.

I do not want to give a disproportionate emphasis to woman's place in the Scriptures; certainly the greatest part of Christ's teaching was to the disciples and the crowds. Yet just as the promises of living water and resurrection are meant for all believers and not just the particular women addressed, may not the same be true of most of the teaching given first to men? Some have pointed out that the apostolic commission of John 20:19-23, Matthew 28:16-20 and Mark 16:15 was given to men only, but does this mean that only the eleven apostles were to "go into all the world and preach the gospel" or that only ten of them (since Thomas was not present when this authority was given) could pronounce forgiveness of sins? I have listened to sermons for over fifty years and have heard countless ministers preach on many of Christ's sayings to his disciples, but I have never heard even one minister warn the majority of his congregation that this was not for them. Are we supposed to keep reminding ourselves in the midst of a sermon that because we happen to have a uterus, a few extra curves and a more complicated nervous system, these words of Jesus cannot be for us?

Christ does not seem to have been concerned with such differences. When a woman in the crowd once called out how blessed were the womb and breasts which had formed and nourished him, he gave a surprising reply: "Yea rather, blessed are they that hear the word of God, and keep it" (Lk. 11:28). He implied that the physical properties of a woman, whether his own mother, or any other, are not the most important part of her. For the ideal disciple, man or woman, the important thing is hearing and obeying God's word. After all, only about one-third of the normal life span can be spent in child bearing, and if this is made the sole aim and purpose of woman's life the remaining years may prove empty and frustrating. Whatever our age, sex or circumstances, God still has a purpose for each life, and it is our privilege and responsibility to be attentive and obedient to his voice.

His Highest Praise   Finally, I would suggest that Christ showed his confidence in women by giving his highest praise to three of them. Others might, and in one case did, misconstrue their actions; Christ saw them for what they really were. To the Syrophoenician woman seeking healing for her daughter, he said, "Great is thy faith!" Others might have thought she was only concerned with getting her girl healed, exercising a selfish persistence at a source to which she was not entitled. Christ saw her action as the result of her understanding of who he was and of a real faith in his power and concern.

The disciples saw Mary's pouring of expensive ointment on Jesus' head as a sentimental extravagance. Christ recognized it as the result of her intuition motivated by her deep devotion and gratitude for what he had done in her life. And he promised that her act would be remembered and preached throughout the world as a memorial to her.

When he saw a poor widow put two mites into the offering box, he called his disciples over and said, "This poor widow hath cast more in, than all they which have cast into the treasury: for all they did cast in of their abundance; but she of her want did cast in all she had" (Mk. 12:43-44). Other people would not have regarded hers as a large offering and, if they had known it was all she had, would probably have called it foolish improvidence. Christ, however, gave her the credit for sacrificial giving of the highest order, and at the same time he established an entirely new criterion for giving: How much have we kept for ourselves?

So the Gospels give us proof that Christ regarded women as worth communicating with, as capable of deep spiritual truth, of exercising strong faith and of setting the highest standards of sacrificial giving.

6
CHRIST'S COMPASSION FOR WOMEN

Another of Christ's most striking characteristics was his compassion. This was exhibited toward all mankind, but we can see instances of it being particularly directed toward women. We have noted it already in his dealings with the three adulterous women. When he raised the widow of Nain's son from the dead, he appears to have done it primarily out of compassion for *her*. It was his compassion for widows, especially, which aroused his great indignation against those who made long, pretentious prayers and then devoured widow's houses (Lk. 20:47). For this, he said, they would receive greater damnation.

When he fed the five-thousand and later the four-thousand men, plus women and children, it was because he had compassion on them (Mk. 6:34 and 8:2). Perhaps he had compassion particularly for the women, who were probably feeling guilty at not having made more provision for their families; but of course they had had no idea this remarkable teacher would hold their attention so long. And what a wonderful picnic it turned out to be for them! The disciples not only did all the serving but even the clearing up afterwards. It would be a day those women long remembered.

Is Divorce Lawful?   His dealing with the question of divorce also reveals Christ's compassion for women, who in his time, it seems, had few rights.

Matthew 19:3-10 tells us that some of the Pharisees attempted to corner Jesus by asking, "Is it lawful for a man to put away his wife for every cause?" According to Alfred Edersheim, there were at that time two main schools of thought among the rabbis on what constituted lawful ground for divorce. Although Mark's condensation of the event omits "for every cause," Edersheim states that "the whole controversy between different teachers turned upon this point. All held that divorce was lawful, the only question being as to its grounds."

The school of Shammai took the phrase "uncleanness" (more literally, "matter of shame") in Deuteronomy 24:1-2 to mean "unchastity" only:

When a man hath taken a wife, and married her, and it come to pass that she find no favour in his eyes, because he hath found some uncleanness in her: then let him write her a bill of divorcement, and give it in her hand, and send her out of his house. And when she is departed out of his house, she may go and be another man's wife.

Martyn Lloyd-Jones, in *Studies on the Sermon on the Mount*, points out, however, that in the time of Moses adultery was punished by stoning and that therefore this "uncleanness" could not refer to that.

The school of Hillel took "uncleanness" in the widest

possible sense, including such things as a wife spoiling her husband's dinner. Rabbi Akiba thought that the words "if she find no favor in his eyes" implied that if a man found another woman more attractive than his wife that was sufficient ground for getting rid of her.

Edersheim states, "In popular practice divorce must have been very frequent, while the principles underlying Jewish legislation on the subject are most objectionable. These . . . were due to a lower estimate of women, and an unspiritual view of the marriage-relation."

Instead of siding with either of these rabbinic schools, Christ brought his questioners back to God's original plan for marriage: that the man should leave his parents, cleave to his wife, and the two should become a new unity, "one flesh," with no thought of anyone else or of breaking the bond.

The Pharisees had a comeback for that. "Why did Moses then command to give a writing of divorcement, and to put her away?" they demanded triumphantly. Christ replied that it was because of the hardness of their hearts that Moses had allowed (not *commanded*, as many rabbis taught) men to get rid of their wives, under certain conditions. In Moses' day things had become chaotic; husbands were turning their wives out on the flimsiest excuses, and with no redress, as Lloyd-Jones tells us:

The men generally held a very low and poor view of women, and they had come to believe they had a right to divorce their wives for almost any and every kind of frivolous and unworthy reason. . . . Of course the ultimate cause was nothing but lust and passion. . . . In the Sermon on the Mount our Lord introduces this subject in . . . immediate connection with . . . the whole question of lust (Mt. 5:27-32). . . . The Mosaic legislation, therefore, was introduced to regularize and control a situation that had not only become cha-

71

otic, but was grossly unfair to the women, and which in addition, led to untold and endless suffering on the part of both the women and the children.

It was no doubt because of this unhappy and desperate condition of so many women that Moses had limited divorce to natural, moral or (perhaps) physical defects which had to be proved in the sight of two witnesses. The wife then had to be given a written statement of divorce, and she was free to marry another man, should there be one who would take her, since her former bond was now completely broken.

Christ did not dispute the fact that Moses had granted this, but said that only fornication really breaks the marriage bond. So if a husband does divorce his wife without that cause, he is making her, and any man she subsequently marries, an adulterer, as well as becoming one himself, of course, if he takes another woman. This view was obviously so startling that even the disciples afterward questioned if it is worth marrying at all if one becomes so irrevocably tied to one woman!

"Come unto Me, All Ye That Labor" One of Christ's most famous sayings, while addressed to a mixed audience, has probably produced a bigger response from the heart of women than any other. During the missionary candidate school I attended, Jessie Gregg, a member of the China Inland Mission who was greatly used of God in women's evangelistic meetings across north China, told us she knew thousands of women who found Christ through responding to his invitation, "Come unto me, all ye that labour and are heavy laden, and I will give you rest" (Mt. 11:28).

Having been engaged largely in academic pursuits up to that time, it seemed to me a rather odd, or even dubious, text through which to find salvation. Since then, however, I have seen its similar appeal to Japanese women. In many countries, in the lower classes particularly, women are harder worked and fare much worse than men, and so respond more eagerly to this word of hope.

When I first went to China, in 1939, our coal-burning ship docked at Nagasaki, Japan, for refueling. We were horrified, when we came on deck after dinner that night, to find that the ccal was coming on board in baskets passed along a chain of women from the barges in which it was brought alongside. Hour after hour, all through the night, this continued, the choking coal dust rising and blackening faces and clothes until the huge bunkers of our ocean liner were filled. I have wondered since if this was just a wartime measure because most of the Japanese men were away conquering Korea and China at the time. But right then, to myself and five fellow brides-to-be on our way to the mission field for the first time, it was culture shock with a vengeance.

So-called Christian England, however, was no better even as late as the Industrial Revolution, just over a hundred years ago. In fact, the position of women there has not, as one might suppose, been one of gradual progress but has varied strikingly with the spiritual condition of the country, and more particularly with how much the Bible was actually read and followed.

During the Reformation, Erasmus and Thomas More wrote of women as reasonable beings, able to contribute with intelligence to society. The latter's daughters studied Greek and Hebrew. The Bible was read with enthusiasm, and a governess of one of the Stuart princesses stated, "Our very reformation of religion seems to be carried on by women." (This quotation and the ones immediately following are from Katharine Moore's *Women*.)

The Industrial Revolution, however, and the Napoleonic Wars, changed things for the worse. Women were gradually drawn from the country districts to the new factories where they were induced to work under appalling conditions. Joseph Corbett, a weaver, wrote in 1833,

My mother worked in a manufactuary from a very early age.... She became the mother of 11 children. She was lamentably deficient in domestic knowledge. As the family increased, so anything like comfort disappeared altogether.... I have known her, after a hard day's work, sit up nearly all night for several nights together washing and mending. My mother's ignorance of household duties: my father's consequent intemperance ... cold and hunger and the innumerable sufferings of my childhood, crowd upon my mind and overpower me.

These women worked in the factories thirteen to eighteen hours daily. "The vast majority of persons employed at night, and long hours during the day, are women. Their labor is cheaper, and they are more easily induced to undergo severe bodily fatigue than men," someone wrote at the time.

Lord Shaftesbury, the great evangelical reformer, described women's work in the mines:

Women always did the lifting, or heavy part of the work, for females submit to work in places where no man or even lad could be got to labor in; they work in the bad roads up to their knees in water, in a posture nearly double; they are below ground to the last hour of pregnancy.

Against considerable opposition, he at last got a law passed in 1842 forbidding the employment of women underground. It is good to know that it was mainly followers of Christ, sharing Christ's compassion, who brought about this badly needed legislation.

As we think of women working in mines or laboring long hours in rice paddies or doing piecework at home at scandalously low labor rates, we can understand how Christ's words "Come unto me, ye that labour and are heavy laden" prove irresistible. Coming to him with weary bodies and hungry hearts, such women find in him a Savior from the heaviest burden, sin, as well as new life and strength to tackle each day as it comes.

Compassionate Warnings Compared to some of the conditions in England and the Orient which we have just considered, the Palestinian women of Christ's day seem to have had a wonderfully easy life, wandering freely around the countryside, for hours and days at a time. We must not forget, however, the cruel and capricious Herods and the Roman invaders; and Christ had a compassionate warning about the difficulties and devastation his contemporaries were soon to face.

As he was telling of the "abomination of desolation" which was going to destroy Jerusalem, he probably noticed a pregnant woman or two in the crowd, for he added, "Woe to them that are with child, and to them that give suck in those days! And pray ye that your flight be not in the winter" (Mk. 13:17). It is hard to imagine most public figures expressing compassion for, or even thinking of, pregnant women in the midst of political crises.

Again, when Jesus was on his way to Golgotha carrying his heavy cross, there were many women among the crowd that thronged after the soldiers and prisoners, and they "bewailed and lamented him" (Lk. 23:27). But Jesus' concern was more for them than for himself. Courteously he addressed them, "Daughters of Jerusalem, weep not for me, but weep for yourselves, and for your children. For, behold, the days are coming, in which they will say, Blessed are the barren, and the wombs that never bare, and the paps that never gave suck" (Lk. 23:28-29).

So to the very end, in the midst of his own great suffering and distress, his compassion never failed, even for these unknown and "unimportant" women.

7
WOMEN AT THE CROSS AND TOMB

The dread day of the crucifixion—the climax of God's great plan of salvation for all mankind—drew near. Surprisingly, the Gospels contain more references to women in connection with this event than with any other. Two of the women did not have direct contact with Jesus, but we mention them because the Holy Spirit has granted them a place in the inspired record.

The first was the maid in the palace of the high priest, where Christ was put on trial (Jn. 18:16-17). She appears to have been an observant girl who recognized Peter as having been in the company of the prisoner within. Here, perhaps, we might say God "used" this girl to bring about the fulfillment of Christ's prophecy that Peter would deny him three times that night and to reveal to Peter his own cowardice and weakness.

The other woman was Pilate's wife, who reinforced the verdict that Christ was righteous, not guilty. She obviously did not want her husband to condemn him, but rather (one hopes her protest indicated) wanted to see that he obtained justice. Pilate, however, out of a mistaken self-interest, took literally her words "have thou nothing to do with that just man," and publicly and ceremonially washed his hands of any responsibility in the matter (Mt. 27:11-26).

Beneath the Cross of Jesus   At the end of the last chapter we took note of the "great company of people and of women which bewailed and lamented" as Christ left the judgment hall carrying his cross through the streets toward Calvary. We do not know how many of these were real believers, but the rest of the women mentioned in the closing chapters of the Gospels were all "of his company" and remained faithful to the Lord in heart and presence throughout the long agony of the crucifixion.

While the Roman soldiers went through the hideous details of the crucifixion, passers-by railed on him; rulers, chief priests, scribes, elders and soldiers mocked him; but a group of women stood by the cross in the grip of grief and love. One of these was his mother, Mary. She was now experiencing, more excruciatingly than she could ever have dreamed, the prophecy of Simeon: "A sword shall pierce through thy own soul" (Lk. 2:35). Right there with her, unafraid of being personally identified with the one receiving a criminal's death sentence, was Mary's sister, Mary the wife of Cleophas, and Mary Magdalene (Jn. 19:25).

In addition, standing by the cross was also "the disciple whom Jesus loved," whom we assume was John. The Lord, in the midst of his own fierce agony, had loving thought and compassion for his mother and put her in John's keeping with the words, "Woman, behold thy son!" and to John, "Behold thy mother!" "From that hour that disciple took her unto his own home" (Jn. 19:26-27). This may seem a strange arrangement to us since we know that Jesus had half-brothers and half-sisters who presumably could have taken care of Mary and also that John had his own mother, who was right there at the scene (Mt. 27:56). Perhaps the main purpose, as in his two former remarks to his mother, was once again to leave no ground for the deification of Mary. The fact that he addressed her as "Woman" yet referred to her as John's "mother" seems to indicate that she was no longer to be regarded as having any unique relationship to him.

As the various phenomena accompanying the sacrificial death of the Son of God took place—the darkness, the earthquake, the rending of the temple veil and the amazing way Christ deliberately ended his life after three hours (instead of the crucifixion's dragging on for several days as was usually the case)—the centurion in charge of the executions exclaimed, "Truly this was the Son of God" (Mt. 27:54). The multitude who had merely come to watch the spectacle returned to the city "smiting their breasts." But, as Matthew, Mark and Luke all tell us, many women remained, beholding from afar the tortured bodies on the crosses. Among these were Mary Magdalene, Mary the mother of James and Joses, Salome and many others who "followed Jesus from Galilee, ministering unto him" (Mt. 27:55). Mark, besides listing the same names adds, "and many other women which came up with him to Jerusalem" (Mk. 15:41). These had all traveled nearly a hundred miles and were in the city to celebrate the Passover. Possibly they had hoped to see Jesus claim the throne of Israel. They had hardly come that distance just to bring spices for his dead body.

When Joseph of Arimathea and Nicodemus took the body of Jesus to a new tomb in a nearby garden, Mary Magdalene, Mary the mother of Joses, and other women from Galilee took note of where he was buried and made plans to return with additional spices as soon as the Sabbath passed (Mk. 15:47; Lk. 23:55-56).

That Terrifying Easter Morning   At very early dawn after the Sabbath, the two Marys, Joanna and possibly some other women, went to the garden, wondering as they hurried along whom they could get to help them roll away the huge stone from the entrance to the tomb. Evidently none of the apostles had thought of going, at least so early.

As these women drew near to the garden, there was an earthquake, and an angel of the Lord rolled away the stone, terrifying the guards (Mt. 28:2-4). The women looked in and saw that the body of Jesus was not there. Then two dazzling angels appeared and spoke to them: "Why seek ye the living among the dead? He is not here, but is risen." The women fled, trembling, and "told all these things unto the eleven, and to all the rest" (Lk. 24:5-9). Unfortunately, to the apostles the women's words "seemed as idle tales, and they believed them not." However, Peter and John did take the trouble to go to the tomb to have a look and saw that the Master's body was no longer there.

Mary Magdalene apparently followed them back to the garden, and, though they returned after looking in the tomb, she, in her desperate grief and her uncertainty about what the angels had really meant, stood outside the opening, weeping. Finally she looked in and saw angels at the head and foot of the hewn-out shelf where the body of Christ had lain. They asked her why she wept, and she replied, "Because they have taken away my Lord, and I know not where they have laid him" (Jn. 21:13). She was still evidently thinking of Jesus as a dead body.

She turned outside again and saw Jesus without recognizing him until, in his own inimitable, compassionate way he said her name, "Mary." Then she flung herself at his feet, and he commissioned her to "Go tell my brethren that they go into Galilee" (Mt. 28:10).

In addition to the reason I suggested in chapter 5, perhaps Christ first showed himself to women rather than men because these women showed personal devotion to the Master himself while the male disciples were preoccupied with thoughts of his kingdom and the positions they would have in it. When, unrecognized, he joined the two discouraged disciples returning to Emmaus, Cleopas told about the crucifixion and added, "But we trusted that it had been he which should have redeemed Israel" (Lk. 24:21), presumably meaning from the power of Rome. Even when the disciples gathered to meet him immediately before the ascension, they still asked, "Lord, wilt thou at this time restore again the kingdom to Israel?" (Acts 1:6). The women, with the possible exception of the mother of James and John, seem more drawn to the Person of Christ than to his kingdom.

Some men may suggest that women's attraction to Christ is due to the unconscious sex appeal of a male figure. It is conceivable that one reason most churches have had a majority of women worshipers, especially in earlier days when extremely few were involved in the business world, is that some women welcomed personal contact with a male figure in the form of the minister. I cannot believe, however, that women are likely to have a similar feeling about the Person of Christ. Women are drawn to him because he understands them perfectly, loves them as individual persons and has demonstrated this love by giving his perfect life for their sins. Search as we may in the Gospels, we never find him belittling or degrading women, but quite the reverse.

Dorothy Sayers describes the situation in a delightful way:

Perhaps it was no wonder the women were . . . last at the cross. They had never known a man like this Man—there never has been such another. A prophet and teacher who never nagged at them, never flattered or coaxed or patronized; who never made sick jokes about them. . . . who rebuked without querulousness and praised without condescension; who took their questions and arguments seriously; who never mapped out their sphere for them, never urged them to be feminine or jeered at them for being female; who had no axe to grind and no uneasy male dignity to defend; who took them as he found them and was completely unself-conscious. There is no act, no sermon, no parable in the whole Gospel that borrows its pungency from female perversity; nobody could possibly guess from the words and deeds of Jesus that there was anything "funny" [or, we might add, "inferior"] about woman's nature.

There is no doubt that men and women cannot understand each other perfectly and completely, just because each has some difference in physical structure and function which the other cannot experience. Christ is the only one who can fully understand both sexes, because he created them: In the image of God, "male and female created he them" (Gen. 1:27). Therefore, as Dorothy Sayers points out, in spite of Christ's example of treating women as ordinary human beings, "his Church to this day" does not quite seem to share his view. The reason its spokesmen would probably give for this, of course, is that the scriptural revelation is not limited to the Gospels. So we must examine the remaining books of the New Testament to find out what took place in the early churches and what the Holy Spirit has added to the inspired text on the subject of woman.

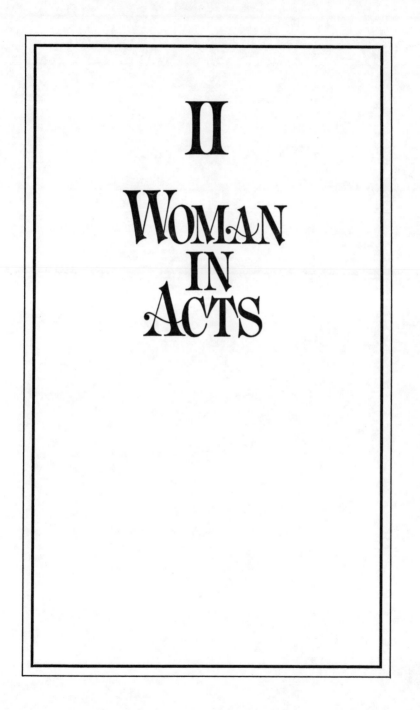

II

WOMAN IN ACTS

8
WOMEN IN THE FIRST CHURCHES

Luke's account of the formation of the early church, recorded in the book of Acts, is certainly one of the most thrilling parts of the Bible. In addition to its general interest and inspiration, it also has some exciting insights about women. I noted thirty-three references to women in Acts, and although this is comparatively few for the size of the book, it is highly significant in comparison with the history of most world religions. These references also indicate a wide range of activity for women within the early church.

Five verses merely refer to famous female figures inconsequential to our study: Pharaoh's daughter, credited by Stephen with saving the life of the baby Moses (7:21); Candace, in whose royal service was the eunuch converted through Philip's witness in the desert (8:27); Drusilla, wife of the governor Felix (24:24); and Bernice, sister of King

Agrippa (25:23), both of whom joined the men out of curiosity about the new religion Paul proclaimed when he made his defense; and lastly, the many-breasted goddess Diana, worshiped as mother of gods and men, whose temple at Ephesus was one of the Seven Wonders of the World and whose worship was threatened by Paul's preaching.

A sixth tantalizing reference mentions a woman famous by association only—Paul's sister (23:16). From it we can only glean that she had a brave and resourceful son evidently in sympathy with his uncle Paul.

The remaining incidents involving women we will consider under eight headings denoting the significance of women's place in and contribution to the early Christian church.

Full Members   *They were full members.* In almost every place where the gospel was preached, women, both Jew and Greek, are mentioned as being among those who believed.

In Jerusalem, "multitudes both of men and women" believed (5:14). We are also told that the disciples "daily in the temple, and in every house, ceased not to teach and preach Jesus Christ" (5:42). This house-preaching would certainly have involved the women very directly in housecleaning and hospitality, and presumably they were fully integrated in the homes and not confined to a separate section as in the synagogues.

Further afield, in Samaria both men and women believed as a result of Philip's preaching (8:12), while at Joppa were Dorcas and many other women (9:36-43). At Lystra lived Timothy's mother Eunice (16:1), a Jewess whom we know was a believer, as was her own mother Lois (2 Tim. 1:5).

At Philippi Lydia, the first Christian convert in Europe, was a charter member of one of the most encouraging churches founded by Paul; and there were other women there also (16:13-15). In Thessalonica there believed and associated with Paul "of the devout Greeks a great multitude, and of the chief women not a few" (17:4). In Berea many believed: "of honourable women which were Greeks, and of men, not a few" (17:12).

The greatest number of women believers mentioned were in Macedonia, but even in Athens, where the response to Paul's preaching was small, a man named Dionysius, important because he was a member of the Areopagus, believed, and also "a woman named Damaris, and others" (17:34).

We are not told why some of these women are described as "honourable." Most commentators assert that it refers to their social status, which seems to give an unpleasant touch of snobbishness to the early church, but we can hope that the term applied equally well to their character as they developed in the Christian life. Certainly Priscilla, a refugee from Rome, played an important part in the founding and establishing of the churches at Corinth and Ephesus; and Paul's later comment that she, together with her husband, "were ready to lay down their necks" for his and the gospel's sake (Rom. 16:4), points to her character rather than her social status.

These women were not merely listeners and believers in the gospel; they were baptized into full membership. Under the Old Testament order only men could partake of circumcision, the outward sign that they were God's people. Some of the Jewish believers from Judea had actually gone and told the new Christians at Antioch, "Except ye be circumcised after the manner of Moses, ye cannot be saved" (15:11), showing how vital a part of Jewish thinking it was. But Acts clearly indicates women's equal place as members of the body of Christ: "When they believed . . . they were baptized, both men and women" (8:12). Lydia was baptized and her household, and also the Philippian jailor "and all his" (16:15, 33).

Thus women who only recently had been recognized as and included in Christ's company, now were able to enjoy full membership in his body, the church. This must have been a wonderful liberation from the thinking of Judaism as expressed in the view of one first-century rabbi, Eliazer, who stated, "Rather should the words of the Torah be burned than entrusted to a woman. Whoever teaches his daughter the Torah is like one who teaches her lasciviousness."

Participants in Prayer Meetings *They joined in prayer meetings.* We are told of this in at least three various locations and circumstances.

The first was immediately after Christ's ascension into heaven, when the one hundred and twenty or so disciples were waiting for the coming of the Holy Spirit whom Christ had promised. We are told that the eleven apostles "continued with one accord in prayer and supplication with the women, and Mary the mother of Jesus, and with his brethren" (1:14).

The second was connected with Peter's imprisonment by Herod after Herod saw that his execution of James pleased the Jewish leaders. The believers were fervently praying in the home of Mary, mother of John Mark, that a similar fate would not soon take Peter from them. We are even given the name of one of the other women there, Rhoda, who went to the door in response to Peter's knocking, after an angel had miraculously freed him from prison in the middle of the night. Rhoda was so overcome with joy at hearing

Peter's voice that she forgot to open the door and ran back to interrupt the praying with the announcement that Peter was outside. The others could not believe the swift answer to their prayers and rather rudely told her, "Thou art mad!" Peter had to keep up a continual, but probably muted, tattoo before they would finally open the door.

Finally, we move to Europe, and the city of Philippi. In spite of its being an important trading center and Roman garrison, there were evidently not enough Jewish men to rate a synagogue (ten was the minimum) and the few worshipers of Jehovah, in this case all women, met each Sabbath at the riverside to pray. Luke tells us, "And on the sabbath we went out of the city by a river side, where prayer was wont to be made, and we sat down, and spake unto the women which resorted there" (16:13). It was well that on this occasion Paul ignored the custom which dictated that a "good" man, and especially a rabbi, should not address a woman in public, for it was as a result of his speaking that Lydia believed, and one of the healthiest New Testament churches was formed in her home. Perhaps it was in response to the earnest prayers of these women that God sent Paul to them.

Spirit-filled Prophets *They were filled with the Spirit and prophesied.* On the day of Pentecost, Luke tells us, "they were all with one accord in one place" (2:1). Presumably these "all" were the same people mentioned in 1:14-15. If so, then the fiery tongues came on the women also.

Luke goes on to say, "They were all filled with the Holy Spirit, and began to speak with other tongues, as the Spirit gave them utterance" (2:4). Some commentators assume that only the Twelve were filled and spoke, but the Greek does not specify males, contrary to the AV's translation of the words uttered by the amazed bystanders: "These *men* are full of new wine" (2:13).

Peter explained the phenomenon taking place this way: "These are not drunken ... but this is that which was spoken by the prophet Joel; ... I will pour out of my Spirit on *all* flesh: and your sons and your daughters shall prophesy, ... and on my servants and on my handmaidens I will pour out in those days of my Spirit, and they shall prophesy" (2:15-18). Thus, it seems probable that Peter was indicating that the women, too, were manifesting the evidences of the Spirit's having come upon them.

Strangely enough, I had never noticed the female element in Joel's prophecy before, and it seems to have escaped the notice of all the commentators as well. Yet surely this prophecy constitutes strong ground for the justification of a spiritual ministry in some form for women. The clear repetition, sons and *daughters,* servants and *handmaids,* seems to leave no doubt of God's intention to include, right from the beginning of the new church age, both male and female among his prophetic or teaching servants. Not only that, but this would seem to be a glorious proclamation that in the new spiritual order just as all are equally saved by Christ's blood so the Spirit will be poured upon them irrespective of seniority, sex or social status; and all will be empowered to minister with his help.

On turning to the Old Testament (Joel 2:15-29), I was interested to note, too, that Joel had called all the people together in a solemn assembly—men, women (including new brides and nursing mothers) and children—that they might all hear and enjoy the promise of the good things to come.

Finally, in Acts 21:9, some other women who fulfilled Joel's prophecy are mentioned: "And the same man [Philip] had four daughters, virgins, which did prophesy."

Establishers and Supporters of Local Churches *They helped establish and support local churches.* The first convert from Paul's preaching in Europe, as already mentioned, was a woman named Lydia. Lydia was apparently a successful businesswoman "whose heart the Lord opened," as Luke beautifully expresses it. She was already a worshiper of God, doing her best to obey him by meeting on the Sabbath for prayer with a few other women.

Since she refers to "my house" and Luke refers to "her household," we assume she was single or, more probably, a widow with a considerable domestic and business staff. On believing the gospel she and her household were immediately baptized, and then with considerable insistence invited Paul and his party to stay in her home. The doubtful propriety with which some in other cultures might view this cannot have been a factor to be considered, probably because of the numerous persons already in her household. However, one commentator, at least, feels Paul must have married Lydia! She was very forthright in her appeal based on whether he judged her "faithful to the Lord"—and evidently she passed the test with Paul.

More believers, including men, were added to their number, and they apparently met at Lydia's house, for after Paul's painful beating and imprisonment for a night and the request of the magistrates that he move on, he went straight to Lydia's house, had a last farewell with "the brethren" and then departed (16:40).

In Athens, as we also saw earlier, one man and one woman, Damaris, were leaders among the believers Paul left after his short visit. In Thessalonica, Berea, Damascus, Joppa, Samaria and Jerusalem, women were also disciples and charter members of the churches there.

Corinth is of particular interest because there Priscilla not only shared in her husband Aquila's business but also had an important place in the church. Paul not only lived in their home for eighteen months but also worked beside them at the same trade, and therefore had ample opportunity to evaluate her life and character. Later he wrote to the Romans, "Greet Priscilla and Aquila my helpers in Christ Jesus: who have for my life laid down their own necks: unto whom not only I give thanks, but also *all the churches of the Gentiles*" (Rom. 16:3-4). Possibly Priscilla had no children and therefore had more time for Christian work. Also, she was probably cosmopolitan in outlook, able to understand the cultural backgrounds of the various believers, since she and her husband had been living and working in Italy until Claudius ordered all Jews to leave Rome.

When Paul finally left Corinth, Priscilla and Aquila accompanied him on the ship to Ephesus and, while Paul went on to Jerusalem, settled there, in yet another new city and country, to undertake the dangerous work of establishing another church in their home. It was while they were at Ephesus that Apollos, the Alexandrian, visited there, eloquently preaching "the way of the Lord [but] knowing only the baptism of John." Priscilla and her husband, having tasted the joy of knowing Christ personally, were anxious that Apollos should have this experience, too, and recognized how much his gift of eloquence and boldness could be used to bring others to Christ. Accordingly, although this man was "mighty in the scriptures" (18:24), Priscilla and Aquila did not let awe or false modesty keep them from trying to minister to him. They invited him to their home "and expounded unto him the way of God more perfectly." Apollos' true greatness is revealed in his gratefully receiving instruction from this lay man and woman team, and he put it to good use, later turning many others to Christ through his preaching (18:24-28).

Victims of Persecution   *They were persecuted for their faith.* No doubt it was because women were so integral a part of and such real assistance to the early church that young Saul of Tarsus had no compunction about dragging them away from home and children to prison and hopefully to death. Luke tells us of Paul's zeal in entering "every house" in Jerusalem, looking for those he regarded as heretics, and even in planning to go to Damascus to drag them bound to Jerusalem for trial (8:3 and 9:2). Paul himself admitted later, "I persecuted this way unto the death, binding and delivering into prisons both men and women" (22:4).

In Antioch of Pisidia, some Jewish women served as persecutors rather than as the ones being persecuted. This incident contains a real touch of irony. After Paul had preached Christ in the synagogue, "the Jews stirred up the devout and honourable women, and the chief men of the city, and raised persecution against Paul and Barnabas." Since the Jews did not allow women in the inner temple court nor permit them in the main area of the synagogue nor even count them in the quorum of persons needed for worship, this act of making them the forefront of opposition against the Christians seems to me a little inconsistent and despicable!

Doers of Charity   *They engaged in charitable work.* It is no surprise to find a woman doing acts of charity in the early church. Rather, it is remarkable that only one occurrence of this is mentioned (especially when we consider how many tens of thousands of women have labored dutifully to produce every variety of wearable and unwearable garment for some Dorcas Society).

Tabitha (or Dorcas) certainly is an example par excellence of practical Christian love, and, interestingly, she is the only woman in the New Testament actually called *disciple*. It seems probable that she helped all in need, not just fellow believers, for when Peter came to her deathbed "all the widows stood by weeping" and showed him the clothes Dorcas had made for them (9:39). After turning them out of the room Peter raised Dorcas from death and "called the saints and widows" (9:41). I find no justification elsewhere in the Bible for assuming that a widow cannot be a saint, so it appears that he called the believers and the other widows Dorcas had helped.

Although the incident is not exactly in the same category, here would be as convenient a place as any to include the reference in Acts 21 to the women who expressed sorrow and sympathy as they accompanied husbands and children in escorting Paul from Tyre to where he was to embark on the dangerous journey to Jerusalem. They all had a foreboding that this would lead to his death and so did all they could to show their love and concern.

Acts mentions one area of practical service which we might think would naturally fall to women, namely, that of "serving tables." Yet surprisingly this was allocated to men, and men with high spiritual qualifications at that. In Acts 6 we read that in the very early days after Pentecost, when the believers were living in a close communal fellowship, there was a "daily ministration." After a while the Grecian Jewish converts complained that their widows were being neglected by the local Hebrews. Was this an imaginary slight, or was it an oversight by the busy apostles to whom those who sold land gave the proceeds for the communal need? We are not told. We only know that the twelve apostles decided they should not let anything interfere with their primary work of preaching and prayer. Instead, they told the believers to choose out seven *men*, full of faith and the Holy Spirit, for this work of "serving tables."

It was the expression "serving tables," together with "daily ministration," which had made me formerly think of the incident in terms of food, just as J. B. Phillips translates it, "in the daily distribution of food." I learned recently, however, that in the Coverdale Bible of 1535 the phrase is rendered as the "daylie handreachinge," and F. F. Bruce assumes it to be the distribution of money from the communal fund. This would certainly make it easier to detect differences of allocations between Hebrew and Greek widows and would better explain why *men* were appointed for the work. In any case, the fact that they were to be full of faith and the Holy Spirit is a reminder that *all* that we do for the Lord is holy, needing our dedicated attention, whether it is serving soup, balancing accounts or whatever.

Recipients of God's Healing Power *They were the recipients of miraculous healings.* Although there is no doubt that she was among the most deserving of all those the Bible records as having been raised from the dead, the mention of Dorcas' charitable acts was perhaps merely incidental to the miracle Peter performed in restoring her to life.

A very different case of the healing of a woman was Paul's healing of a demon-possessed slave girl at Philippi, who had the gift of clairvoyance and could tell fortunes with apparent accuracy. Paul appears very human here, and probably many of us could identify with him in the motive which prompted him to heal her! Instead of being full of compassion for this girl in her sad condition, as we can imagine Christ would have been, Paul was irritated by the nuisance of her constant following and calling out after his party as they went to the place of prayer by the river. Although the AV says "grieved," which could be taken in another sense, the original meaning is rather "vexed," or, as J. B. Phillips puts it, "She continued this behavior for many days, and then Paul, in a burst of irritation, turned round and spoke to the spirit in her, 'I command you in the name of Jesus Christ to come out of her!' " (16:18). The girl was instantly delivered, and lost the power of fortunetelling.

Perhaps Paul had been aware that driving the evil spirit out of her would mean trouble from her masters, both for the slave girl and himself, as indeed proved to be the case when he and Silas were cruelly beaten and thrown into prison. This, however, led to the remarkable conversion of the jailor and all his house. We do not know what happened to the slave girl, but, since she already had the insight that Paul and Silas were messengers from the most high God and were able to tell the way of salvation, we may hope that she truly believed and that her sister in the faith, Lydia, was able to buy her from her masters, since she was no longer of any particular value to them. If not, her fate does not bear thinking about in the face of her masters' anger and their frustration at the loss of such an easy and considerable income.

Responsible Sinners   *They were held accountable for sin.* The only remaining reference to a woman is a sad and frightening one: that of Ananias and his wife, Sapphira (5:1-11). One might have imagined that it was the wife's deceitful scheme to save a little money, but the Bible tells us clearly that it was merely "with her full knowledge" that Ananias planned and practiced the deception.

Here we have the Adam and Eve situation reversed. Paul laid the greater blame for their original sin on Eve (1 Tim. 2:14), but Peter indicated plainly that it was Satan who put this scheme in the husband's heart and blamed Sapphira merely because she "agreed" to the plan—and that in spite of the fact that later, in his first letter, he would tell wives they should be in subjection to their husbands.

But God held her equally culpable because she had evidently not condemned the sin of her husband and had prepared to tell a lie to support his falsehood. Therefore, when it comes to a moral issue, a woman cannot be blindly obedient to a husband and shelter under the "weaker sex" label. We must face the solemn fact that since woman has been given a significant place, and equal membership, in the body of those redeemed by Christ's blood, she must also recognize that God requires the same high moral standard from every disciple, man or woman, since there is in his sight neither male nor female.

Can we find God's ideal woman in the book of the Acts? Was it Lydia, successful businesswoman and a charter member of the church at Philippi, a woman whose heart the Lord opened? Or equally capable and hardworking Priscilla, able to teach the great biblical scholar Apollos more fully about Christ? Or Dorcas, constantly busy with her needle for the poor widows? (She would certainly seem to be the choice of most commentators!) Or Mary, John Mark's mother, who hospitably opened her home? We are given no clue about which of the women in Acts is God's ideal. But we can be reasonably sure it was not Sapphira.

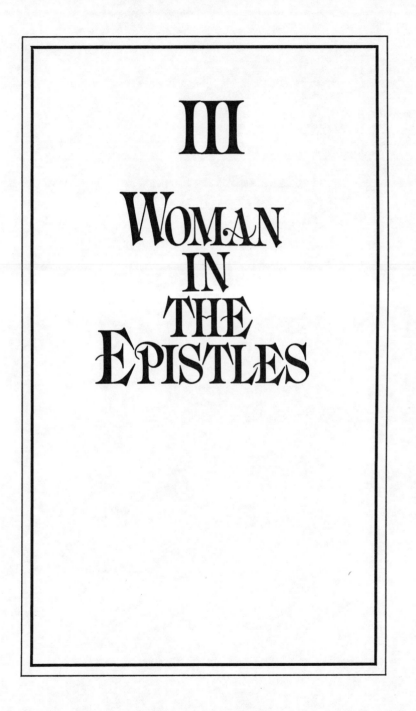

III

WOMAN IN THE EPISTLES

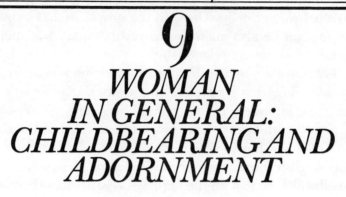

9
WOMAN IN GENERAL: CHILDBEARING AND ADORNMENT

This section proved a much less pleasant, and much more difficult, study than that in the Gospels and Acts. In the former we found Christ's amazing tenderness, courtesy and interest in women and their spiritual growth while in Acts we saw the exciting historical account of the conversion of various women and their active place in the early church. In the Epistles, however, we find a few restrictive instructions for female believers, suggestive of an inferior status, and we see that Paul occasionally has some unpleasant things to say about woman in general; for example, that it was the first *woman* who was deceived by the devil. In the letter to the Romans he mentions female as well as male sexual perverts while in the ones to Timothy he speaks of "silly women laden with sins" and "old wives' fables." This sounds rather different from any of Christ's words about women. Paul does, however, send warm and appreciative greetings to individual women whose help in the gospel he has experienced, and he also makes some revolutionary statements about the marriage relationship.

There are two main difficulties in studying woman in the Epistles. The first is determining what exactly the writers said, and intended, in the original languages. Since some of the AV renderings have given rise to some of the confusions, I had hoped at first to ascertain this from the various English translations of the Bible, but this proved impossible. We have it on the highest authority that there are in Paul's letters "some things hard to be understood" (2 Pet. 3:16). Part of the difficulty arises from the concepts dealt with, but part also from the language. Donald Guthrie in *New Testament Introduction* tells us that Paul "inclines away from literary Greek towards the vernacular, yet is not a good example of that. He is too individualistic, too given to frequent diversions of thought, too often apt to express himself in broken syntax. In a sense, the style is as adaptable as the man." I certainly can make no claim to an exhaustive study since I know little Greek and since this book was researched amid a busy yet often circumscribed life as a missionary wife and mother with traveling, speaking engagements and various odd jobs and residence in four countries. However, I think I have been able to indicate most of the main views on the subjects dealt with in this section.

The second difficulty arises from the very nature of letters. While we have no problem deciding that the message of David's letter to Joab—"Set ye Uriah in the forefront of the hottest battle . . . that he may be smitten, and die" (2 Sam. 11:15)—was limited to one occasion, when we read Paul's letters of instruction to Timothy the issue is not quite so clear. For example, Paul says, "Drink no longer water, but use a little wine for thy stomach's sake and thine often infirmities" (1 Tim. 5:23). Is this command for everyone with a stomach ailment or infirmity? Some people regard *1 Tim., 2 Cor.* and so on merely as convenient tags for finding verses, giving no thought for the persons to whom the letters were addressed. They regard every instruction of Paul as binding on the church today, using the same logic as well-meaning persons who affirm these lines: "Every promise in the Book is mine; Every chapter, every verse, every line." But surely some thought must be given to context.

While in Christ there is neither male nor female, as he himself often demonstrated and as Paul explicitly states in Galatians 3:28, the fact remains that God did create two complementary biological sexes; thus it was natural for the new churches, established in the midst of a completely heathen environment, to seek guidance on marital, social and spiritual spheres from their missionary, Paul. But whether every detail of his answers applies to all Christians of all times is not always easy to determine; or whether, when he speaks about woman, he is referring to all women or merely to wives, since every woman in those days was expected to marry young. (A girl was considered to be of age at twelve-and-a-half years.)

One might think that the more detailed instructions about woman in the Epistles would make it possible to discern "God's ideal woman" there. Yet in them she sometimes appears rather different from God's supposed ideal in Proverbs 31. These variations could be due to differences between an agrarian and an urban culture and the desired qualities of a wife in each. But this again points to the probability that God does not have a final blueprint of the ideal woman. Further, since in addition to generalizations about woman in the Epistles there are also instructions to specific groups (older and younger women, virgins, wives, widows), it seems legitimate to assume that "the exemplary Christian matron," favored by many commentators, is not necessarily God's ideal. Nor is it invariably true, as one states, that a woman "only in connection with her husband attains her proper dignity and worth." These qualities may be found in a single person, too, and in one place Paul advocates the unmarried state for both males and females.

Since the references to woman in the Epistles are made by different writers, and for varying purposes, we will study them under the specific categories mentioned above. But first we will consider some aspects of woman in general. As I studied the verses dealing with woman I began to realize that one rarely hears most of them preached on. It is curious that some pronouncements about woman are almost completely disregarded by Christians today while a few are treated as having great weight. Finally I saw a pattern: Things said just about woman usually are not interesting or do not seem important to male theologians. Instructions dealing with her relationship to man, on the other hand, are regarded with the utmost gravity.

Childbearing I am considering the childbearing function of woman first for two reasons. It is the most obvious and unique physical ability of woman and the main purpose for which many people consider her to have been created. Also it leads to a good illustration of the difficulty in understanding some of the verses about woman.

The verse in question here is 1 Timothy 2:15: "Notwithstanding she [the woman] shall be saved in childbearing, if they continue in faith and charity and holiness with sobriety." I was hesitant to consider this in isolation from its context, but there is so much uncertainty about this verse that many commentators deal with it in that way (or not at all) since, curiously, it comes at the end of a section often headed "Instructions for Worship." Also some of the points mentioned in that paragraph are the subjects of later chapters in this book. Suffice it to say here that Paul begins by urging men to pray everywhere with uplifted hands, then speaks on women's dress and status (in the church?). He does not allow the woman to teach or be dictatorial to the man: "For Adam was first formed, then Eve. And Adam was not beguiled, but the woman being beguiled hath fallen into transgression: but she shall be saved through her [or the] childbearing, if they continue in faith and love and sanctification with sobriety" (1 Tim. 2:12-15, ASV).

The problems in verse 15 are obvious, and Bible translators have been rather free in manipulating it to make it say something that sounds sensible to them. One of the simplest techniques is changing the plural into the singular. Instead of *they* we have in the RSV "Woman will be saved through bearing children, if *she* continue . . ." with a footnote to say the Greek is plural. The New International Version (NIV), the latest translation by conservative scholars, has both in the plural: "Women will be kept safe [footnote: 'be saved'] through childbirth, if they continue in faith. . . ." The NEB has "Yet she will be saved through motherhood [footnote: '*Or* saved through the Birth of the Child, *or* brought safely through childbirth']—if only women continue in faith . . ." and a footnote alternative, "if only husband and wife continue in mutual fidelity."

These quotations indicate the major problem of this verse. What is the "saving" that is promised, conditionally, to women? Is it spiritual salvation, which they can only earn through bearing children and having, in addition to faith, love, holiness and propriety? Or is it a promise of safe delivery during childbirth provided she, or she and her husband, have faith, love, holiness and sobriety?

Modern theologians and translators tend to think this verse refers to the dangers of childbirth since the first view creates an obvious theological problem. J. B. Phillips' paraphrase has "I believe that women will come safely through childbirth if they maintain a life of faith, love and gravity."

The trouble with this theory is that it does not appear to accord with the facts of life. Those of us who have lived in more primitive (and usually non-Christian) societies have observed that tribal women often have easier deliveries than their more "civilized" (and sometimes Christian) sisters. A missionary doctor friend of mine has suggested that the oriental practice of squatting for some forms of work, for resting and for elimination purposes may also make for easier delivery.

Again, while waiting to sail for China I spent three months helping in a Christian home established for unmarried expectant mothers. During that time, although most of the twenty-five girls certainly did not meet Paul's specifications, all except one had uncomplicated deliveries, easily handled by midwives.

Conversely, most of us have known some godly Christian women who have experienced great difficulty, and even death, in childbirth. In the Bible, Rachel died in childbirth right after Jacob had built the altar at Bethel and the whole family had cleansed themselves and thrown away their idols, Rachel having harbored her father's family images for twenty years. Surely at this time she was most likely to be pleasing to God.

Some men are sure the word *saved* must be taken in a spiritual sense and that Paul must be referring to the birth of Christ since he is the true means of salvation. As we have noted, the NEB gives as an alternative reading "saved through the Birth of the Child." Donald Guthrie, however, in *The Pastoral Epistles* says the passage cannot refer to the birth of the Messiah because the Greek article is generic, referring to the whole process of childbearing rather than to one particular instance.

Walter Lock, in the *International Critical and Exegetical Commentary,* believes that Paul means "they shall be spiritually saved" not merely physically preserved because Paul is still thinking of the idea expressed in verse 4 that God "will have all men to be saved and to come unto the knowledge of the truth." A stronger ground for this meaning could be the paragraph which ends with this verse on childbearing. Paul's quick mind jumps ahead, not always spelling out the logical steps. He has said he does not let women teach, or dominate, "the man" since Adam was formed first, then Eve, and "Adam was not the one deceived; it was the woman who was deceived and became a sinner" (NIV). Does Paul then remember God's words to Eve about bearing children, and intend a note of encouragement that Timothy may pass on to the church women: Just be good, and all will go well? Or is there an ominous hint that woman is the specially wicked half of humanity and must perpetually pay for her sin with painful childbirths? We shall consider this view in depth later. For now it is enough to state that this opinion has been held, and is implied in the very complicated paraphrase of the Amplified New Testament: "Nevertheless (the sentence put upon women [of pain in motherhood] does not hinder their [souls'] salvation) and they will be saved [eternally] if they continue in faith and love and holiness, with self-control; [saved indeed] through the Child-bearing, that is, by the birth of the [divine] Child."

So strong has been this idea that at first many people, especially ministers, were highly critical of the use of analgesics for women during childbirth on the gound that it would nullify God's "curse" on them and perhaps even endanger their salvation. The latter threat must have been especially important since the former argument seems never to have been advanced against power mowers, tractors and other labor-saving devices calculated to reduce considerably the sweat on men's brows, and thus the "curse" put upon them!

Whatever view one takes of the difficult first part of the verse, the problem remains: This "saving" appears to be dependent on some mature Christian virtues in the woman; and I have found no one who tries to explain this. A typical modern commentary on the passage is that of Paul F. Barackman:

2:13-15 One of the difficult passages in these letters. But we may note these facts. First, Paul's concern was mainly with married couples at this point. Secondly, for Paul the Scripture ... supported his argument by the priority of Adam's creation, and the initiative of Eve in the first sin. Thirdly, generally speaking, verse 15 may be taken to mean that woman's honor is found in her intended sphere, taking her place in the home and exemplifying Christian virtues.

This certainly leaves some things unexplained, including why only mothers are to experience the "curse" on women.

Another highly regarded modern theologian, William Hendriksen, boldly assures us:

The complete thought is as follows: if the women members of the church will abide in faith, love and sanctification, meanwhile exercising proper self-control and reserve, they will find their joy and salvation in bearing children to God's glory, yes, in all the duties and delights of Christian motherhood.

This still leaves us with a problem. Where did Martha and Mary, and probably Mary Magdalene, plus countless single and childless women since them find their joy and salvation? It seems to me that the commentators who maintain that no one really knows what this verse means are nearest the truth.

One other possible explanation has occurred to me since reading A. Cohen's *Everyman's Talmud*. In it he tells us that the rabbinic teaching of the Pharisees was that Satan performs three functions: He seduces people; he accuses them before God; he inflicts the punishment of death. He particularly accuses people before God "only in times of danger." Thus, "At the time of childbirth the angel of death (i.e. Satan) becomes the accuser of the mother" (Eccles. R. III 2.). Another teaching was that certain classes of persons are particularly susceptible to attack by evil spirits and need special protection: an invalid, a woman in confinement, a bridegroom and a bride.

Since Paul had studied under Rabbi Gamaliel of the Hillel school, whose teaching, according to Edersheim, "placed tremendous emphasis upon Jewish oral traditions," and since Paul himself was, as he tells us, a Pharisee "taught according to the perfect manner of the law of the fathers" (Acts 22:3), these teachings would have been well-known to him. Thus when he mentioned Eve's being deceived by Satan his mind may have jumped to Satan's accusing women before God at childbirth. In this way he could legitimately suggest that if a woman had faith, love and holiness she would have nothing to fear when Satan accused her before God. This seems more logical than the idea that a woman must live a mature Christian life if she is either to be saved spiritually or to come safely through childbirth.

All we can be absolutely sure of, however, is that childbearing is a function of women and that faith, love, holiness and self-control are very important characteristics for her, as for every believer.

In contrast to the complexities of 1 Timothy 2:15 another reference to childbirth is Paul's sublimely simple statement, "God sent forth his Son, made of a woman . . . that we might receive the adoption of sons" (Gal. 4:4-5). What an incredible honor for humanity's supposed second-class sex! God could so easily have created a second Adam in baby form, to be legally adopted into a Davidic family. Some early Moslems even believed that God would miraculously cause a special baby to be born from a male, and that is why their men traditionally wore baggy pants tied at the ankle —to catch the baby when it suddenly and miraculously arrived. But in fact it was to a humble woman's body that God chose to entrust his sinless Son.

Through a woman sin first came into the world, but God in his love and mercy planned that through a woman also should come the Redeemer for the sin of the whole world. Through faith in this woman's perfectly human yet perfectly sinless seed all may be adopted as children into God's family. We can assume that the particular girl chosen for this honor must have been close to God's ideal, but as we saw in our study of the Gospels there are few details about the young Mary, except her thoughtfulness, knowledge of the Scripture and a complete willingness for God's will.

The Epistles contain a few other references to childbearing, but these can be more appropriately studied later under the topic of widows remarrying.

Adornment, Dress and Disposition   Next to her ability to bear children, probably the most obvious topic associated with woman is dress and adornment. And both Peter and

Paul express views on this subject. In 1 Timothy 2:9 Paul states that women should adorn themselves "modestly and sensibly in seemly apparel, not with braided hair or gold or pearls or costly attire but by good deeds" (RSV). Women of his day did go in for elaborate hairdos. Some braided their hair with gold thread and jewels. Others dyed it, powdered it with gold or added blond hair imported from the Germanic tribes. Many wore wigs. This caused quite a problem for the Pharisees in determining, for the purposes of Sabbath keeping, what part of a woman's attire was apparel and what part was an ornament which constituted an unnecessary Sabbath burden. In the Talmud we find this ruling:

A woman may go out on the Sabbath [in the courtyard of her house only] wearing plaits of hair, whether of her own hair or of another woman or of an animal; or with frontlets or other kinds of ornaments sewn to her headgear; or with a hairnet or false curl, or with wadding in her ear or shoe or prepared for a sanitary purpose.

Some of the Greek mystery religions had regulations about women's dress similar to those in the New Testament. One inscription reads: "A consecrated woman shall not have gold ornaments, nor rouge, nor face-whitening, nor head-band, nor braided hair, nor shoes, except those made of felt or the skins of sacred animals."

Even the British Parliament tried proscribing women's adornments. In 1770 it enacted the following:

All women of whatever age, rank, profession, or degree, who shall after this act, impose upon or seduce and betray into matrimony any of His Majesty's subjects, by virtue of scents, paints, or cosmetics, artificial teeth, false hair, Spanish wool, iron stays, bolstered hips, or high-heeled shoes, shall incur the penalty of the law now in force against witchcraft and like misdemeanors, and the marriage under such circumstances shall be null and void.

In comparison to this the scriptural limits are mild indeed, yet surprisingly not one commentator I have read is in favor of taking them literally. One pontificates that pearls and other adornments are "not to be understood as any further prohibited than they are inconsistent with seemly apparel." W. M. Stratham in *The Pulpit Commentary* seems to go even further from Paul's view:

As God is the God of beauty, and nature is clothed with the garments of glory and beauty, so here we have the true idea carried out in religion. Women are "to adorn themselves," God's most beautiful work in creation, the human frame, is to be fitly apparelled: for to this day art knows no higher subject than the human face and form. But—modesty is to be the spirit of all adornment.

Martin Luther, I am told, said that if a husband desires a wife to adorn herself she should do so.

I am still not completely persuaded, and do not remember ever buying myself any jewelry except two one-dollar necklaces to coordinate some colors in my clothes. But judging by Christmas and birthday presents through the years, my family and Christian friends are convinced I need a little sparkle added to my seemly apparel.

Peter also has ideas on what constitutes the best-dressed woman. He states, "Let not yours be the outward adorning with braiding of hair, decoration of gold, and wearing of [expensive?] robes, but let it be the hidden person of the heart with the imperishable jewel of a gentle [meek] and quiet spirit, which in God's sight is very precious" (1 Pet. 3:3-4, RSV). So it may begin to seem that we do have part of a blueprint for the ideal woman. Good works are the outcome of the new birth in any person, however, and both Peter and Paul elsewhere exhort *men* to be meek and self-controlled in the face of unjustified criticism and ill-treatment. Meekness was Moses' great characteristic. Christ proclaimed himself meek and lowly in heart and also declared

"Blessed are the meek" when addressing his male disciples. We cannot regard these qualities as uniquely required of female Christians, therefore; rather, they are the Lord's ideal for every believer.

Few commentators claim that Paul's restrictions apply to what a woman was to wear in church, although the whole paragraph has often been labeled "Instructions for Worship." No doubt this is because what Paul described as the desirable "adorning" of women would hardly be limited to worship time. It was to have modesty, sobriety (meaning not a long face but "habitual inner self-government," as one scholar puts it) and good works rather than expensive clothing and jewelry. This is an area where many women in Western evangelical churches have departed somewhat from the apostolic pattern; and the lady in Proverbs was certainly expensively attired. So it seems to most men that this is a relative matter, perhaps depending on the family income and the husband's wishes. But let us not forget the positive side of the apostolic patterns and the importance of the adornment of the inner woman.

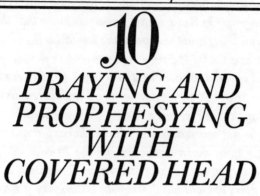

10
PRAYING AND PROPHESYING WITH COVERED HEAD

Probably the logical consideration after ornaments and clothing is Paul's discourse in 1 Corinthians 11 in which, according to the AV, he says, "Every woman that prayeth or prophesieth with her head uncovered dishonoureth her head: for that is even all one as if she were shaven" (v. 5).

I have spent long hours considering this difficult passage. If Paul had just said, "God wants all women to have their heads covered when they pray and prophesy," and left it at that, there would be no problem. Instead, he precedes and follows the above statement with various arguments, the logic of which is difficult to discern. For instance, to be shaved does not in the least seem the same as having a head full of uncovered hair. But we had better look at the whole passage:

(2) Now I praise you, brethren, that ye remember me in all things,

and keep the ordinances ["traditions," ASV and others] as I delivered them to you. (3) But I would have you know that the head of every man is Christ; and the head of the woman is the man; and the head of Christ is God. (4) Every man praying or prophesying, having his head covered, dishonoureth his head. (5) But every woman that prayeth or prophesieth with her head uncovered dishonoureth her head: for that is even all one as if she were shaven. (6) For if the woman be not covered, let her also be shorn: but if it be a shame for a woman to be shorn or shaven, let her be covered. (7) For a man indeed ought not to cover his head, forasmuch as he is the image and glory of God: but the woman is the glory of man. (8) For the man is not of the woman; but the woman of the man. (9) Neither was the man created for the woman; but the woman for the man. (10) For this cause ought the woman to have power on her head because of the angels. (11) Nevertheless, neither is the man without the woman, neither the woman without the man, in the Lord. (12) For as the woman is of the man, even so is the man also by the woman; but all things of God. (13) Judge in yourselves: is it comely that a woman pray unto God uncovered? (14) Doth not even nature itself teach you, that, if a man have long hair, it is a shame unto him? (15) But if a woman have long hair, it is a glory to her: for her hair is given her for a covering. (16) But if any man seem to be contentious, we have no such custom, neither the churches of God. (1 Cor. 11:2-16)

Perplexities in Paul's Arguments If a covering on her head signifies that a woman is "under the power of her husband" as the AV margin suggests, why wouldn't a covering on a man's head appropriately indicate his subjection to God? And what about an unmarried woman? Who is her head? Isn't any woman believer a part of the church of Christ, whose head he is (Col. 2:18)? Conversely, God is called the husband of his people in the Old Testament, and the church (men and women collectively) the bride of Christ in the New. So again, why shouldn't all Christians have their heads covered to demonstrate this relationship?

Next comes the argument that since Adam was created first and then the woman from and for him she should show her subjection to him. Yet Adam was the only man to be "before" the woman. Every other man has been born from and extremely dependent for a time on a woman, as Paul suddenly remembers; and the inconsistency of his previous statements seems to strike him in verses 11 and 12. He then invites his audience to judge for themselves, a suggestion which perhaps is a helpful hint for us today.

Then, too, it is not clear if Paul wants all women to be veiled all the time in a worship service, or only married women, or only the women who pray and prophesy while they are in the act of doing that. Perhaps such women had begun to remove their veils for just that purpose so that they might be heard more clearly.

What really is his main reason for advocating this covering? Is it for God's sake? I grew up in a denomination where all girls and women wore hats in church, and the purpose seemed to be to show reverence for God. Even women tourists were required to cover their heads while sightseeing in the church whether a service was in progress or not. Or was it rather to demonstrate male headship for man's own satisfaction? I have found some commentators who implied so: "Before man, the lord of creation, woman must have her head covered at worship, since that is the proper way for her to recognize the divine order at creation." Or was it for another, quite unexpected reason?

In the midst of his argument Paul puts this puzzling sentence: "For this cause ought the woman to have power on her head because of the angels." At first this left me cold.

I care very much whether I am pleasing to the Lord, and do not want in any way to offend fellow believers or the unconverted; but must I consider the angels also? For a moment it seemed almost comical to imagine angels peering down at some of the monstrosities which in our western countries have gone by the name of ladies' hats. In fact, each time I came on furlough from the Orient I found these "creations" very distracting in church and usually sat near the front to avoid having them in eye range. Surely these were not what Paul had in mind as coverings! And could the church today be at fault for almost entirely neglecting the angels with whom Peter also seemed well-acquainted?

Paul then jumps from the argument for women's heads being covered to the merits of short and long hair for men and women, and here this rather ambiguous statement appears: "Doesn't nature itself teach that for a man to wear long hair is degrading?" We have a double problem here. First, how long is *long*? Paul did not always wear his hair very short, for Acts 18:18 tells us that at Cenchreae he had his hair cut short because he was under a vow. Second, what is meant by *nature*? In the animal world it is often the male which has the longer hair or feathers, for example, lions, peacocks and roosters.

Furthermore, if left to "nature," a man's hair usually grows as long and beautiful as a woman's, as has been seen in the hippie culture. And if long hair in men is objectionable to God, why were the Nazarites forbidden to cut theirs? And why did God tell Aaron and his sons to wear "bonnets" when they entered the tabernacle if men's uncovered heads are to the glory of God? Paul himself seems to end up conscious that his reasoning may not have been too convincing, for he says that if there are those who still want to argue about the matter all he can say is that this is the custom in the existing churches.

With such confused thoughts I obviously needed help from the commentators. It was a comfort to find that as conservative a scholar as Donald Guthrie speaks of "the usual Pauline abruptness, digressions, and . . . habit of losing the line of his argument altogether." J. S. Glen notes the peculiarity of Paul's arguments in this passage, including his appeal to custom and nature, which "does not reflect the Paul who in the high points of doctrinal interpretation exhibits the richest evangelical insight. The extremity of tone suggests an urgency to be met more than an issue to be clarified." Actually, there are nearly as many views on this passage as there are commentators, and we will now consider some in detail.

Conventions of That Day   *The Pulpit Commentary* contains quite a wide range of views from that of David Thomas— "There are some things in these verses that perhaps no one can rightly interpret, and that may have been written from personal opinion rather than Divine inspiration"—to that of C. Lipcomb, who professes great admiration for Paul's arguments, claiming he is outstanding among the apostles for his "insight into the natural economy of the universe."

Both here and elsewhere few care to comment on hair length, but all agree that the "covering" Paul speaks about is a veil. I wondered why the church had changed from this to hats until I found that Calvin in one place refers to the veil as "the badge of celibacy," so I suspect it is because of both Moslem and Roman Catholic use of the veil that Protestants have eschewed it. Most commentators assume that a veil was used by Corinthian women as a token of marriage. Some would have it that all Greek women wore veils, others that only the wealthy did; some say there were two kinds of veils, a long one covering face and bust, worn in exceptional circumstances (mourning, marriage, going on a dangerous journey), and a more common short one, worn the rest of the time, concealing hair, ears and forehead only.

According to J. V. Fitzmeyer women could be present at Greek religious assemblies bareheaded, and thus Christian women were not innovating when they attended Christian gatherings without a head covering. Others believe that at some pagan altars women did cover their heads. However, there were one thousand priestess prostitutes at the temple of Aphrodite in Corinth, and some say that they, and also slaves, were forbidden to wear veils on pain of torture. So perhaps Paul wanted no confusion to arise between these and the Christian women, and therefore decreed synagogue tradition should be followed in the Christian churches. After all, the Corinthian church was already involved in drunkenness and gluttony at their "love feasts" (as mentioned next in 1 Cor. 11), and with unveiled women present outsiders might expect even greater debauchery. This would not explain, however, why Paul seems to limit the veil-wearing to women praying and prophesying, unless they alone had begun to remove them for that reason.

The Bible nowhere else states that women must be veiled and here again we find commentators not quite agreeing on what the biblical custom was. One says that "young girls were more apt to be veiled than married women," but most state that married women were always covered.

Another suggestion is that their new emancipation had gone to the heads of the Christian women and they had discarded their veils as a sign of independence from their husbands. Others even suggest that some of the women had shaved their heads in order to obliterate sex differences in view of Galatians 3:28. One of the chief problems in the passage, however, is the uncertainty about whether Paul is referring to men and women in general or to a wife's relationship to her husband, and we will discuss this further in the chapter on wives. We will limit ourselves here to the matter of women having their heads covered to pray and prophesy.

The Power on the Woman's Head   If Paul were only concerned that Jewish or Greek customs not be hastily overthrown, would he have added verse 10, "For this cause ought the woman to have power on her head because of the angels"? I found some interesting and surprising explanations for this difficult verse. One honest and brave man, David Thomas, wrote, "Who shall divine the meaning of verse 10? . . . To me it is utterly incomprehensible." Those who can only think in terms of male headship twist this word *power* to mean *under* the power of another, as the AV margin states. This word is used sixty-six times in the New Testament, however, always in the sense of power of choice and liberty of doing as one pleases. It is the word Paul used earlier in this same letter concerning a wife and husband's each having power over the other's body (7:4) and also in the admonition "Take heed lest by any means this *liberty* of yours becomes a stumbling block to them that are weak" (8:9). No classical writer uses it in any other sense than this.

Sir William Ramsey in his *Cities of St. Paul* states in this connection: "Most of the ancient and modern commentators say the 'authority' which the woman wears on her head is the authority to which she is subject—a preposterous idea which a Greek scholar would laugh at anywhere except in the New Testament where (as they seem to think) Greek words may mean anything that the commentators choose."

John Lightfoot also believes the woman's own authority is meant here.

With this in mind, Jane A. McNally in *The Place of Woman in the New Testament Church* comes up with a novel idea. She views the construction of the whole passage as being comparable to a teeter-totter, verse 10 being the point of balance: Women have the authority, as each sees fit, to choose whether to veil at worship or not. "One end of the see-saw is her obligation not to bring dishonor to her husband by appearing in the guise of a harlot (3-9); and the other her right to pray to God unveiled (11-15)." When the proprieties are such that they weight the former end heavily, Paul would advise her to make her decision in the light of verse 6, which is meant to express what public opinion might say.

Some commentators who admit that grammatically this word *exousia* means "power" and not a sign of someone else's authority mention a view held down the centuries from some of the early fathers and rabbis, namely, that women need "power," or a veil with magic properties, as protection against the evil angels who would try to seduce them. This idea is based on Genesis 6, but since Christ said the angels neither marry nor are given in marriage (Mt. 22:30) presumably they have neither sex organs nor urges. This is the view expressed in the Talmud regarding good angels, whereas evil spirits can propagate themselves! In any case, two commentators point out that Paul only used this particular term for good angels, and most assume that it refers to those angels thought by the Jews to be present at public worship. "Angels are delegated special duties, and one of them is . . . in connection with prayer. It was said: 'After all the places of worship have completed their services, the angel who is appointed over prayers gathers up all the devotions which had been offered in all the places of worship, forms them into crowns and sets them upon the head of the Holy One' " (Exod. R. xxl.4).

A further suggestion is that "the angels" refer to the seraphim who, out of reverence, veil their faces with their wings in God's presence. But if women and seraphim are to be veiled, why not men, since, according to the psalmist and the writer to the Hebrews, they are at present a little lower than the angels?

Another interesting but complicated view has recently been advanced by Dick and Joyce Boldrey in an article in *Trinity Studies.* They note that Paul makes use of the pun in his various references to "head." Also the Greek *exousia* ("power") in some ancient texts reads *kalumma,* the Arabic word for "veil," the root of which is a common verb meaning "to have power, dominion over," and thus is the equivalent of the Greek word *exousia.* They state: "We opt that Paul used the combined meaning, and may have left the word in Aramaic, as is suggested by Tertullian's citations of verse 10, one time translated 'power,' another 'veil.' . . . So the *veil* which symbolizes the effacement of man's (humanity's) glory in the presence of God, at the same time serves as a sign of the *exousia* [power] which is given to the woman."

The Boldreys then conclude,

Paul used the physical symbols "head" and "veil" to convey two spiritual realities. The first is that human beings are created not in their own image but God's, and should therefore show his glory, not their own, when they worship. The second is that in Christ males are not superior to females; they both have "power on their heads" to worship God. For "we all, with unveiled face, reflecting the glory of the Lord, are being changed into his image from glory to glory. . . . For God . . . has shined in our hearts to give the light of the knowledge of the glory of God in the face of Christ." (2 Cor. 4:6)

Tentative Conclusions   Merely reading English translations of 1 Corinthians 11 would hardly enable one to reach a conclusion like the Boldreys'. Is there anything in the text itself which can guide us without our having all this background knowledge?

The fact that Paul refers to tradition, nature and custom, and invites readers to "judge in themselves" ("judge for yourselves," NASB) seems ground for regarding his instructions here as something not necessarily binding on us today. One writer notes that 1 Corinthians is the only letter where Paul does not seem quite sure of himself. Paul admits that one or two of his judgments lack the authority of a clear ruling by Jesus, and although Paul believes he interprets the Spirit's wisdom he will not go beyond the phrases "but in my judgment" and "I think I have the Spirit of God." Although Paul does not use those phrases in the passage we are considering, most commentators agree that the wearing of a veil concerns a custom of dress which was merely local and temporary.

That it was more than mere custom among the Jews, at least at some period between the first century B.C. and the sixth century A.D., is evident from a study of the Talmud. For a Jewish wife to be seen in the street with her head uncovered was grounds for divorce without even the return of the marriage settlement money, a usual provision for women in the case of divorce for less heinous reasons.

The following have their marriage dissolved without receiving what is due them under their Kethubar: *a woman who transgresses Jewish law, such as going into public with uncovered head, spinning in the street or conversing with all sorts of men; a woman who curses her husband's children in his presence; a loud-voiced woman, which means one who talks in her house and her neighbors can hear what she says. (Keth. vii. 6)*

There is also a footnote to say that at marriage a bride covered her hair and it was considered immodest for her to expose it. Cohen also explains that the ordinary term for marriage is *Kiddushin* denoting "sanctification." It is so called because "the husband prohibits his wife to the whole world like an object which is dedicated to the sanctuary." On the other side of the coin, the penalty for anyone else uncovering a woman's head in the market place was 400 zuz, equal to 100 temple shekels.

Joachim Jeremias in *Jerusalem in the Time of Jesus* tells us there were women so strict that they did not even uncover their heads in the house:

Women like Quimhit, who, it was said, saw seven sons admitted to the high priesthood, which was regarded as divine reward for her extreme propriety: "May it (this and that) befall me if the beams of my house have ever seen the hair of my head." Only in her wedding procession was a bride seen with uncovered head, and then only if she were a virgin, not a widow.

If these conditions prevailed in Paul's time, one can readily understand his acute uneasiness that some women were removing their veils to pray and prophesy. We should remember, too, that he had ended the previous chapter with the words, "So whether you eat or drink or whatever you do, do it all for the glory of God. Do not cause anyone to stumble, whether Jews, Greeks, or the church of God—even as I try to please everybody in every way. For I am not seeking my own good but the good of many, so that they may be saved" (1 Cor. 10:31-33, NIV).

Julian McPheeters points out this:

Although the problems in the Corinthian church may seem far removed from those in the present day church, Paul solves them by principles which are eternal. One of these has to do with accommodating one's teaching and preaching, within limits, to the habits and customs of the people in order that the fullest impact of the Gospel message may be realized.

"Women in matters of dress should conform to the demands and usage of the public sentiment of the community" is the way Hodge sums it up. (Would he still stick by that today, I wonder, when "anything goes" in most communities?) So, if women's hair in Palestine and at Corinth was considered unseemly, by all means cover it up. In Japan, the back of a woman's neck was for a long time considered sexually stimulating. Forty years ago in certain parts of China, to see a woman's naked foot or her arm above the elbow was thought immoral.

Incidentally, most Chinese women did not wear hats, while the men did. And in the early days of missionary work that great pioneer, Hudson Taylor, felt that missionary men should wear the pigtail required of Chinese men by their Manchu rulers, in spite of Paul's remarks in this passage. This was certainly along the lines of Paul's determination to be all things to all men that he might "by all means save some."

Campbell Morgan wisely states,

As we study this passage, let us beware of the slavery of tradition. Beware lest we let something important in the long ago govern our thinking in the present time. Yet let us remember the possible importance of secondary things, because the church is ever witnessing to the world.

With this in mind, when we arrived home on our last furlough, I reluctantly parted with the necessary dollars to purchase a hat. On Sunday morning when I appeared with it on, after years in the Orient without one, my husband's reaction was, "*Boy*, you look funny!" Needless to say, I happily followed the present custom at home and have not worn one since.

A New Interpretation   Such had been the state of my best thinking on the topic until I read an article in a recent issue of the *Westminster Theological Journal* which throws considerable new light on the theme of this chapter. Since it appears to make Paul's words in this passage much more logical and unified, I feel some of it must be included, although it is difficult to summarize a thirty-page article without doing injustice to the scholarship behind it.

The main point of the writer, James B. Hurley, is that the real Greek meaning of verse 5 is not covered hair, but loosened hair. He tells us there is little information available to us about veiling customs in the early church. The Greek pottery which shows elaborate hairstyles and no head covering dates well before Christ. The Talmud stretched over seven centuries so we cannot now be sure what customs were current in Paul's day. Moslems introduced veiling after the writing of the Koran, which was well after the New Testament era, and may have influenced Jewish custom. Jewish men wore a long rectangular mantle with the ends over the arms of the wearer, and this shawl, or Tallith, was "spread as a sign of reverence over the head of the Jewish man when he prayed. . . . The purpose was that the person might 'appear white before God.' "

Was Paul trying to do away with this custom when he speaks of it being dishonoring for a man to pray covered (11:4)? Hurley says the Greek (*kata kephales echon*) does not contain the word *shawl* or *covering*. The only time Paul uses this word is in verse 15 where the Greek word *anti* has usually been translated "for" or "as" instead of given its usual meaning of "instead of." To give its full meaning the verse should read, "A woman's hair is a divinely given sign of her role. Her hair is given her instead of a shawl or veil."

As for the word in verse 5 describing the woman, which

has always been translated with the idea of being uncovered or unveiled, Hurley says it is the same root word as the Septuagint uses in Leviticus 13:45 to describe the leper whose disease has been diagnosed: "He shall let his hair hang loose" as a warning to people of his uncleanness; and also in Numbers 5:18, where a woman accused of adultery was to have "her hair loosed" (RV), or "let down" (Berkeley), thus being set apart from the community until proved innocent or guilty. If innocent, her hair was put up again, if guilty (since in New Testament times the Jews did not have power to inflict capital punishment), she had her head shaved.

Hurley claims that if women were really veiled as supposed, there would have been no need for Paul and Peter to speak against gold-braided hair, for it would not have shown. The custom at that time, begun with the dancing girls, was to put the hair in from eleven to twenty-one braids, with a teardrop or tiny circle of gold every inch or so down the length of the braids, creating a striking shimmer of gold with every movement. The fact that both apostles prohibit this indicates it had already appeared in the churches. Hurley thinks, therefore, that most women were worshiping without veils, but wearing their hair up, pinning or folding the braids on top or at the back of their heads as was done at their marriage.

I had already seen in *Manners and Customs of Bible Lands* that a bride on her way to the bridegroom's house allowed her hair to be loose and flowing, but on arrival older women arranged it, presumably in this marital style. But contrary to Hurley's view the author of that book states that the flowing locks were hidden under a thick veil. "From this time on custom would dictate that her face was not to be unveiled in public."

Hurley points out that Paul had earlier chided the Corinthians for thinking they were already "reigning" with Christ; and probably some of the women, on the ground of Christ's words that in the resurrection they neither marry nor are given in marriage and Paul's words that in Christ there is neither male nor female, had let their hair loose or down thereby to proclaim their new status.

He suggests this would horrify some in the congregation, leading to a controversy in which both a "hair-up" party and a "loosened hair" party might cite Paul for support. "One can envision a [third] party arising which would advocate wearing the shawl. . . . In the midst of this controversy Paul was asked his opinion. . . . He would not want to alienate any but rather win all parties to his side."

So Paul begins his argument from a hierarchy—God, Christ, man, woman. Thus any man praying with his hair done up like a woman dishonors himself by indicating he is under the authority of a man and dishonors Christ whom he should reflect in his relation to his own wife, that is, "Christ is dishonored when one who should be under none save Himself and God publicly proclaims that a man is over him."

As to the wife, the husband would be dishonored in his wife's rejection of his authority; she would also dishonor herself by loosening her hair, for she thus would put on herself the public sign of an accused adulteress. This would be the equivalent of a confession and therefore she should be shaven. "Paul is concerned that in the midst of a woman's exercising the gifts of prayer and prophecy . . . she must continue to maintain her proper relation to her husband." But what about women being co-heirs with Christ (1 Pet. 3:7) some might ask? Paul answers this in verses 10-12, Hurley tells us.

Like others, Hurley recognizes the difficulties of verse 10, but agrees with Ramsey that it refers to a woman's own authority. His proposition is that Paul refers to angels four times in this letter, in each case in connection with problems at Corinth. In 6:1 he had said that Christians will judge both the world and angels in the future reign with Christ (so why couldn't they settle problems among themselves satisfactorily now?). The Corinthians had thought themselves already equal with the angels, showing no sexual distinctions, speaking with tongues of angels (13:1). The divinely structured hierarchy places women under the husband's authority but of no other being.

It is as we consider the exalted place of women within the order of creation, together with the Corinthian boast of their relation to the angels that we come to a proper understanding of Paul's remark in 11:10 . . . which marks a transition in Paul's development. Having stressed the subordination of woman within the marital relation, Paul moved to develop a more positive side.

Hurley then states that a woman's hair marks her as a woman; its style marks her either as accepting her role in creation or rejecting it. The biblical place of woman (unlike that of most pagan societies) is above all of creation, barring her husband. The hair done up on her head

must therefore be understood as a sign of tremendous authority, as well as a sign of a particular relationship to her husband . . . a sign of her proper authority as vice-regent with her husband over the rest of creation; it marks her as a woman, part of mankind, and over the angels. That Paul's word is surprising in this context which had previously stressed subordination is no doubt to be interpreted as part of his design . . . sympathetically apologetic, designed to win women to obedience.

In verses 11 and 12 Paul develops the theme of the inter-relatedness of men and women. Though God had designed an "economic subordination" for women, this does not mean men are independent and women dependent; rather, they are mutually dependent. "At creation women were in one sphere equal with men, and in another subordinate. In the initiation of the new creation they were equal with their husbands in the sphere of charismatic gifts, and subordinate within the family sphere."

Hurley then concludes that Paul would thus address himself to the three parties back in Corinth:

You asked me to judge whether it is proper that a woman pray to God uncovered. I've told you enough that you can . . . judge for yourselves. God's plan in nature shows you the way. A man is shamed if he has long hair, while that same long hair brings glory to a woman. You can see that hair is given to be a sign of the distinction between men and women. This natural sign of long hair is also sufficient covering and there is no need for a shawl.

If anyone still wants to argue about the need for a covering, he should know that neither we nor the churches of God have any other custom than that women should pray and prophesy with their heads covered . . . by their hair.

As already noted, this view of Hurley's does make for a more unified argument in this whole passage. One criticism might be that, like many others, this author, while mostly speaking of the husband and wife relationship, in a few places seems to apply his ideas to all men and all women. Also it is hard to see why Christ is dishonored if a man appears to be under the authority of another man. In this temporal world many men are in positions of subordination to employers.

It is confusing, and a little irritating, to find such divergent views about how a woman is to appear in church. I must confess to having to resist a small initial impulse to think, "A plague on both of you, translators and commentators!" But we should appreciate those who have given themselves to understanding the original languages of the Scriptures, and pray that there will be more who approach them with an open mind and not with preconceived ideas and wishful thinking, more who can fully evaluate the possibilities in the original words of the writers.

As I ponder what the Lord really does want of women with regard to praying and prophesying with covered heads, my most reassuring thought has been the verse, "Man looketh on the outward appearance, but God looketh on the heart" (1 Sam. 16:7). Men do judge by outward appearance, and so to a certain extent we should govern ourselves by this for the sake of the gospel.

If one woman feels, however, that this passage in 1 Corinthians as found in most translations is binding on her, and out of loving obedience to the Lord she covers her head to pray and prophesy, surely he will accept it as from her heart. And if another truly loves the Lord, and with no idea of disrespect and no desire to draw attention to herself in a land of bareheads or to waste precious money on silly hats, prays and speaks uncovered, will God not judge her by her heart and not her head?

Does God really desire to see the good old Salvation Army or missionary "bun" or other long-haired style on wives or on all adult women? Or is it enough for us to give adequate indication that we are women and not men and that our heart's desire is to please him? One cannot help feeling that if the matter were really of vital importance he would have made sure there was no possibility of mistaking his preference.

WOMAN IN CHURCH

Perhaps more important than her dress and headcovering is the question of a woman's conduct in church. Looking first at 1 Corinthians 14:33-35 we read,

(33) For God is not the author of confusion, but of peace, as in all churches of the saints. (34) Let your women keep silence in the churches: for it is not permitted unto them to speak; but they are commanded to be under obedience, as also saith the law. (35) And if they will learn any thing, let them ask their husbands at home: for it is a shame for women to speak in the church.

In English, and taken in isolation, these verses seem quite clear. Yet just before, in chapter 11, Paul had gone into great detail about why women should have either their heads covered or their hair up when they pray and prophesy. Would he waste time on this discussion if he was soon to tell them they must not prophesy at all? So think some com-

mentators. Others, however, insist that after "further reflection" Paul changed his view!

We must remember, too, that both the prophet Joel and
the apostle Peter had said, "And it shall come to pass in the
last days, saith God, I will pour out my Spirit upon all flesh:
and your sons and your *daughters shall prophesy,* . . . and on
my servants and on my *handmaidens* I will pour out in those
days of my Spirit; and they *shall prophesy*" (Acts 2:17-18).
Was Paul contradicting them?

How thankful I am for Peter's word that in Paul's letters
"are some things hard to be understood." I certainly have
no wish to be among the "unlearned and unstable who
wrest the scriptures to their destruction," but have earnestly
and prayerfully tried to find out (1) if Paul meant exactly
what the English translation seems to say, (2) if there is a
reasonable explanation for the apparent contradiction and
(3) if there is a legitimate reason for some of the things
commonly done by Christian women today, particularly on
the mission field, which seem contrary to some of Paul's
injunctions. Some tentative conclusions from this search
will be recorded in the next few chapters.

What Is an Official Church Service?   Turning to the commentaries for light, I found one which recognized that the
gift of prophecy is given to women but said it is only meant
to be exercised in private. Yet in 1 Corinthians 11 Paul talks
about disorderliness at the communion service and uses the
expression, "when ye come together in the church." The
AV heads the whole chapter "Rules for divine worship"
while various commentaries similarly use such expressions
as "Conduct in Public Worship."

Another commentator suggests that the passage about
women praying and prophesying does not refer to "official

services in the church." But what exactly was "an official service" in New Testament times? Paul describes one in chapter 14: "When ye come together, every one of you hath a psalm, hath a doctrine, hath a tongue, hath a revelation, hath an interpretation. . . . If any man speak in an unknown tongue, let it be by two, or at the most by three. . . . Let the prophets speak two or three. . . . For ye may all prophesy one by one, that all may learn, and all may be comforted" (1 Cor. 14:26-27, 29, 31). That is certainly different from most official church services today. In fact, it seems a very informal type of fellowship meeting and therefore all the more strange if a woman with the gift of prophecy must be silent there.

Another (an Episcopalian) states, "It is evident that in this primitive Christian worship great freedom was allowed." But gradually the churches "advanced" to abolishing free prayer, limiting participation in the service to a presiding minister. That this must be a man was, of course, a foregone conclusion to him.

What Kind of Speaking Did Paul Mean?   The most important clue to solving the problem of the apparent contradiction is the meaning of the Greek word translated "speak" in 14:34. Typical of most commentators, who judge only by the western form of church service, is one who notes that "of course it is public speaking which is here intended, as the context implies."

The translators of the NEB were evidently of that opinion and thought to clarify the matter by saying that "women should not address the meeting. They have no licence to speak, but should keep their place as the law directs. If there is something they want to know they should ask their husbands at home. It is a shocking thing that a woman should address the congregation."

Campbell Morgan, however, points out that this Greek word (*laleo*) is used over three hundred times in the New Testament, usually with the sense of talking, chattering, questioning, arguing; and he feels that that is the meaning with which Paul is using it here. Since Paul begins with the thought about confusion, and tells the wives to ask their husbands at home if they have any questions, this seems a much more likely meaning than if he is interjecting the matter about asking questions at home into the middle of instruction about not addressing the congregation. A friend who works among Jewish people says that even to-day he has often heard the president of a synagogue bang on the pulpit and shout to the women's section to be quiet.

Julian C. McPheeters says,

Another disorder in the worship of the Corinthian church, besides the tongues problem, was the disturbance made by the wives talking in undertones to their husbands. Women were not subject to educa-tion in the ancient pagan world. Although the Greeks had the high-est standard of culture, they did not educate their women. Wives were dependent on their husbands for knowledge. The talkative-ness of women in church called for disciplinary measures. The women are directed to seek at home the information they desire. Con-trary to the pronouncements of some, Paul here says not one word against women's participating in the service of worship.

In a Jewish synagogue the women are seated separately. We do not know if this custom carried over into the Chris-tian meetings at first and therefore whether the women were whispering to their husbands or to each other. Cer-tainly in early church history they were seated separately. In pre-war China, too, women and men sat on opposite sides of the church. And since in most pagan religions there is little sense of worshipful reverence and since most of the women of inland China were illiterate, it was natural that in the young churches, when much that was entirely new to the people was preached, there was murmuring and questioning—not to mention children and dogs running around, babies being breast-fed and even peddlers coming in looking for customers.

To further illustrate the kind of situation quite unthinkable to anyone who knows nothing but a western church building, I remember my shock at an incident one Sunday morning at the beginning of the typhoid season early in my career in China. The church in our city had been bombed flat the previous year by the Japanese, and the Christians were meeting in a rented upstairs room. In the course of the service a dear old Chinese elder announced that a Christian doctor and two nurses had walked in from the military hospital, two miles away, to give innoculations. So at the close of the worship service, while the baptized believers had communion at the front of the room, the inquirers and children were to get their shots at the back. Just a few benches separated the two groups.

While there was much more justification for this procedure than for the scandalous behavior of some of the Corinthians at their communion services, I think it illustrates how entirely different the concept of worship in most of the pagan world is from that of centuries-old western churches (which is all that most commentators have experienced). So it is highly possible that it was about chattering and lack of outward reverence on the part of the newly converted Corinthian women that Paul was speaking here. Donald Guthrie also holds this view.

Another possibility, to which the Boldreys subscribe, is that since the word *laleo* has already been used two dozen times in this chapter in connection with *glossai*—the two words together referring to "babbling" in tongues—the meaning is the same in the two verses about women (vv. 34-35). Paul has twice before, in 14:28 and 30, said that people should "keep silent" when confusion would otherwise occur from several people wanting to speak at once, and this is a continuation of the same idea. Paul is not implying that these men are to remain silent forever, but only when their speaking would constitute an interruption.

Are There Other Explanations?   In the Codex Bezae and in some other early manuscripts the verses about women keeping silent appear at the *end* of chapter 14 or else as a marginal gloss. Some even regard it as "an interpolation by a later hand," probably at the end of the first century when women were being downgraded by the church fathers. Moffatt suggests that messengers from Corinth, who were troubled by the women's behavior there, asked Paul to add the item to his letter! Since there is no manuscript which omits these verses completely, however, we assume their authenticity.

Some suggest that verses 33 and 34 are actually a quotation from a letter the Judaizers at Corinth wrote to Paul. In fact, Coneybeare and Howson use quotation marks for about twenty verses in 1 Corinthians, and Sir William Ramsey states, "We should be ready to suspect Paul is making a quotation from a letter addressed to him by the Corinthians when he alludes to their 'knowledge' or when any statement stands in marked contrast either with the immediate context, or with Paul's own known views."

Some neatly dodge the issue by saying that the gift of prophecy ceased after the New Testament Scriptures were complete and therefore the question of women prophesying is now irrelevant. Such an idea of prophecy is rather limited, however, and seems different from Paul's. Earlier in chapter 14, in explaining the superiority of prophesying over speaking in tongues, Paul says, "He that prophesieth speaketh ... to edification, and exhortation, and comfort. He that speaketh in an unknown tongue edifieth himself; but he that prophesieth edifieth the *church*" (vv. 3-4). Surely the church in every age needs edification, exhortation and comfort. (Also, if prophecy is meant to edify the church, it would be pointless for women to exercise the gift in private.) It would be strange, too, for the Holy Spirit to cause Paul to tell the Corinthian believers to "desire spiritual gifts, but rather that ye may prophesy" (14:1) if this gift was soon to be taken away. Martyn Lloyd-Jones says about prophecy, "Prophets actually taught the law and applied and interpreted it, in addition to foretelling." Others hold a similar view. Furthermore, Peter at Pentecost had claimed that they were now in "the last days" in which God had promised through Joel that he would send his Spirit on all flesh, men and women alike, and they would prophesy. Since Christ has not yet returned, aren't we still in those "last days"?

James Hurley explains away the apparent contradiction by referring back to 14:29, which reads in the NEB, "Of the prophets, two or three may speak, while the rest exercise their judgment upon what is said. ... It is for prophets to control prophetic inspiration." Women could certainly prophesy but were not to take part in discussing and evaluating the messages to explore their meaning and make sure they were not contrary to the true gospel. That would be "assuming the anomalous role of judging men ... [a] violation of created authority structure." It is hard to see why, if the Holy Spirit were indeed poured out on men and women, the resulting utterances had to be examined so critically, but evidently Paul had found he could not trust everyone who claimed to be guided by the Spirit. One would think the Spirit could give women as well as men true discernment, but perhaps Paul felt that they had little scriptural background as well as that it is insufferable for a man to be criticized by a woman. Evidently the male believers did not appreciate this from each other either, for a professional ministry soon eliminated any opportunity for public sermon evaluation.

Others have a similar idea that the women Paul refers to were merely wanting to take part in discussion, something men sometimes did in the synagogues. Jean Héring in his commentary states,

There was no question therefore of imposing silence on women who spoke in a state of inspiration to deliver a message. This contingency is expressly dealt with and passed as permissible in 11:5 where women were ordered to have their heads covered, and no exegete has ever doubted that the point there concerns women speaking in church gatherings. There is a clear distinction between a preaching woman who has a right to bring a message and a woman present as an ordinary member of the congregation. It goes without saying that the reason for this [partial] silence [imposed on women in the congregation] must be sought solely in a concern not to violate the rules of propriety . . . at the time. We are then in the realm of the relative. Calvin was well aware of this.

We must note that this writer says "no exegete" has doubted this. There are certainly many ordinary men who can only see in these verses an absolute and eternal divine principle that women can have no speaking ministry in the church. Calvin, however, does allow one exception. Stating that God has committed the office of teaching exclusively to men, he adds,

If anyone challenges this ruling by citing the case of Deborah and

other women of whom we are told that God at one time appointed them to govern the people, the obvious answer is that God's extraordinary acts do not annul the ordinary rules by which He wishes us to be bound. Thus, if at some time women held the office of prophets and teachers and were led to do so by God's spirit, He who is above all law might do this, but being an extraordinary case, it does not conflict with the constant rule.

One cannot help wondering how Calvin would determine if a woman *was* truly "led by God's spirit."

Was Paul Quoting the Oral Law? Together with the view that this "speaking" refers to women's chattering and interrupting the service, I find the most satisfying explanation for the seeming contradiction of 1 Corinthians 11 and 14 in some information I have recently gathered concerning the oral law of the Jewish scribes which developed after Ezra's return from the captivity. Since this throws light on a number of the passages relating to women (and much more) it may be helpful to understand its origin and its impact on the Jewish mind.

For various reasons the position of Jewish women deteriorated considerably during the captivity. First, the Jews began to follow the Persian practice of seclusion of women. Second, the sex vices of the Gentiles who dominated the Jews had filled the Jewish leaders with a disgust which tended to extend to all women. Eve's fall in Eden came to be thought of as sexual lust. Third, perhaps because women were regarded as being so frequently ceremonially unclean, during menstrual periods and after childbirth, they were not counted as part of the quorum of ten needed to establish a new synagogue or even to hold a service.

How did the synagogue originate? With the temple gone, the Jews had to find a substitute center to avert national extinction. Ezra assembled the elders of Judah a number of times, and the solution they evolved gradually became summarized in the word *Torah*, a Hebrew word meaning "teaching" or "direction." A. Cohen notes, "For the exiles it denoted the body of doctrine, *written and oral*, which had come down from past ages. . . . We may assume the Jews in Babylon had in their possession the Mosaic revelation. . . . They also had some of the prophetic writings and the Psalms."

It was the Pentateuch, however, and the oral commentaries surrounding it which were considered God's great revelation, the prophets and wisdom literature being slightly less highly regarded. Thus David says, "How I love thy Torah" (Ps. 119:97). And Ezra is described as "a ready scribe in the Torah of Moses. . . . He set his heart to seek the Torah of the Lord, and to do it, to teach the statutes and judgments" (Ezra 7:6, 10). The word translated "seek" means to deduce or interpret the text, and the majority of the teachers (scribes) who developed from Ezra's approach came to regard this system of interpretation or commentary to be as important as the text itself.

Ezra's assembly of the elders was succeeded by the Sanhedrin, composed of priests and laymen, including the scribes (later entitled *rabbis*). The Sanhedrin gradually divided into two parties. One was the Sadducees, who held a position which they regarded as fixed for all time by the written code of the Pentateuch and inseparably bound up with the temple ritual. The other, the Pharisees, held that the oral Torah was an integral part of the written Torah, enclosing it by additional precautionary measures for the purpose of avoiding unintentional infringement. Some of the Pharisees' leaders saw in the freedom of interpretation allowed by the oral law an invaluable instrument for making the Torah adaptable to varying circumstances. (It did in fact enable the Jewish religion to continue after the destruction of Herod's temple while the Sadducees faded out of existence.) However, this also laid the Pharisees open to the charge of casuistry.

Interpretation of the Torah became a science and only men who were duly qualified to expound the text could speak with authority and receive the name of *Teacher*, later *Rabbi*.

After the Exile, all the people spoke Aramaic as their first language, and most could not read the Hebrew Scriptures. (One high priest is on record as having to be read to.) Thus much of the instruction in the synagogue schools (for boys only) would be oral, and memorized by them. This instruction included both the oral and written Torah. It was probably these oral traditions Christ was referring to when he said, "Ye have heard that it was said by them of old time . . . but I say unto you" (Mt. 5:21-44). Certainly "Thou shalt love thy enemy, and hate thy enemy" was not from the Old Testament.

It was not until after the time of Christ that this oral law appeared in written form, first as the Mishnah, then as the Talmud. The latter was created as commentaries of various rabbis over a seven-hundred-year period were added together to form the Palestinian and Babylonian Talmuds, the rabbinic schools in Jerusalem and those in Alexandria each making their own compilations. Strangely, both the Mishnah and Talmud refer frequently to women, and not always in complimentary terms.

One section of the Talmud gives "the tradition of the elders" in the following way:

Women, slaves and children are exempt from the study of the law. A woman who studies the law has a reward, but not equal to the reward a man has, because she is not commanded to do so: for no one who does anything which he is not commanded to do, receives the same reward as he who is commanded to do it, but a less one. [Curious reasoning, and almost the opposite of what Christ taught.]

Though the woman has a reward, the wise men have commanded that no man should teach his daughter the law for this reason, that the majority of women have not got a mind fitted for study, but pervert the words of the law on account of the poverty of their mind. The wise men have said "Everyone that teacheth his daughter the law is considered as if he taught her transgression." But this applies only to the oral law. As to the written law, he is not to teach her systematically; but if he has taught her, he is not to be considered as having taught her transgression.

A certain Rabbi Eleazer said, "Let the words of the law be burned rather than committed to women." It was this oral tradition which forbade women to speak in the synagogue, and it used such expressions as "It is a shame for woman to let her voice be heard among men" and "The voice of woman is as filthy nakedness." Even to hear a woman singing in private was considered unchaste.

This is very different from Old Testament practice, where many women sang God's praises and prophesied. Nowhere is there any command to women to be silent. So when Paul says, "It is not permitted unto them to speak; but they are commanded to be under obedience as also saith the law . . . for it is a shame for women to speak," he is literally quoting the oral law. The translators of the AV probably had no knowledge of this rabbinic law and in search of some justification for Paul's mention of "the law" could only come up with the suggestion of Genesis 3:16 in their marginal note. This has colored the thinking of most theologians ever since. Now that much more data on Jewish traditions and practice is available, it is easy to see that this could be the explanation for Paul's words.

In support of this, J. Stanley Glen writes,

What evidence do we have that Paul clung [to some of these traditions] in spite of all that he said of the freedom which the believer has in the Gospel? . . . [In silencing the women at Corinth] much as his action may have been justified in the light of local circumstances, he expects of these what any rabbi would expect of Jewish women in an ancient synagogue. For although it was probably correct that the women were indulging in ecstatic babbling, as Paul's use of the verb laleo *suggests, and that for the sake of decency and order in worship they had to be restrained, the character of his injunction reflects Rabbinic practice . . . "as even the law says." The law here in question is not the Pentateuch but the tradition that required women to be silent in the synagogues, and confined them to certain areas apart from men. . . . It was this law which, if women desired to know anything, required them to ask their husbands at home—now taken by Paul from synagogue practice and applied to Christian women in Corinth.*

Referring to the way that Paul maintains a patriarchal subordination of the woman to the man, Glen states,

Even within his Christological understanding of their interdependence, an unresolved problem seems to remain. The subordination is derived not from the familiar answer previously given to irresponsible freedom: "All things are lawful, but not all are expedient." It is derived from extrabiblical tradition that occupies a place alongside the Gospel, which is somewhat exceptional for Pauline theology.

Glen sees this as "not unlike [the position] claimed for circumcision and dietary laws by his opponents in the Galatian controversy." There Paul disposed of them as "traditions." But in the case of the women

he seems to be clinging to a little of the law, which, according to his argument in Galatians and Romans, should have been overcome. This is not to say that the women in Corinth were right, and Paul wrong, only that his answer in the light of the Gospel was as yet incomplete. It had been worked out for the problem of the Jew and the Gentile, but not yet for the male and female, slave and free.

I know there are those who will say that Paul's words that "in Christ there is neither male nor female" refer only to her "spiritual privilege" of being saved, not to her "spiritual activity" or her social relationships; and also that such a view as Glen expresses threatens the doctrine of the divine inspiration of the Scriptures. With regard to the first, if the loss of distinction between sexes is spiritual, then the church, of all places, should be the place where equality exists. The second objection will be faced in the next chapter.

Meanwhile, how should God's ideal woman behave in church? Certainly she should listen in courteous silence to whoever is speaking, as do also the men of the congregation today. Also, if she is a wife and mother, she should serve no "roast preacher" to the family after a service, although if some heresy was taught she will be wise to point this out. If she has questions, she may ask her husband at home, though in these days many women have had more Bible study and done more Sunday school teaching than their husbands.

It is obvious from Paul's words in 1 Corinthians 7:13-16 that sometimes wives were Christians and husbands were not, and Peter implies the same thing in 1 Peter 3:1. From whom were these to get answers? We can be thankful that today it is not considered immodest for a woman to question the speaker afterward or to phone the minister and that a wide range of Christian books is also available.

Whether the ideal Christian woman is ever justified in opening her mouth in church in a prophetic manner or in testimony to the saving power of Christ will be considered more fully after we study another passage of Scripture.

12
WOMAN'S CHURCH ROLE: MUTE BENCHWARMER?

The other verses bearing on the conduct of women within the church are 1 Timothy 2:11-14: "(11) Let the woman learn in silence with all subjection. (12) But I suffer not a woman to teach, nor to usurp authority over the man, but to be in silence. (13) For Adam was first formed, then Eve. (14) And Adam was not deceived, but the woman being deceived was in the transgression." This English version certainly seems to limit a woman to being a perpetual benchwarmer, forever learning but never having an opportunity to pass her knowledge on, a bottomless cup never destined to overflow with the good news of Christ to others.

Paul gives no indication in these verses as to *where* women are to be "in silence." Earlier in the paragraph he says men should pray "everywhere." But he could hardly expect women to observe a continual silence in their homes and in all other places. Since he begins the paragraph with a list of prayer topics, it is usually assumed he means in some kind of Christian gathering. But is he referring to all meetings or only to that ambiguous "official church service"?

What Did the Words Originally Mean?   In most English translations Paul sounds not as if he is dealing here with the matter of chattering or babbling but as if he does not want women to do anything with their mouths, perhaps not even to sing, pray or prophesy, and certainly not to ask questions or teach. D. Edmond Hiebert, however, tells us that the word translated "silence" (*hesuchia*) has the basic meaning of quietness, tranquility, the absence of disturbance, and is the word used in 1 Timothy 2:2 for "quiet life" and in 2 Thessalonians 3:12 in the phrase "to work in quiet fashion and eat their own bread" (NASB). Therefore, he concludes, "Clearly the term does not prohibit all speech, but does call for calm, nondisruptive conduct." In other words, it is much the same idea as in 1 Corinthians 11.

Hiebert also quotes R. C. Nichol's observation that Paul here uses the word for "authoritative teaching . . . the activity of the accredited teacher, and implies the teacher's position of authority over the taught." Therefore for a woman to engage in this kind of teaching would be "a direct violation of her position of subordination."

It is not clear whether the phrase "usurping authority over the man" ("a man" or "men," according to some translations) refers to men in general or to a husband. Many commentators regard it as covering the whole male sex. Actually, the word translated "usurp authority" in the AV would more accurately be rendered "dictate to" or "domineer over." It does not suggest the idea of women snatching a prerogative given by God only to men. This word is used nowhere else in the New Testament. Originally it meant an independent actor, but it became a popular term used to indicate any autocratic personality. The quality it implies would hardly be desirable for any Christian, male or female.

If, as Hiebert suggests, the "teaching" prohibited was only that of an accredited teacher, we are given no indication by either Christ or Paul about how a Christian becomes "accredited." Possibly Paul had in mind the academic training of the scribe, which lasted a number of years before he was "ordained" a teacher and could receive the title of *Rabbi*. "Only ordained teachers transmitted and created tradition derived from the Torah which according to Pharisaic teaching ... was regarded as equal to, and indeed above, the Torah. ... Their decision had the power to bind or to loose for all time the Jews of the entire world. ... They were the guardians of a secret knowledge, of an esoteric tradition," Joachim Jeremias tells us. Certainly there were no women with such qualifications; and if that is what Paul is referring to, then it would appear that women moved by the Spirit could still prophesy to comfort or edify fellow believers.

Many men, however, quite naturally favor the idea of complete silence for women and sound like they enjoy expounding this passage. Listen to William Hendriksen:

Though these words and their parallel in 1 Corinthians 14:33-35 may sound a trifle unfriendly, in reality they are the very opposite. In fact they are expressive of a feeling of tender sympathy and basic understanding. They mean: let a woman not enter a sphere of activity for which by her very creation she is not suited. Let not a bird try to dwell under water. Let not a fish try to dwell on land. Let not a woman yearn to exercise authority over a man by lecturing him in public worship. For the sake both of herself and the spiritual welfare

*of the church, such unholy tampering with divine authority is for-
bidden.*

*In the service of the Word on the day of the Lord a woman should
learn, not teach, she should be silent. . . . Moreover this learning in
silence should not be with a rebellious attitude of heart, but with
complete submissiveness.*

Quite apart from his view of women, which we will examine later, and also the fact that Paul does not mention
"the day of the Lord," this writer gives a rather horrifying
picture of a Christian preacher. Surely the average minister
is not "yearning to exercise authority . . . by lecturing" his
congregation.

This, and the description of the accredited teacher as "a
master to be heard and obeyed" (Hiebert), hardly describes
what Christ commissioned his disciples to be and do. He
told them to "feed my sheep" and to preach the good news
of freedom from sin, of release for the captives and of rescue for the sheep who have gone astray. He gave an invitation—"Come unto me, and I will give you rest"—not a lec-
ture. Granted lectures have their place, but is it at worship
and evangelistic services? The tragedy is that early in the
history of the church ecclesiastical professionalism silenced
not only women but also men, so that today we often hear
nothing but a monologue from the minister.

One can well understand that this sometimes seems the
only way to have things done "decently and in order," yet
we must beware of Christianity developing that "elitism"
which characterized the evolution of all the major religions
and which was especially apparent in the priestcraft of
medieval Christendom, so well described by Robert Brow in
his book *Religion*. The outbreak of home Bible studies and
body-life emphasis at the present time is no doubt a swing of
the pendulum in the opposite direction.

Should Women Never Be Heard in a Mixed Audience?
To return to 1 Timothy 2:11, could the "learning in silence"
required by Paul really mean, as some men claim, that there
should never be women speakers in a church service, that
missionary women should never report on their work to
mixed audiences in their home church, that women should
not be heads of Sunday school departments, teach classes
with both sexes in it or give a testimony to a mixed audience—all of which are done to some extent in many
branches of the Christian church at home and abroad today? Hendriksen's description of "the service of the Word
on the day of the Lord" seems to deny women any divine
sanction for even teaching a Sunday school class of their
own sex.

As I studied this passage of Scripture in Japan and before
I had heard of the probable meaning of "teach," I was
forced to take a serious look at my own work. In the beginning, all my contacts had been with college and high school
girls, but gradually other invitations had come. For example, for some years I had, at the invitation of the pastor,
been teaching an English Bible class in a Japanese church
as an evangelistic outreach. The majority of those attending
the class were male university students, mostly non-Christians, although a few from a nearby seminary also came.
This was certainly not an "official church service" and I do
not think I "lorded it over them." But was Paul saying that I
should not be teaching male students anything (even Latin
to seminarians?) or only that teaching them the Bible was
wrong, even though some of these students would never
look at it in any other situation?

Should I be taking my turn, with the rest of the Christian
college faculty, as a chapel speaker? At first, I had spoken
more in the line of testimony, on Christian journalism or on

international communism and its methods of infiltrating Christian groups as I had seen it at the London School of Economics and Political Science in pre-war years and later in China. But there is a limit to that kind of subject.

Looking at that passage, I concluded that Paul might not be happy to see me on that platform. But more important: Was God equally displeased? Availing myself of James' promise, "If any of you lack wisdom, let him ask of God" (1:5), the next time I was asked to speak in chapel I refused, having a good excuse for that date, and prayed that God would guide in whether I would be asked again. The request was repeated soon after, and, without telling him why, I asked my husband if he would like to speak instead of me. "When you are out there anyway, why should I go all that way?" was his response. (A three-hour round trip was involved.) The man who asked me to speak in chapel is now president of one of the outstanding Bible colleges in the States, and the Japanese pastor one of Japan's best evangelists; so all things considered, I felt this was God's assurance that I was doing his will.

Are there other reasons which can legitimately be added to this admittedly subjective ground for what may appear to be the ignoring of a scriptural injunction? One explanation for Paul's statement might be that at Corinth and Ephesus, where Timothy was working when Paul wrote to him, the main deities were the goddesses Venus and Diana. This apparently resulted in most obscene and disorderly "worship." So possibly the women there had little idea of propriety at first, and any participation by women in the Christian services might be misunderstood by outsiders.

It was a time when the majority of pagan women were illiterate, and the few who were not were often of doubtful morals or notorious in other ways. Cara Afrania, for example, a Roman Senator's wife and herself an attorney, was so vehement in her court arguments that the Senate decided to bar all women lawyers from the courtrooms forever! Calvin also mentions this woman as an outstanding example of the lack of "the modesty that becomes a female."

Pythagoras had said, "Three things are greatly to be feared: fire, water, and woman"; and Seneca that "woman and ignorance are the two greatest calamities in the world." Jewish women, as we have seen, had a very inferior place in the synagogue and were not allowed to teach the smallest children, even their own.

With mingled contempt and fear of women prevalent, it seems unlikely that many men would be drawn to Christianity if women were in positions of leadership; and Paul's greatest concern was for the spread of the gospel. We have other instances where he accommodated himself to local conditions in spite of its being against his general principle. Although he had "no small dissension" with Jewish believers who taught that all Christians must be circumcised (Acts 15:1-2), he circumcised Timothy before going on a missionary journey because the Jews of that area knew Timothy's father was Greek (Acts 16:3). Thus, though he believes in principle that there is no longer Jew and Gentile, male and female in Christ, perhaps for the sake of the gospel he is accommodating himself to local thinking.

Commentators' Views Change with Time   As I studied all the commentaries in the Tokyo Christian College library, I noted how the remarks differed according to the age in which they were written. This reveals that some of the most learned, orthodox and dedicated interpreters of Scripture are nevertheless strongly influenced by their environment.

One of the early fathers, Chrysostom "the golden

155

mouthed," succinctly sums the whole matter up by saying, "The woman taught once and ruined all."

Calvin, writing in 1546, in one place upholds the injunction that women should not teach, not so much on the ground of divine edict as of logic and propriety: "Unquestionably, wherever even natural propriety has been maintained, women have in all ages been excluded from the public management of affairs. It is the dictate of common sense that female government is improper and unseemly."

Some of the nineteenth-century commentators express great concern for the temptations women might fall into if they take part in a meeting. One feels that public speaking or asking questions is "calculated to foster woman's vanity," especially if the question is "keen and pert"! Some wax eloquent on woman's susceptibility to guile and persuasion, and P. Fairbairn, writing in Edinburgh in 1874, is almost lyrical in describing some male characteristics and capabilities:

She [woman] lacks, by the very constitution of nature, the qualities necessary for such a task, . . . the equability of temper, the practical shrewdness and discernment, the firm, independent, regulative judgment, which are required to carry the leaders of important interests above first impressions and outward appearances, to resist solicitations, subtle entanglements, and fierce conflicts, to cleave unswervingly to the right.

There must have been some wonderful men in Scotland in 1874!

While agreeing that many men have a superior power of objective and analytical thinking, I cannot help feeling that the above writer forgot for a moment that the human heart, male and female, is "deceitful above all things and desperately wicked." How many men are there in the Bible of whom his description would be accurate? Through patriarchs, judges, kings, prophets and disciples, we see men who made serious errors of judgment. While the situation might have been worse had women held any positions of responsibility, the history of the church has not been conspicuously bright in spite of its all-male leadership. Mary Baker Eddy and a few others apart, from Gnosticism right down to modernism and the heresies of certain well-known bishops, the onus for departing from scriptural truth lies rather heavily on masculine shoulders.

Some more recent commentaries make no attempt to prove the inferiority or innate inability of women, perhaps because a half century and more of coeducation and women's increasing participation in public life have proved that some women, at least, can fulfill responsibilities creditably, and even make excellent teachers.

William Barclay has come a long way from Chrysostom: "This is a passage which cannot be read out of its historical context. It springs entirely from the situation in which it was written. It is written against a double background." He discusses first the Jewish background, which we have already touched on, adding that in Jewish law a woman was not a legal person; she was a thing, entirely at the disposal of her husband or father, forbidden to learn the law, having no part in the synagogue service. For her even to read the Scripture in that place would be to "lessen the honor of the congregation."

Dealing next with the Greek background, Barclay notes that a respectable Greek woman led a very confined life, living in her own quarters where none but her husband came and not even appearing for meals. He also speaks of the conditions in Greek religions which we have mentioned, maintaining that if a woman had taken an active part the church would inevitably have gained the reputation of being the resort of loose and immoral women. He concludes,

We must not read this passage as a barrier to all women's work and service within the church. We must read it in the light of its Jewish background, and in the light of the situation in a Greek city. And we must look for Paul's permanent views in the passage which tells us that the differences are wiped out, and that men and women, slaves and freemen, Jews and Gentiles are all eligible to serve Christ.

Do Such Views Undermine the Infallibility of Scripture?

Do such views in any way undermine the doctrine of the infallibility of Scripture? We firmly believe the Bible is the Word of God. We open it and read, "Let the woman learn in silence with all subjection. But I suffer not a woman to teach, nor to usurp authority over the man, but to be in silence." That "I" is God speaking, we may conclude, and certainly we need to be very sure of our ground before in any way weakening the force of these words.

Just a few verses before, however, the text says, "Some . . . concerning faith have made shipwreck, of whom is Hymenaeus and Alexander; whom I have delivered unto Satan that they may learn not to blaspheme" (1:19-20). Is that God speaking, and is this a divine eternal principle for dealing with those who lose their faith? Or is it Paul telling Timothy about something he has done?

Dealing with the theory that the intent of the instructions for women may be limited to the time in which they were written, the large majority of commentators, as we have seen, are quite sure that this is true with regard to the wearing of pearls and veils. Are there other clear scriptural injunctions about which the church in general holds such a view? Paul ends both letters to the Corinthians and the first to the Thessalonians with a command to greet one another with a holy kiss, but as nominal Christians began to enter the church this practice was so abused that it was finally forbidden. Paul also told the Philippians that "at the name of Jesus every knee should bow" (Phil. 2:10). I have been present in churches where some took this as a literal command and genuflected at every mention of the word *Jesus*, yet all the evangelicals I know ignore this. A little further on in 1 Timothy, Paul commands, "Drink no longer water, but use a little wine for thy stomach's sake" (5:23)—a command about which most Bible-believing Christians are silent!

Other instances of Paul's commands which are not usually followed today are "Owe no man anything" (Rom. 13:8), which could conceivably include mortgages and credit cards. Then, "I exhort . . . first of all, supplications, prayers, intercessions and giving of thanks, be made for all men; for kings, and for all that are in authority" (1 Tim. 2:1-2), yet in many fundamental churches it is rare to hear these authorities prayed for. Also, Paul's requirement that overseers and elders must have well-controlled children (1 Tim. 3:4) often seems ignored.

There are, I believe, two further examples of greater importance. The first is Christ's command to his disciples that they should wash one another's feet. This seems very specific, but there is no evidence in the Scriptures that they actually did this. Only the widows put on the church roll seem to have been required to do it (1 Tim. 5:10). Very few churches today practice this, probably because a change in footwear, paved roads and improved transportation have made it unnecessary.

The second concerns the letter on conduct sent to Gentile converts by the council at Jerusalem. After much heated discussion, the participants finally reach a conclusion. James then wrote that it was the considered opinion of all the apostles "and of the Holy Ghost" that Gentile believers did not have to be circumcised but that all should abstain "from meats offered to idols, and from blood, and from things strangled, and from fornication" (Acts 15:29). Leviticus 3:17 is emphatic on one of these points, too: "It shall be a *perpetual* statute for your generations throughout all your dwellings, that ye eat neither fat nor blood." Yet I have never heard of a Bible-believing church which teaches this requirement today. And I know many ministers who relish a rare steak or a roast of beef dripping with bloody juices, although there is no later word in the Scriptures to indicate that these things have been abrogated.

All these examples of omission by the church would not necessarily justify ignoring 1 Timothy 2:11. As the study of hermeneutics indicates, however, and some commentators such as Donald Guthrie have pointed out, "Reserve must be exercised in deducing universal principles from particular cases." Few churches teach and practice baptism for the dead, for instance, although Paul speaks of it with apparent approval (1 Cor. 15:29).

Is it not possible, then, to reason that Paul also was just telling Timothy, "Personally, I don't allow women to teach" (Phillips), and then stating his reasons? He does not claim this is God's permanent command, nor demand that Timothy follow his example. In fact he tells Titus that older women should teach the younger, and in other letters he mentions the names of women who have helped him as co-workers in the gospel.

Most English versions of the Bible printed in paragraphs have 1 Timothy 2:8-15 as one paragraph. It is curious that almost all men ignore the injunction to lift up their holy hands in prayer, insist that women *may* wear pearls and look attractive, and largely bypass verse 15 with all its problems about being saved through childbirth; yet they take the intermediate verses, 11-14, at face value as God's basic eternal rule. Then they have to wriggle their way around Galatians 3:28, the instances of women prophesying and having positions of leadership, and Priscilla teaching Apollos with such beneficial results. They also have to close their eyes to Joel's and Peter's declaration that God promised that in the last days he would pour out his Spirit on sons and daughters and they would prophesy and to the evidence that this did happen at Pentecost.

Of course, the fact that Paul refers back to Adam and Eve in 1 Timothy 2:13-14 does suggest a universal element in the matter. So to evaluate this subject fully we must examine the validity of the reason Paul gives for not letting women teach. We will look at this and related texts dealing with the basic nature of woman in the next two chapters.

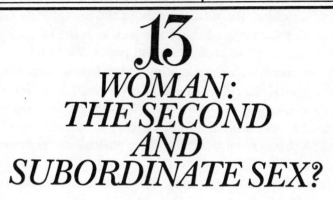

13
WOMAN: THE SECOND AND SUBORDINATE SEX?

There were several phrases in the biblical passages we studied in chapters 10—12 with which we did not deal fully. They are ones which many theologians have taken to indicate the basic inferiority and subordination of all women to all men—deriving either from creation itself or else from the Fall—and they are in fact involved in the reasoning behind some of Paul's restrictions. Though some men think these phrases refer only to a wife's relationship to her husband, since the word *woman* is used we must first consider whether these phrases have a more general sense.

What Is the Meaning of Headship? In 1 Corinthians 11 we read, "The head of the woman is the man.... [The man] is the image and glory of God: but the woman is the glory of the man. For the man is not of the woman; but the woman of the man. . . . Nevertheless neither is the man without the woman, neither the woman without the man, in the Lord. For as the woman is of the man, even so is the man also by the woman; but all things of God (vv. 3, 7-8, 11-12).

Many men think the meaning of the first sentence is obvious: Man is the ruler. The Boldreys, think, however, that *Paul was punning on the word "head." . . . Rosh the Hebrew word for head is often translated in the Septuagint by arche the Greek word which may mean "rule" but just as often means "beginning." In this context Paul speaks of Christ "the head of the body, the church: who is the beginning, the firstborn from the dead" (Col. 1:18). To be the "head" is related to being "first" . . . but priority of time neither necessarily nor universally leads to priority of rank. . . . When Paul spoke of woman's head being the man, he was emphasizing man's temporal priority and woman's derivation from him; this is further substantiated in verse 8.*

Most, however, view man's "headship" as proof that he is boss and the woman his subordinate, and believe that man is to be uncovered in worship to demonstrate the distinction. One writer in the *Pulpit Commentary* tells us that Paul opted for the Greek method of worshiping with uncovered head for men, as opposed to the Jewish wearing of the Tallith, because "the Christian who is in Christ may stand with unveiled face in the presence of the Father." But isn't a woman believer also "in Christ"?

Many commentators like the idea of man being in God's image and having his glory. (Paul mentions only the man in this regard, but Genesis includes the woman.) One man in the *Pulpit Commentary* states, "Man reflects God; woman, in her general nature in this earthly and temporal dispensation, reflects the glory of man." Isn't man's nature also in "this earthly and temporal dispensation"?

When one thinks of the varieties of men's uncovered

heads in the average church today, in what way do they reflect the glory of God? I have sat behind tribesmen who, when they removed their turbans, had heads visibly alive with vermin; others with eyes encrusted with discharge from various diseases. By faith I saw them as sons of God, heirs with Christ, people changed into his likeness; but not merely because they belonged to the male sex and had their heads uncovered.

Woman the Glory of Man   With the exception of James Hurley's recent article, no commentator I have read has attempted to explain how exactly woman is the glory of man, though one suggests "she is as moonlight to his sunlight"—which does not sound very glorious. Usually the commentators are more specific about the part of their own sex; for example, man is the image and glory of God "in face and form" or "in his powers of thought, creativity and ability to rule."

I found no clear explanation for this puzzling thought of Paul's until I encountered Hurley's article. Hurley begins with Paul's hierarchy of God—Christ—man—woman, assumes that the woman is under the authority of her husband and tries to show that her hairstyle demonstrated this fact. With regard to the words that the man is the image and glory of God, and the woman the glory of man, Hurley points out that Paul is not citing Genesis 1:26, which says "image and likeness":

Man in his authority relation to creation and to woman, images the dominion of God over creation (a central theme of the whole of Gen. 1) and the headship of Christ over his church. The woman has a corresponding but different role to play. The woman is not called to image God in the relation which she sustains to her husband; she is rather to show loving obedience.

Then he comes to the term *glory*, which is used both of the man and the woman. Concerning this he says,

Man is relationally the glory of God as he is in appropriate relation to him: under God, thereby pointing to God's dominion, over the remainder of creation, thereby reflecting dominion. In such a relation man is free to be what he truly is, and shows truly what he is meant to be. A woman is the glory of her husband as she stands in a proper relation to him and demonstrates the truth concerning her created role.

In the sense developed above, and within the marriage relationship, the role of image is an active one while that of glory is passive. In this sense therefore the man ought to be designated the image and glory of God, and the woman the glory of man.

As mentioned before, this does present Paul's words as a more unified argument and may be what he was thinking. Whether Hurley's idea of "headship" is really justified by the Genesis account of creation or whether the Boldreys' version is right is hard to determine without a careful study of Genesis. This husband and wife relationship which Hurley suggests is hardly an exact parallel with that of Christ and God. Christ left equality with the Father (Phil. 2:6) to come to this earth as God manifest in the flesh and has returned to reign in heaven as King of Kings and Lord of Lords. It is true that while on earth he submitted to the Father's will, but he also said, "I and the Father are one" and "If ye have seen me, ye have seen the Father." This is hardly the passive role Hurley posits and, in fact, Paul had started out comparing the woman to man relationship as like Christ to God; so it hardly seems justifiable then to make the man image *both* God and Christ.

Subject Because of Eve   A related text is 1 Corinthians 14:34, which the AV inaccurately translates as "but *they are*

commanded to be under obedience, as also saith the law."
More correctly the NASV puts "Let the women subject
themselves" and the NEB says that the women "should keep
their place." The Greek word used here (*hypotasso*) was originally a military term denoting inferior rank, and in the
papyri it was used for "appendages" to documents. The
Greek voice, however, indicates that this is something the
women are requested to do themselves, not something
others are to impose on them. Even if the law had said so
(which some regard as doubtful, as we shall see later), had
not Paul said elsewhere that Christians are no longer under
the law?

With regard to 1 Timothy 2:11-14, Hendriksen rejects
the view that these directions about women might be based
on contemporary conditions, insisting rather that they are
based on an eternal principle. This does appear to be Paul's
view: "Let the woman learn in silence with all subjection. . . .
For Adam was first formed, then Eve. And Adam was not
deceived, but the woman being deceived was in the transgression."

Literally this is "has become a transgressor" (Greek perfect expressing an abiding state—Guthrie). One commentator tells us this would better be translated by the English
past tense, but, according to W. Lock, Paul's idea was that
"the woman 'passed into and has remained in the position
of the transgressor.'" And Lock adds, "Possibly a quote
from the Jewish oral law, scornful of women, makes the
perfect tense more natural."

Not only the rabbinic schools but many theologians after
them, as well as most pagan religions, of course, have been
firmly convinced of the inferiority of women. In these
verses Paul's reasoning is that woman was made after man,
from man and for man, and she was deceived by the devil

while he was not. So some men have seen two basic principles implied here: first, that woman was created second and therefore subordinate to man; second, that woman is the weaker and more sinful sex. James Strachan tells us, *According to rabbinic casuistry, Adam was created first and sinned second, Eve was created second and sinned first. Therefore let woman recognize that she is both weaker and worse than man, and let her never attempt either to teach or control him! The premise of this argument—in which the rabbis to their shame delighted—finds no confirmation either in science or experience.*

If true, this last statement is certainly encouraging for women. But of primary importance, before the findings of science or experience, is whether there is ground for such a view in the Scriptures. It is interesting that J. B. Phillips, who spent much time studying the New Testament documents to make his paraphrase in modern English, also sees these views of Paul as having a rabbinic source, while at the same time coming to believe the Scriptures to be divinely inspired:

It was not until I realized afresh what the man [Paul] had actually achieved, and suffered, that I began to see that here was someone who was writing . . . by the inspiration of God himself. Sometimes you can see the conflicts between the pharisaic spirit of the former Saul (who could write such grudging things about marriage and insist on the perennial submission of women) and the Spirit of God who inspired Paul to write that in Christ there is neither Jew nor Greek . . . male nor female.

What Is Woman? In Scripture God did create two sexes, however, and obviously with some purpose. So we shall now try to discover what a female really is—primarily from Scripture, but with a brief glance at science and experience to see whether Strachan's statement is justified. We must go further back than the New Testament and scientists' and theologians' opinions to find what woman is. Is she a female human being, a part of humanity who happens to have certain biological and psychological differences from the male? Or is she an entirely separate and secondary species made just for the need of man? The answer to this important question is in the scriptural account of creation.

Our problem in understanding the Genesis account fully is that the Hebrew word for mankind is the same as that later made into a personal name for the first male, Adam. So we cannot always tell which meaning is intended; translators vary, some rendering "Adam," some "man." Genesis 1:26-31 says:

God said, Let us make man [kind] in our image, after our likeness, and let them have dominion over the fish of the sea, and over the fowl of the air, and over the cattle, and over all the earth. . . . So God created man [kind] in his own image . . . ; male and female created he them. And God blessed them, and God said unto them, Be fruitful and multiply . . . and subdue it [the earth]: and have dominion. . . . God saw everything that he had made, and, behold, it was very good.

We have a summary of this again in Genesis 5:1-2, and here modern versions bring out the meaning more clearly: "In the day when God created man, he made him in the likeness of God. He created them male and female, and he blessed them and named them Man[kind] in the day when they were created" (NASB). The New Berkeley Version has "He created them male and female. He blessed them and called them human at the time of their creation."

From these passages it seems clear that God created humanity, male and female, in his image, and gave them both dominion over the earth. Many theologians and rabbis ignore these, however, and look only at Genesis 2 where we find a more detailed account of the creation of man first and then woman. There we are told God formed man of the dust and then "breathed into his nostrils the breath of lives [plural in Hebrew]; and man became a living soul [being]" (v. 7).

After an unspecified period of time but still within "the sixth day" evidently, "God said, It is not good that man should be alone; I will make him an help meet for [lit: *corresponding to*] him" (v. 18). The animals were next brought before the man and he gave them names, "but for Adam there was not found an help meet for him" (v. 20). So God caused a deep, anesthetizing sleep to come over him. For some unexplained reason (possibly Jewish tradition) most English translations state that God took one of the man's "ribs," but according to Archdeacon Wilberforce this same word occurs forty-two times in the Old Testament, and is nowhere else translated "rib," but "side," "sides," "corners" or "chambers."

From whatever was taken from the man God made a woman, and brought her to Adam. McNally suggests that in great excitement he exclaimed something like: "At last! This is me!" Not another animal, but "bone of my bone and flesh of my flesh!" There is no suggestion woman was weaker physically or inferior because she appeared last. She could have been the crowning glory of creation since not until after her appearance does it say, "God saw everything that he had made, and, behold, it was very good" (Gen. 1:31). It is possible he delayed the formation of the woman so that the man would really experience a need for her and appreciate her the more when God gave her to him, rather than that she was a mere appendage or afterthought.

After the woman's formation the Bible continues, "Therefore, shall a man leave his father and his mother,

and shall cleave unto his wife: and they shall be one flesh"
(Gen. 2:24). They originated from one flesh, were separated into male and female, and in the divine provision of
marriage would again become one flesh. There is nothing
about the man ruling over the woman, only that he leave his
parents and cleave to his wife; together they would form a
new independent unit.

This divine pattern has rarely been followed in pagan
societies, or even Jewish and Christian in some areas.
Rather, the wife is taken into the husband's home to be
ruled by the mother-in-law and other males in the family.
Lange expresses the superiority of God's plan thus:

*With a stroke of the pen, the Biblical view of the world places itself
above the aboriginal doctrines of every heathen people, and all
national pride. . . . In a few lines it records the equality by birth of
the male and female sexes, the mystical nature of true marriage, the
sanctity of the married and domestic life, and condemns the heathen
degradation of woman, sexual lawlessness, and also the theosophic
and monkish contempt of sexual nature.*

What Is Woman? Biologically   All are aware of the ana-
tomical differences in the normal male and female body.
But that they are not separate species is evident from the
fact that some are born with a mixture, such as internal
female organs but a penis and empty scrotum outside. Or
what appears like a penis may prove to be an enlarged clit-
oris and the scrotum fused labia. That these are not so rare
as some suppose is indicated in the rabbinic teaching that
"one of doubtful sex" and "one of double sex" were included with women, slaves, children, deaf-mutes and so
forth, and thus not required to go to the temple for the
three great feasts.

We are not told in Genesis how God dealt with the part

he took from the man to form the woman, nor are we sure of what it consisted. Could part of it have been the X chromosome? Of the 46 chromosomes in the human body only two vary according to sex, although 23 are contributed by each parent. The female normally has two X chromosomes, the male an X and a Y. Some male criminals of low mentality and strong aggressive traits examined in prisons recently have been found to have two Y chromosomes, but there is no firm proof yet that chromosomes determine masculine or feminine traits.

Traditionally, society has tended to stereotype male and female, whereas modern genetical research recognizes a great range of types neither clearly male or female. From this Margaret Evening concludes that biological sexuality is not a major factor for "a new creature in Christ." "All human beings are a combination of both sexes and wholeness implies the accepting of one's femininity (the Anima) as a man, and one's masculinity (the Animus) as a woman."

Bernard Ramm, on the other hand, states that every cell in the body is coded masculine or feminine at conception. "If to be a woman or to be a man is a *total way* of existing, then the categories of 'superior' and 'inferior' are secondary. The issue then is that man lives his life in a *masculine* way, and the woman lives her life in a *feminine* way. The real issue is what is the Biblical doctrine of the feminine role, and what the Biblical doctrine of the masculine role?"

It would still seem possible to say that the masculine "way of existing" has been far superior to the feminine in many cultures! Apart from the husband-wife relationship, how do we live in a masculine and feminine way? The average day of a man and a woman high school teacher or doctor in the West would be lived very similarly, though granted their view of, and reaction to, their respective students or patients might differ a little; and he might shave his face and she her legs. On the whole, however, these two would live much more similarly than the male doctor and a man from a primitive tribe of West Irian. About the only thing the doctor would have in common with that man would be the power to impregnate.

Many today fear to indicate superiority or inferiority in relation to sex, and instead put the emphasis on "role." Actually this is neither a scriptural term nor a scientific one. While it sounds like a nice theory, useful in the problems of family, business and church relationships, doubt is now cast by some psychologists on its universal application to all men and all women. Not all agree, of course. Clyde Narramore claims, "When God created a companion for the first man in the garden of Eden he endowed her with the attributes of beauty, gentleness, love, a sensitive nature, and an understanding heart. These have become symbols of womanhood. They form the framework for development of every little girl." Nowhere does the Bible contain this prescription for girls, however, nor are any of these characteristics actually attributed to Eve.

While many have thought that male and female characteristics are inherent in the coded cells of the fetus, the theory is now advanced that they are conditioned by cultural upbringing. John Money, member of the National Institute of Mental Health's Task Force on Homosexuality, holds that there are only four imperative differences between the sexes: Women menstruate, gestate and lactate; men impregnate. These are basic powers or functions which cannot be interchanged (and will certainly affect action to some extent). Role is a much more elastic term, its connotation for the sexes being apt to change considerably in different ages and cultures.

Money's view is based on numerous observations and experiments. In addition to hermaphrodites, he cites the case of a family with identical twin boy babies. When these were circumcised, the penis of one was burned off by a surge of electrical current in the cauterizing needle. The parents were advised to bring this baby up as a girl, with the help of plastic surgery. Nine years later "she" seems psychologically to be a girl and behaves very differently from the identical twin brother. Such instances are creating doubt in some scientists' minds that major sexual psychological differences are immutably set by the genes at conception.

No one is yet sure what causes a fetus to be male or female, many conjecturing that it is determined by the time in the menstrual cycle at which conception takes place. Others suggest environmental stress is the factor. The father's sperm determines the sex, and if seven weeks before conception the Y-bearing sperms are damaged, the resulting fetus will be female. Statistics at Bristol University are even pointing to such things as prolonged smog, or sudden deluges temporarily softening drinking water, as being connected with sudden regional increases in female births.

From experiments conducted on animals, Money believes that in the normal process of sex differentiation, if the genes order the production of the hormone androgen the embryo becomes a male; otherwise it becomes a female. One interesting finding is that androgen not only shapes the external organs, but also "programs" parts of the brain, so that some types of behavior may come more naturally to one sex than the other. For instance, both males and females can "mother" children—the necessary circuits are there in the brain—but the "threshold" for releasing this behavior is higher in males than females. This is certainly an interesting conclusion from experiments with animals.

We also hear sometimes of human widowers who successfully "mother" their children; and many more widows, as well as wives of military men, who of necessity have had to take over "the managing of affairs" for varying lengths of time, and with some success. The two world wars also saw women undertaking almost all types of work on the home front, as well as many serving with the military forces.

What Is Woman? In Experience   After the first four years of life, Money thinks, there is little hope of breaking down the sex-role stereotypes which will usually have been established by parents and friends by then. But from war experiences noted above and my own school days (very different from America), I doubt this is so. In England then co-education was rare, so in my schools teachers and students were all female. Most of us were unaware the male was "the head." I hardly knew any males, having no brothers, no church young people's group. Females far outnumbered males in Europe then, and our education and training were not for the purpose of competing with men, but to prepare us for an interesting, useful life of benefit to community and country and at the same time ensuring economic security.

Maybe the "threshold" was higher for us, but we managed to have presidents of clubs, captains of sports teams, and so on. One girl I sat next to in high school was elected a member of Parliament, and a few years ago was made a life peer for her contribution to the country in the industrial relations field. Three of my class of thirty-five became doctors. The one who took me to the meeting where I found Christ has "manned" a clinic in an isolated area of India for many years, with only one nurse to help her. Another had the rare distinction of winning a math scholarship to Oxford University where there were few women in those days.

The publication marking the school's 80th anniversary records many interesting occupations. One of our earliest alumni was Dr. Edith Brown, founder of the famed Ludhiana Christian Medical College and hospital in India. One girl, a year my senior, is an architect who has worked in England, West Africa, Arabia and now India. Many are working in different parts of the world, some as missionaries, I am glad to say. Another is a lawyer, one a national broadcaster, one Principal of the Goodhousekeeping Institute which entails a wide national ministry. Others are journalists, agricultural specialists, as well as the more ordinary social workers, probation officers, teachers at all levels of education, nurses, doctors, secretaries, wives and mothers.

I realize now that we had a very fine, highly qualified and dedicated faculty who, though all were unmarried, must have felt they had some useful purpose in life. May I stress again that there was no idea of "competing with men," for no men teachers would have thought of teaching in girls' schools.

It was the same when I began my career as medical social worker in a Christian hospital for women and children in the slums of London. (Many women in those days were too embarrassed to go to a man doctor, partly because it was the Depression and they had no decent clothing, and the only free treatment was at the big teaching hospitals where there was always a group of observing male students present.) The two doctors, former missionaries, who started this little hospital were women, as were the visiting specialists and dentist, and also pharmacist and nurses. I began my Christian ministry to adults by taking my turn giving short evangelistic messages in this hospital's out-patient waiting room, and taking devotions in the wards. Our head was not a man, but Christ.

To summarize what a woman is, then, we find from Scripture that she is a human being made by God in his image, of the same bone and flesh as man, a counterpart for him, and together they are to have dominion over the earth. From science, observation and experience we further know there are three biological functions possible only to woman, and which determine some of her "roles" at certain times and circumstances; but at least some of her characteristics and roles may be the result of upbringing and training rather than inherent biological necessities. In any case, it appears that "roles" are not so much genetically determined as some theologians claim. And, therefore, there is a strong possibility that when Paul spoke of the headship of the man he was referring only to the marriage relationship.

Is Woman Subordinate Because Second? Most theologians and many others are quite happy with the rabbinic teaching that because Adam was formed first he was therefore naturally superior to Eve. As McNally points out, we do not know if the first human was solely male or hermaphrodite. But even if he were all male, creation was in ascending order, from creeping things, to animals, to man, to woman.

God created woman because man was incomplete or in a "not good" state without her. Paul Tournier in *To Understand Each Other* says that it is a mysterious fact that no one comes to know himself through introspection or in the solitude of his personal diary but only in his meeting with other persons. "That is why in the beginning of the Bible God says it is not good that the man should be alone. Man here means human being: It is not good that the human being should be alone." A human being needs fellowship; he needs a partner, a real encounter with another. He needs to understand others and to sense that others understand him.

Tournier claims, "Such is the very intention of God in instituting marriage, according to the Bible. Alone, a man marks time and becomes very set in his ways. In the demanding confrontation which marriage constitutes, he must ever go beyond himself, develop, grow up into maturity."

Many of the early commentators would regard this as heresy, for most believed Paul taught that since woman was created "of and for man" then the priority of man's creation places him in a position of superiority. Because she has been made as a "help" for him, that obviously means she is to be a kind of servant, someone to wait on him and someone for him to ejaculate into, as Muslims and many others have believed. "The woman is expressly the man's 'helper' which underlies her inferior position." She is certainly not meant to constitute a "demanding confrontation" to help the male to maturity!

Actually this Hebrew word *ezer* (help, succour) used of Eve in Genesis 2:18 is often used to describe God himself, the "helper" of his people. (See Ex. 18:4; Deut. 33:7; Ps. 27:9 and many other passages.) "It indicates one who comes to another's aid, ... and occurs in the Bible sixteen times of a superior, five times of an equal, but never of an inferior. Adam needed someone like himself; Eve, derived from his very being, supplied that need as his equal, as himself. This is a practice of oneness, not of subordination," the Boldreys tell us.

How different this view is from Calvin's: "The reason women are prevented from teaching is that it is not compatible with their status, which is to be subject to men, whereas to teach implies superior authority and status." It would be "a mingling of earth and heaven" for women to teach. He admits that even men teachers are subject to kings and magistrates, but says there is no absurdity in man's commanding and obeying at the same time in different relationships. This does not apply to women, however, "who by nature are born to obey." Calvin considered that this was the law God imposed on them from the beginning: "The teaching of Moses is that woman was created later, to be a kind of appendage to the man, on the express condition that she should be ready to obey him." Calvin not only held that this subordination was innate in woman's creation but also that God inflicted it upon woman by way of punishment. He sees this as rather a contradiction; but it must mean the subjection was less agreeable after the fall, he concludes. (I will deal with the latter in the next chapter.)

Even Clyde Narramore, who has wide experience and has given helpful counsel to thousands, after a good chapter on the unmarried woman says in *A Woman's World*, "Woman was not made for herself, but to complete the man." Is the implication that man *is* made for himself? Are not each made for God? Otherwise a single woman must constantly have the frustrating feeling that somewhere there is her Mr. Right whom she somehow cannot locate or else that she was born useless, with no purpose in life.

Hendriksen, in the quotation given earlier, also seems to have the idea that woman is a somewhat subhuman sort of creature when he likens her to a bird trying to swim under water or a fish trying to live on land. Why not use another human as an illustration, for example, a woman's trying to

179

preach or teach is as contrary to her nature as a man's trying to breastfeed a baby? But no, he likens women to something near the bottom of the creaturely scale.

It was a revelation and shock, at first, to read some theologians' views of women (the worst have been subject to editorial cutting), and I wondered if they wrote them thinking only other men would read them. Certainly I had never heard such things in sermons. I have found Paul Tournier's book, referred to earlier in the chapter, helpful in understanding some of the differences between men and women, however. He says men usually think in general theoretical terms, unrelated to people. They may expound magnificent theories, such as how the world should be governed or how to achieve universal peace, a pollution-free environment and so on, while if one of their wives were present she would probably say, "What about carrying out the garbage or taking an interest in your son's learning difficulties?" So probably most of these commentators had no real women in mind as they were expounding these passages. I, on reading them, immediately think of missionary women I have heard who are excellent speakers and of some men I know who would feel uncomfortable in the pulpit or before a Sunday school class.

In the introduction to the Bible study *Learning to Be a Woman*, K. G. Smith says some rather strange things. "Woman can only be called virtuous [in the sense of Prov. 31] when she has come to understand . . . her role in life as God intended. . . . Woman as God designed her can only be understood and appreciated as she is viewed in her position beside man." Then the author states frankly that his "entire study has been cast as it were in the framework of a man's point of view. After all, that's where a woman lives her life."

I suppose because until very recently women have been

in the minority in North America and therefore most have been married, men there have no conception of how such statements can affect a single girl who with no man beside her may be running an orphanage, a girls' school or a home for the blind in a foreign country or even having the responsibility of a widowed mother at home. It seems cruel and untrue to say that all the Christian women doctors, dentist and nurses at the little hospital I worked at in the slums of London could not be understood or appreciated, that they did not have "the secret of a woman's understanding herself" and even could not be "called virtuous," just because they did not live beside a man.

Certainly sex can be a beautiful experience. God himself planned it in love for his creation. But he did have a few other things in mind for his people to do. As we saw in the study of the Gospels, Christ rebuked the bystanders for evaluating his mother merely in terms of womb and breasts, and he did not tell Martha and Mary they ought to be married to be able to understand themselves. Paul actually said it was better not to marry, but devote oneself without distraction to serving the Lord.

Gladys Hunt's *Ms. Means Myself* has a good description of the spiritually liberated woman who has had a personal encounter with God:

If you were to ask her, "Are you most conscious of being a person or a woman?" she would affirm her personhood. Healthy women are conscious of being persons, as men are. They are persons who are women, not women trying to find personhood. It seems accurate to say that men make women most conscious of their womanhood, and I suppose the reverse is true as well. But an unhealthy woman is one who has no sense of self except as she exists in the eyes of men.

How true that is! I heard recently of a senior in high school who wasted and worried away her whole final year fearing she would not get a date for the graduation Prom. Sure enough, she didn't.

It has been a blessing for me to be acquainted with many men of spiritual, intellectual and administrative greatness, through membership in two large interdenominational missions, fellowship with IVCF in several countries and visits to many Christian conferences and well-known churches. God is obviously equipping and using these men for their varied work. But in some of these places one could also meet some women of higher caliber than some men. Why the rabbis should regard all men as automatically superior to all women just because Adam was created before Eve is hard to understand. Perhaps they took too seriously the law of primogeniture, sacrosanct in many countries but which God many times ignored, choosing Jacob above Esau, Joseph above his eleven brothers. Moses, Gideon, David, Solomon—none of them was the oldest in his family.

The Jewish people actually owed their existence to a few women God chose to use. Sarah was responsible for them in the beginning. They were not descended from Abraham's firstborn, and he had children by Keturah after Sarah's death. In Egypt it was the midwives who first thwarted Pharaoh's plan to exterminate the Hebrews; and then Moses' mother and sister with great courage and ingenuity saved his life so that he was able later to lead the people to freedom. Deborah and Jael delivered them from the mighty oppression of Jabin. Through Huldah God chose to reveal his will to King Josiah and the high priest, thus bringing about what was probably the greatest spiritual revival in the history of the Jews. Esther with great bravery and initiative saved the whole Jewish nation from extinction.

So we may conclude that priority of birth, or even creation, does not automatically and necessarily mean superiority in any other way. *The International Standard Bible Encyclopaedia* has some surprisingly strong words on this subject: *Man's historic treatment of woman, due to his conceit, ignorance or moral perversion, has taken her inferiority for granted, and has thus necessitated it by her enslavement and degradation. . . . Her inferiority, subjection and servitude . . . are the severest possible arraignment of man's intelligence and virtue. Natural prudence should have discovered the necessity of a cultured and noble motherhood in order to produce a fine grade of manhood.*

As we have seen, God has not always chosen to promote the firstborn to positions of great responsibility, nor has he always chosen to keep women in positions of subordination. It may also be well to remember that Christ promised that many who are first in this life will be last in the life eternal, and many of the last here will be first there (Mt. 19:30).

WOMAN: THE WEAKER AND MORE SINFUL SEX?

In addition to his view that the woman was made on the express condition that she be ready to obey the man, Calvin also felt that since she had seduced the man from God's commandment it was fitting that she should be deprived of all her freedom and placed "under his yoke." He admits that it could reduce women to despair to hear that the whole ruin of the human race was imputed to them, "for what will be the judgment of God upon them!" But Paul seeks to comfort them (in 1 Tim. 2:13-15), and make their condition bearable by reminding them that although they are suffering temporal punishment, the hope of salvation remains to them, Calvin declared. Paul, however, in Romans 5: 12-14 designated Adam as the cause of sin's entering the world.

Fairbairn had much the same view, although he seemed

to see the Fall as Eve's stepping out of her subordinate place and Adam's listening to her, rather than their eating the fruit God had forbidden:

Adam was first formed, then Eve. Thus did God give clear testimony to the headship of man . . . [to his right to stand under the law only to God] while the woman, being formed for him, stands under the law to her husband. And simply by inverting this relative position and calling—the helpmate assuming the place of the head and guide—was the happy constitution of paradise overthrown, and everything involved in disorder and evil. For this sorrowful violation of the primeval order with its disastrous results, the apostle fetches his second reason for fixing . . . the social position of women. "And Adam was not deceived, but the woman being altogether deceived fell," . . . a grand though mournful example, at the commencement of the world's history, of the evil sure to arise if in the general management of affairs woman should quit her proper position as the handmaid of man.

We saw in the last chapter that the Genesis account of creation gives no indication at all of the woman's being placed "under the law to her husband." The suggestion that her sin as the result of being deceived was worse than her husband's seems at first a strange argument to us, since we are inclined to think of sin done in ignorance as less culpable, even if not so regarded legally. In fact Paul himself, in 1 Timothy 1:13, states that he had been a blasphemer and persecutor, "but I obtained mercy because I did it ignorantly in unbelief." In other words he had been deceived by the devil, or his Jewish leaders, as to what Christianity was and had fought against Christ and murdered his followers. It is hard to see how Eve's succumbing to the reasoning of the father of lies was really worse, except perhaps that she was doing it from a state of perfection while Saul of Tarsus was a member of a fallen world.

Is Woman the Weaker Sex?   In his commentary on the Pastoral Epistles Donald Guthrie sees this point, saying, "The serpent deceived the woman, the woman did not deceive the man but persuaded him. Logically this should have made Adam more culpable, but Paul is concerned primarily with the inadvisability of women teachers, and he may have had in mind the greater aptitude of the weaker sex to be led astray."

This idea of women being more easily led astray is a favorite theme with many commentators. It is usually stated as a fact without proof, Eve's action being taken as typical of all womankind. It does not seem to be universally true in experience, however. In a recent Gallup Poll in Canada, for example, people were asked, "Do you believe that religion can answer all or most of today's problems—or is it largely old-fashioned and out of date?" In reply forty percent of the women questioned believed that it can answer most problems while only twenty-eight percent of the men thought so. Which group appears to have been most led astray? (Of course, *religion* is a very wide term, but in Canada the majority of people would still think of it as denoting Christianity.) Again, as has been mentioned already, by far the greater number of Christian heresies have been introduced and supported by men.

Then if Adam sinned with his eyes open, so to speak, just how was he better than Eve? Some have proposed that he only agreed to her suggestion out of a feeling of noble loyalty, determined to "cleave" to her whether in heaven or hell. It would be interesting to know what would have happened to the human race if only Eve had eaten the fruit, but it is profitless to speculate.

Included in the idea of woman's inferiority in the minds of many rabbis, theologians and the majority of mankind is that mentally and morally she is the weaker sex. Her "very creation" makes her unsuitable for teaching, according to Hendriksen, and the ancient rabbis used that as the reason for not teaching her the Torah. Paul does not state this specifically, but it is possible he implies it. One of the commentators in the *Pulpit Commentary* says, "This facility of deception on her part seems to suggest to the apostle her inferiority to men in strength of intellect, and the consequent wrongness of allowing to women an intellectual supremacy over men." Another presumes it is "the *ideal* woman and *ideal* man" which are meant. "It is because the man is supposed to have more brain and soul than the woman that he is the master." But he adds that he knows "not a few cases where the woman is greater in intellect, heart, and all moral goodness" than the husband.

Even if it were true that all women are a little weaker in intellectual capacity than all men, should that necessarily exclude them from taking part in any Christian ministry? In 1 Corinthians Paul tells his readers, "I came with no superiority of eloquence or of wisdom when I announced to you God's revealed truth. . . . My message and my preaching were not in persuasive, learned oratory, but rather in evidence of the Spirit and power, so that your faith might not rest on human wisdom but on divine strength" (1 Cor. 2:1, 4-5, Berkeley). So if God poured out his Spirit on his daughters and handmaidens wouldn't the results be the same? Great human intellect is not essential.

Further, Paul has said in 1:27-29, "God hath chosen the foolish things of the world to confound the wise; and God hath chosen the weak things of the world to confound the things which are mighty . . . and things which are despised, hath God chosen, yea, and things which are not, to bring to nought things that are: that no flesh should glory in his presence." What has been considered more foolish, weak, despised and unmentionable throughout the ages than woman? Therefore it is possible that God could be consistent with his character and intentions by calling and using women in the service of the gospel.

Another man, however, thinks that the "primeval order" —that woman was made for man—governs all her relationships, not only in the family and the church but also in the state. Someone else believes that "the way woman was worked upon by the tempter was emblematic of a natural disposition which unfits her for taking a public position."

As for woman's supposed inability in "the management of affairs" and her facility in being swayed by others, there have been countless cases which have disproved this as universally true, just as there have been a number of men who have had these two failings. Two examples of female competence must suffice here.

The first is a woman mayor in London, Ontario. According to one reporter's account,
since she assumed the mayor's chair, London's city council has experienced a refreshing decline in bickering, meddling, and time wasting. Backslapping has all but vanished. . . . Chunks of parkland have been saved from developers. "Nonestablishment" community groups have been astonished when the mayor came to convince them they had open access to city hall. Businessmen and developers have come to have a grudging respect for Jane's competence.

She also bicycles to work, or hitches a ride with the fire chief rather than piling up a big expense account.

I certainly don't believe men have the monopoly on bickering, meddling and time wasting; if all the council had been women, conditions might not have been better! In addition to this woman's competence, perhaps the presence of both sexes brought out the best in each. Surely God made us complementary not only for the sex act but for many other situations as well. Tournier says, "It is from woman, and under her influence, that man can acquire a feeling for persons. Civilization built by man alone would remain abstract, cold, technical and dehumanized."

Even more astonishing is the effect that the first woman medical student in the English-speaking world, Elizabeth Blackwell, had on her fellow students and professors at Geneva Medical College, New York. From D. C. Wilson's biography, *Lone Woman*, we learn that she felt God calling her to this work but met with every kind of difficulty as she pursued it. Every medical college kept its doors firmly closed against the intrusion of women. Finally the Geneva administration let the students vote, saying if even one was negative they would not admit her. Treating it as a hilarious joke, the students voted unanimously for this unknown monstrosity. The effect of her attending was that they began to behave like gentlemen in class, instead of drowning out the professors with uproar and dirty jokes, as had been the custom particularly in anatomy classes.

Elizabeth felt a divine command to alleviate suffering among women, and she took each step of her preparation with prayer. Even those she intended to help, however, usually spoke evil of her, imagining her to be like a notorious female abortionist in New York at that time. She had the greatest difficulty renting a room from scandalized landladies, and even women from the slums of New York's Ward Eleven, with a population of 54,000 and no medical facilities whatever, were slow in coming to her free clinic.

She eventually founded the New York Infirmary, providing the first possibility for women to intern in the United States and for nurses to train. Some of her unusual practices were to bathe patients, keep careful records and insist on the patient's name and doctor's signature being put on prescriptions. Elizabeth even had the then ridiculous idea that a surgeon should wash his hands and instruments before operating and that each patient should be put on a fresh sheet. The usual practice for a surgeon when operating was to wear his oldest frock coat which gradually became so full of dried blood and puss, it would stand up by itself.

Elizabeth Blackwell also helped found the first women's medical college in her native England. There her friend Florence Nightingale, only through the unhappy circumstances of war, was finally able to introduce the idea of women nurses and "revolutionize the whole health program of the British army." Florence's ideas were later incorporated into the military forces of many countries, including those of the north in the American Civil War, and have probably saved hundreds of thousands of lives since. How many men who experienced hospital care or the benefits of preventive medicine in the many battlefields of the world during this time honestly believe it would have been better to die rather than to have women think up such ideas or leave their "God-appointed place in the home" to become nurses?

It appears, then, that not all women are inferior in intellectual or administrative ability, nor are all easily swayed from a right purpose.

Is Woman More Sinful? When Paul used that perfect tense to describe Eve as becoming and continuing a transgressor, did he mean all that the rabbis implied about woman? It is hard to tell, but let us examine what Genesis states about the Fall. Satan, "the wiliest of all the field animals" and evidently bent on spoiling God's creation, came with subtle lies and half-truths to tempt Eve to disobey God's order. She evidently believed him and was tempted to try the fruit on three counts: It was good for the body, the eyes and the mind. These are the basis for most temptations, it seems, for both men and women; but Eve was certainly the first to take the fruit. Whether she actually ate it first is not absolutely clear but sounds probable. The Berkeley Version has "she took of the fruit and ate; she also gave to her husband, who ate with her. Then the eyes of both were opened" (Gen. 3:6-7). Was Adam alongside all the time, and could he have stopped her? We do not know.

The majority assert that God's later edict was Eve's punishment—that in pain and sorrow (although literally it is "labor," exactly the same word as is used later of the man) she would have many pregnancies and that "thy desire shall be to thy husband, and he shall rule over thee" (Gen. 3:16). Many have said that this means she would have an "inordinate sexual desire for a husband bordering on disease"! A few, however, have suggested that the latter part of God's words to Eve is "descriptive rather than prescriptive," that is, that God was explaining what would be the historical result of being the fallen wife of a fallen man. The Jerusalem Bible has "He will lord it over you," not something God usually approves of. "This was not a new enactment, but a prophecy of the treatment that should come to her," says H. A. Thompson.

In her thesis Jane McNally has an interesting quotation on the word translated "desire":

Drs. Bushnell and Starr follow the Septuagint, Peshitta, Samaritan Pentateuch, Old Latin, Sahidic, Bohairic and Aethiopic Versions in rendering the Hebrew word not "desire" but "turning." In the sixteenth century an Italian Dominican monk, named Pagnino,

*published his translation of the Hebrew Bible. Influenced by the
teaching of the Talmud–the bane of the Jewish race–he rendered the
word "lust" or sensual desire. The offensiveness of this rendering
becomes apparent when we apply it to Genesis 4:7 where God says
to Cain, "Unto thee shall be his desire, and thou shalt rule over
him" . . . In the word itself there is no suggestion of libidinousness.
. . . It seems to the author that Dr. Bushnell's rendering, "Thou art
turning away (from God) to thy husband, and he will rule over
thee," is well supported.*

The Boldreys also hold this view and believe that Eve
usurped *God's* authority, not Adam's, by suggesting he eat
the fruit.

Perhaps it is because the Bible mentions that after the
Fall Adam and Eve discovered they were naked that lustful
sex has been associated with the Fall. As we have already
seen, the oral law thought of the Fall as originating in intercourse between the serpent and Eve, and taught that the
poison she thus derived was then transmitted to the rest of
the human race. Some rabbis later amended this theory,
saying the poison was removed from Israel by obedience
to the law but remained with the Gentiles. Early church
fathers, too, particularly Augustine, continued some of this
idea that sex is evil.

Even in 1972, the religion columnist of a Canadian newspaper, writing on the subject of the ordination of women,
reported that the Anglican Bishop of Dorchester "naively"
said, "Women, unlike men, radiate sex, and their temperament is inappropriate in church. . . . Their ordination
would introduce distractions and earthiness into worship."
This view, according to the columnist, is based on "the arguments of Scripture and theology rather than sociology and
psychology"! It may be the argument of some theologians,
but I find no Bible verse expressing such an idea.

Most of us women really do go to church to worship God and learn more about him. There more than in any other place we probably think of ourselves less as women and more as human beings saved by Christ's loving sacrifice. One of the preachers I am privileged to hear frequently is my husband; but I do not ever remember my thoughts being turned to sex while listening to his sermons which are usually interesting and helpful; and certainly not while listening to any other preacher, good, bad or indifferent.

That statement by the bishop reminds me of something a wife said to Charles Shedd: "It seems that all my husband ever thinks about is sex. He interprets every move I make as a mating move. Do *all* men figure *all* of life by sex symbols *all* the time?" Shedd then made a wise observation:

When you examine this sort of thing carefully, you observe an important fact. Man's seeming obsession with sex does not prove that it means more to the male than the female. On the contrary, it may mean the opposite. His sex drive is more of a surface, physical thing. Yours is likely to be much deeper, a matter of spirit and soul. He is more easily aroused. Your stirrings come from farther away inside yourself.

This is how God made us, male and female, and yet how few of us really understand the differences between us and the opposite sex and act in the most helpful way to the other. I am told on good authority that even while preaching men may be sexually aroused; that is the way they are made, and women would be more restrained in dress and action if they realized this. On the other hand, it hardly seems fair for the bishop to impute *his* reactions to the women, label their temperament "inappropriate in church" and claim that the ordination of women would introduce "earthiness into worship." That is already there in his mind and makeup.

One cannot help wondering why the church has not advocated completely separate worship services for men and women if women are so distracting. But since they have been content to have two-thirds of the congregation female, in spite of the disturbing effect, surely just one (probably middle-aged) female in the pulpit would not be really disastrous. She could be robed or dark-suited, like Margaret Heckler who "conducted her first primary campaign in Massachusetts wearing a grey flannel suit at every appearance. It was designed to allow her to blend into the grey male political arena, so voters would be forced to forget she was a woman." While in training for the China Inland Mission we women candidates had to wear staid uniforms calculated to see us safely through the worst areas of London in our evangelistic endeavors. Seeing me in it, my fiancé would sometimes teasingly say he was tempted to break our engagement!

We will look at one more "Christian" view of woman, that of Tertullian, whom W. S. McBirnie calls "the first great genius, after the Apostles, among Christian writers." He certainly had a gift for making his meaning unmistakably clear! He thought women should "dress in humble garb, walking about as Eve, mourning and repentant . . . that she might more fully expiate that which she derives from Eve—the ignominy and odium of human perdition." Addressing women in *De Cultu Feminarum* he says,

Do you not know that you are each an Eve? The sentence of God on this sex of yours lives in this age: the guilt must of necessity live too. You are the devil's gateway: you are the unsealer of that tree: you are the first deserter of the divine law: you are she who persuaded him *whom the devil was not valiant enough to attack:* you *destroyed so easily God's image, man. On account of your desert–that is death–even the Son of God had to die.*

I find no Scripture saying that God will judge me for sins

committed by others before my life began or that women are the sole cause of evil in the world. But, thank God, Christ did die for us women as well as for all men who will receive him. Since the church is usually composed of a majority of women and since prisons are very sparsely inhabited by them (thirty men to one woman in England last year, while in North America just over ten percent of the inmates are female), does this mean that woman has to some extent learned her lesson or availed herself of God's provision more readily than man? Admittedly, though, there may be many things displeasing to God which do not rate a prison sentence.

Paul Tournier has some interesting observations about the greater proportion of women in the church:

In the whole area of sex, as in many others, . . . women are in a general and overall sense, more upright than men. Or, at the least, the man is in general more conscious of his sins than the woman is of hers. He is very conscious of his sexual lust, of his lying to his wife or to his competitor, of his cheating on income tax; perhaps this is one reason why he goes to church less willingly than his wife. He feels less at ease there. He feels a little pharisaical in thus publicly parading his piety, for he very well knows what is not right in his real life, and what he does not feel capable of putting right.

Perhaps this is also a reason why in church we see men who are generally less virile, less taken up in life's struggles: civil servants, teachers, men who can more easily lead a life apparently spotless. Like such men, women generally are less conscious of their sins.

He then gives as an example a mother-in-law who is cruelly jealous of a daughter-in-law, yet may convince herself she is acting in love and is a fine Christian!

His statement about a man's knowing "what he does not feel capable of putting right" would certainly be a good explanation of why many Japanese men who accept Christ disappear from the church after a year or so, given the close-knit web of big business and age-old custom in that country. But is Tournier referring to people in the West who are just nominal Christians, or does the same hold true for born-again men? I would hesitate to class them all as "less virile" and as liars and cheats.

Tournier has insight into human nature born of much counseling, but it seems to me that sins like lying, adultery and cheating, because they are, or have been until very recently, regarded by the general public as unethical, may cause a twinge in even a comparatively untender conscience. Such things as jealousy, pride, bad temper, prejudice regarded as principle and so on, require a real meeting with the Lord in humility and love, by both men and women, before they are appreciated for the horrible things they really are. The scribes and Pharisees were men who neglected this, and thus were frequently rebuked by Christ, while women were not (as far as we know from the record of the Gospels).

We can add the views of two rabbis, views which agree with many of the Christian theologians, and also with the pharisaic spirit. Jesus Ben Sirach said, "From woman was the beginning of sin, and because of her we all die," and, "No wickedness comes anywhere near the wickedness of a woman." Philo was more specific: "The woman, being imperfect and depraved by nature, made the beginning of sinning and prevaricating; but the man, as being the more excellent and perfect creature, was the first to set the example of blushing and of being ashamed, and indeed of every good feeling and action." I find it hard to discover in this statement any trace of that masculine trait Tournier speaks of, that is, that "the man is in general more conscious of his sins than the woman is of hers." Philo's conviction seems

to have been not so much of his sin but of the greater imper-
fection and depravity of woman, a view shared by many of
his fellow men through the centuries.

Does the Common Pagan View Prove Anything? Donald
Guthrie in his comments on 1 Timothy 2:11-15 notes that
the equality of the sexes received little recognition in ancient times, mentioning that Greek and Hebrew thought
were equally unsympathetic to the idea. He continues,

*The entire subjection of women mentioned by Paul relates primar-
ily to public worship as it was then enacted, and reserve must be exercised in deducing universal principles from particular cases. The
idea, however, of women's subjection is not only engrained in the
conviction of the mass of mankind [which would not of itself be a
justification for it, he allows] but also appears to be inherent in the
divine constitution of the human race.*

Perhaps adding a few illustrations to the ones I have
given earlier will help to emphasize the universality of this
idea.

Aristotle, for instance, said, "Because all women are
worthless, it is better to marry a little bride. She will do less
harm than a big bride." Solon, "for the convenience of all
conditions of men," listed what was available to them in the
way of women in the Greek states. First were wives, who
presumably were off limits to other men. They were kept
for the purpose of bearing legitimate children, existed for
the most part in ignorance and seclusion, and did not even
sit at table with their lords. From earliest childhood these
women had been allowed "to see as little as possible, hear as
little as possible, and inquire as little as possible." Second,
were the Hetairai, aliens or freed slaves who could not
marry Greek citizens. They were the only free women in
Athens, and were often courtesans to male citizens. A few

were of outstanding achievement and talent, and scorned marriage because of its enforced ignorance. With little stigma attached they could be unveiled and attend affairs with men whose wives were restricted to the inner house (in some respects quite similar to Japanese men and geisha until recently). It is thought that Damaris was one of these since no other type of woman would be at the Areopagus. Another group were public entertainers, often imported slaves who played the flute and danced at banquets; at the height of these affairs they would often be auctioned off to the highest bidder. Then there were concubines, slaves made members of the household with the knowledge of the wife. Lastly there were prostitutes procured by the state. The revenue from these enriched the public treasury, and so maintaining them was considered "a public-spirited measure." Not one of these situations for women sounds pleasant.

Further east, Siam had a proverb: "Teach a buffalo before a woman." From Hindu gurus we have such statements as "A woman's education should not go beyond the oven" and "A woman's object of worship is her husband."

W. M. Thompson, speaking of the Arabs in *The Land and the Book,* says that such a concept as the woman in Proverbs would be a moral impossibility to an Arab. The men dislike even to mention the women of their household. As examples of their "mildest and least offensive" proverbs about women he gives: "The only religion for a woman is to stay at home." "Everything is easy but women, and the mention of them." Another advises not to let women folk live in the upper story or learn to write; "treat them roughly and accustom them to hear 'No' for 'Yes' will make them insolent." A parting blessing often used by Arabs was,
May the blessings of Allah be upon thee.

199

May your shadow never grow less.
May all your children be boys and no girls.

This dislike of girl babies seems almost universal, and if men had discovered earlier what produces a boy baby the human race would have been in danger of dying out! As it was, women have often been blamed unmercifully, and divorced, for not bearing sons, although we now know it is the male sperm which determines sex.

For further evidence of the worthlessness with which girl babies have been viewed, consider this letter written in the year 1 B.C. by an Egyptian working in Alexandria to his expectant wife: "If it is a boy, keep it; if a girl expose it." This was a common practice, of course, and it is noteworthy that the early Christians did not expose their children and even began to rescue some who were abandoned.

The value which females were accorded until quite recently in China is well illustrated by Marie Monsen in her book *The Awakening*. She makes the horror stories of present day anti-abortionists seem pale by comparison. Monsen tells how in the early 1920s she and another missionary were teaching some Bible study courses to heathen women. She began to speak about infanticide.

Suddenly, in extreme amazement one of the women said: "Can't we do what we like with our own children?"

We talked about it a little longer. Then they broke down:
"Oh, I have killed three."
"And I five. . . ."
"I took the lives of eight of my children."
"And I of thirteen, but they were all girls."

All of the others had probably been girls, too, and only two out of the 16 women in the class did not confess themselves guilty of this.

Why is this conviction about the inferiority of women, and the fear or contempt with which they have been viewed, "engrained in mankind"? Why do Asians, for instance, believe the *Yin* stands for earth, moon, darkness, evil and the female sex, and the *Yang* for sun, heaven, light, goodness and the male sex? It could be that it is "inherent in the divine constitution of the human race," and I am quite prepared to believe that God in his inscrutable will has ordained it so. Yet as I read some of the Christian commentators' explanations and justifications for this phenomenon, I cannot help but feel that they sound more like the views and attitudes of the rabbinic and pagan worlds than like the words and actions of Jesus Christ.

As I pondered this problem and looked at commentaries on Genesis, I was struck with the words spoken to the serpent, "I will put enmity between thee and the woman" (Gen. 3:15). H. C. Leupold pointed out "the eminent propriety about having the one at whom the devil aimed his attack to be the one from whom his downfall emanates. Furthermore, by leaving open the question of from just which woman the Savior was to be born, God mocks the tempter, always leaving him in uncertainty as to which one would ultimately overthrow him, so that the devil had to live in continual dread."

I had always assumed the devil is more or less omniscient, but I have talked to several ministers recently who say this is not so. Otherwise, he would never have driven Judas to betray Christ and thus bring about the salvation of the world. So it has occurred to me that possibly because of Satan's dread of and hatred for the unknown woman through whom his downfall would come, he may have largely been responsible for the fear, contempt, degradation and rejection to which women have been subjected down through the ages. Even though Christ finally came to vanquish sin and the power of the devil, and placed women in a more favorable light, it has taken nearly two thousand years for this engrained conviction to begin to be erased.

We have noted previously that a Jewish male was taught to thank God daily that he was not born a Gentile, a slave or a woman. With this in mind Paul "asserted that these categories, with their antithetical privileges and priorities characteristic of fallen humanity and maintained by the law were abrogated in Christ" (as the Boldreys suggest). According to most English versions, Paul had declared to the Galatians that "there is neither Jew nor Greek, there is neither bond nor free, there is neither male nor female: for ye are all one in Christ" (Gal. 3:28). The Boldreys point out, however, that "most English translations fail to show the interruption caused by *arsen kai thelu* ('male and female') and thus miss its importance in the text." The series "neither . . . nor" has been interrupted by the use of "and" and the technical terms *male* and *female* (not man and woman) are used, so that it seems to be a direct quote from Genesis 1:27. They suggest the translation should be this:

There is neither Jew nor Greek.
There is neither slave nor free.
There is no "male and female."
For all of you are one in Christ Jesus.

"In other words, in Christ humanity transcends the male/female division. . . . For men and women, this implies the war between the sexes is over."

Thus any discrimination on the ground of being "female" is ended among Christians. True, we are still each individual men and women, with characteristics which will determine our actions at certain times, especially within the family. But the logical conclusion would appear to be that in the Christian community or church, especially, there can be no justifiable discrimination merely on the ground of sex.

If the female sex ever was the more guilty of sin, Christ has now removed that guilt forever. If it was weaker morally and intellectually, he delights to show his strength through such human weakness. He does not regard *woman* as a separate category any more than *slave* or *Gentile*; he sees each person as a redeemed soul, an essential part of his body, the church.

What Is Abrogated by the Gospel?   I finally found one recent commentator who has made on this subject some penetrating observations which deserve to be quoted at length. This is J. Stanley Glen in *Pastoral Problems in 1st Corinthians.* Referring to the tradition of the greater inherent sinfulness of women, which some think is indicated in 1 Timothy 2:14, he notes that both the Old and New Testaments are singularly free from texts derogatory to women, the most likely one in the Old Testament being Leviticus 12 where the birth of a girl baby rates twice as long a period of ceremonial uncleanness as a boy.

L. L. Hastings, however, in *The Wonderful Law*, suggests that this may have been for the purpose of preserving the balance of the sexes by "assuring that the births in families composed mostly of girls would be less frequent than in those in which boys predominated, and that because of this regulation 112 Jewish males were born to every 100 girls." Someone else has concluded that the eighty day period of separation was actually a boon to womanhood and provided a baby girl with a better start in life through a longer period of constant care by the mother—certainly a happy result from a law taken to indicate that greater defilement is caused by girl babies.

The idea of "uncleanness" resulting from childbirth was held by the Roman and Anglican churches until recent times. It appears in the latter's prayer book as the "Churching of Women." Dyson Hague tells us in *Through the Prayer Book* that it was

a quaint survival of a very ancient custom that was common both in the Eastern and Western church, possibly an echo of Old Jewish doctrine and practice. The idea was that the defilement of childbirth prevented a woman from going to church . . . without some sort of purification service. So all through the middle ages an English mother after childbirth came to the door of the church wearing a veil like that worn at confirmation. After several psalms and prayers the priest led her by the hand into the church, chanting in Latin "Enter into the temple of God that thou mayest have eternal life. . . ." The whole service was evidently intended to show the woman was being readmitted to the privileges of the church.

It is hard to see why doing what she was supposed to be created to do should be the means of separating her from the church.

Glen comments,

The conception of the greater sinfulness of women was not, however, incorporated into the theology of late Judaism in a consistent way, and so does not influence the main thrust of its doctrine of sin to any extent. In this respect Paul is not exceptional. His extra-biblical traditions relevant to women were not incorporated into his primary doctrines, even in his thought of Adam in relation to Christ, where contrary to what we might expect, there is not even an allusion to Eve [1 Cor. 15:21-22]. These traditions lie, as it were, alongside his primary doctrines, and alongside his Gospel, unassimilated by them, so that his conception of women, as of slaves, is not essentially challenged.

The problem that emerges concerns the extent to which the subordination of women, even within Paul's Christological interpreta-

tion, is justified. From the evidence reviewed, doubt has been expressed regarding the origin of such subordination, viz., its derivation from extrabiblical tradition. In other words, before the question of the place of women in the church can be answered, we have to answer the prior question of whether we recognize the traditions which were mainly responsible for Paul's view of women. Are these traditions properly regarded as coming from the canon of Scripture? Or if they do come within the canon of Scripture, do they fall within the category of those things which are abrogated by the Gospel? This latter question prompts another—one which makes us conscious that the whole matter of the place of women in the church depends on our doctrine of the Scripture: what are the things abrogated by the Gospel, and how are they abrogated?

A very interesting question indeed! It reminds me again of the apostolic injunction that believers must refrain from blood and things strangled. How and by whom has this been abrogated? Glen goes on to suggest that the issue cannot be evaded, as Calvin tried to, by saying that Paul's words in Galatians 3 refer only to Christ's "spiritual kingdom." Glen thinks Jew and Gentile were meant to be reconciled in their outward relationships as well as in spirit:

The Gospel is a power that shattered and continues to shatter slavery, not only as a spiritual and mental form of bondage, but as an institution. And no less can be expected of that slavery which historically has been of greater scope, and of much more serious and tragic consequences than the formal institution of slavery itself—the subordination of women to men. . . .

What we have to consider, therefore, is whether in a Christological interpretation of the relation between the male and female we should speak of the subordination of the latter at all. For if the subordination is mutual, as Ephesians 5:21 so clearly indicates in its exhortation to be subject the one to the other, we should recognise it. To do otherwise, and on Rabbinic grounds for the sake of maintain-

ing the legalistic authoritarianism of a patriarchal order, is to undercut the Gospel. At this point, of course, most men will find it hard to surrender the last vestige of masculine pride which this order sustains, and to see their relation to women governed exclusively by the Gospel . . . of grace. Their masculine pride, confronted by the agape of the cross, will perhaps die harder than religious pride, which is represented by the righteousness of the law.

It takes a man to say that, and no doubt some will consider him a traitor to his sex, but it was a surprise to find other men with similar views much earlier. Theodore Weld, assistant to the great evangelist Charles G. Finney, said more than a century ago, "The devil of dominion over women will be one of the last that will be cast out" of man. Seth Cook Rees, one of the founders of the Pilgrim Holiness Church, believed one of the marks of the ideal church is no distinction as to sex and had his wife as co-pastor. "Nothing but jealousy, prejudice, bigotry and a stingy love of bossing in men have prevented woman's public recognition by the church. No church that is acquainted with the Holy Ghost will object to the public ministry of women" was his opinion.

If the reasons given by Paul to Timothy for not letting women teach—that she was born after man and was deceived by Satan—were completely unknown before, then we would certainly assume that they were a revelation of God to Paul. If they were repeated elsewhere in Scripture, that would make a stronger case. But since they are a clear reference to Rabbinic teaching, it does seem possible the comment may be of no greater weight to us today than was Paul's quotation to Titus that "The Cretians are always liars, evil beasts, slow bellies" (Tit. 1:12-13) and that he should act accordingly. At least one commentator suggests that in the Greek the first words of 1 Timothy 3 ("This is a true saying") could belong equally to the end of chapter 2 and no one has found evidence of such a saying about bishops. Chrysostom was also of that opinion.

Where does this leave God's ideal woman? My guess is that she will not be concerned with trying to prove any personal equality with men, although she will be ready to help alleviate known discrimination and hardship to others. I may seem to some to be trying to prove equality in this book, but my aim is rather to indicate that individuals should be judged on their capacities and not their sex. The purpose is really twofold: first, to defend Christianity from the claims made today that it has downgraded women and to show that it is in fact some ecclesiastics and commentators, as well as almost all of paganism, which has done this—not the Founder of the Christian faith nor the general trend of the Scriptures; and second, to find evidence that many great women missionaries were not necessarily out of God's will. These will be dealt with in a following chapter.

I think the ideal woman's concern will be, in the spirit of Christ and the words of Paul, "Let each esteem other better than themselves" (Phil. 2:3). She will be aware of her own weakness and tendency to sin and will therefore seek the more to depend on Christ and abide in him. She will with humility seek to glorify Christ and try to make him known by others, since in that same chapter to Timothy Paul says that God wishes all to be saved and come to the truth.

With regard to the ministry of a church (perhaps largely from custom), I think that generally speaking both men and women prefer to listen to a man preach, and his public ministry will normally have a wider impact than a woman's. I do not see how a mother with children, or even most wives could give their time to the twenty-four-hour-a-day duty expected of most ministers. On the other hand, I cannot find in Scripture that that is necessarily the church pattern God had in mind. If a woman has a clear assurance of God's leading and no desire to "lord it over" anyone, it seems difficult to deny the validity of an audible ministry for her in Christian gatherings and in personal witness, since God himself has chosen to use many women in this way as the next three chapters will show.

The later rabbis taught it would "lower the honor of the congregation" to have a woman read the Scriptures in the synagogue although provision had been made for it in the early days. But does it necessarily lower God's honor? Certainly woman was first to sin, but Christ has now offered himself the full sacrifice for all sin. There is no need for a temple building or priesthood. Paul said to *all* believers, "Your body is the temple of the Holy Ghost.... Ye are not your own, ye are bought with a price: therefore glorify God in your body, and in your spirit, which are God's" (1 Cor. 6:19-20). Also, "Ye are the temple of the living God; as God hath said, I will dwell in them and walk in them" (2 Cor. 6:16). Verse 18 of the same chapter makes it quite clear that this is addressed to both women and men.

Once one has grasped this amazing and humbling truth that hour by hour our body is the temple of God, then a man-built church on the day of the Lord does not seem quite the awesome place a human priesthood would like us to believe. That good bishop may feel that woman's temperament is earthy and unsuitable in church, but whatever we once were, however weak and however deep in sin, God assures us: "Ye are washed ... ye are sanctified ... ye are justified in the name of the Lord Jesus" (1 Cor. 6:11). He deigns to make us his temple, holy, "perfect through my comeliness which I have put upon thee, said the Lord God" (Ezek. 16:14).

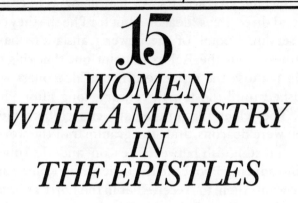

15
WOMEN WITH A MINISTRY IN THE EPISTLES

Having considered at length the role to which Paul may or may not have intended to restrict women, we will now look at some women mentioned by name in the Epistles who were obviously more than benchwarmers.

Remarkably, most of these references occur in Paul's greatest doctrinal document, his letter to the Christians at Rome. This important theological statement about sin and salvation addressed to believers in the prestigious capital city was entrusted to a woman named Phoebe, who carried it the several hundred miles from Corinth to Rome—an arduous, even dangerous journey in those days. And some consider this "a responsibility only given to someone of official standing."

Phoebe   In the Greek text Phoebe is called a *diakonos*, a word which appears twenty-two times in the New Testament. In eighteen places the AV translators render it "minister" and three times "deacon," but for Phoebe they change it to "servant." Some of the newer translations have put "deaconess," but the Boldreys point out that this is misleading because the separate office of deaconess was not established until the fourth century, long after Phoebe's death. They claim that in the early church both men and women were deacons, and "the grammar of the word does not even distinguish between 'deacon' and 'deaconess.' "

In introducing Phoebe to the believers in Rome Paul says that he wants them to "receive her in the Lord, as becometh saints, and that ye assist her in whatsoever business she hath need of you: for she has been a succourer of many, and of myself also" (Rom. 16:2). Many have imagined from this that she must just have given him hospitality, done his laundry and possibly run a soup kitchen, and that she needed a little cash for this. But actually the word translated "succourer" in the AV and "helper" in other versions is the feminine form of *prostates* (Latin *patronus*), "the title of a citizen in Athens who took charge of the interests of clients, and persons without civic rights." It literally meant "one who stands before, a front rank man, a chief, leader of a party, protector or champion," according to Liddell and Scott's lexicon. Phoebe was therefore obviously a woman of means and position and may have acted as Paul's "patron." He was therefore asking the men and women believers in Rome to "stand by" her, to be at her disposal in any way she required, since she had "stood forth" as a leader or supervisor. It is the same kind of consideration he asks for other church leaders and elders in 1 Thessalonians 5:12-13 and 1 Timothy 5:17.

With the thought of Phoebe as a deacon in mind, let us look at 1 Timothy 3:1-12, where Paul is advising Timothy on the kind of people he should (or should not) appoint to positions of leadership in the church. He refers first to overseers ("bishops" in the AV), deacons and women ("wives" in the AV). I, like many other people, because of this translation imagined Paul to be referring to the wives of the overseers and deacons. Hendriksen states, however, *That these women are not the wives of the deacons, nor all the adult women of the congregation is clear from the syntax: "The overseers therefore must be . . . ; deacons similarly [must be] . . . women similarly [must be]. . . ." One and the same verb (i.e., "must be") co-ordinates the three, the overseers, the deacons, and women. Hence these women are here viewed as rendering special service in the church, as do the elders and deacons. They are a group by themselves.*

Hendriksen does not see these women as constituting an "office of the church," endowed with equal authority with men deacons, but rather as "servants or assistants" who perform ministries "for which women are better adapted." Like most commentators, he does not specify what these might be. The early church held that the women deacons of 1 Timothy 3:11 introduced women to the overseer, assisted in the baptism of women and visited the women's part of the homes.

Father Jean Daniélou, in his *Ministry of Women in the Early Church,* also agrees with this. He assumes that baptism was by immersion, that the whole of the body was anointed with oil before the ceremony and that for women candidates this had to be done by a deaconess. (A priest might only anoint the head where women were concerned.) He quotes the rule of an early monastic order, which states, "When she who is baptized comes out of the water, the Deaconess shall receive her, instruct her, and look after her, to the end that the unbreakable seal of baptism may be impressed

211

on her with purity and holiness." He tells us there was an Ordination of Deaconesses in the Eastern church, the *Apostolic Canons* giving the following instructions:

Thou shalt lay thy hands upon her in the presence of the Presbyters, the Deacons, and the Deaconesses, saying, "Thou who didst fill Deborah, Hannah and Huldah with the Holy Spirit, thou who in the Temple didst appoint women to keep the holy doors, look upon thy servant chosen for the ministry, and give to her the Holy Spirit that she might worthily perform the office committed unto her."

Canon 15 of the Council of Chalcedon added that "a woman may not be ordained under 40 years of age." However, there does not appear to have been complete agreement about this ordination of deaconesses, the Council of Orange (441) decreeing that "deaconesses should not be in any way ordained." The problem was finally resolved when deaconesses were absorbed into the nunneries. The order was suppressed in the Latin church in the sixth century, not until the twelfth century in the Greek church.

Modern theologians are just as divided on their views of Phoebe and these other women. Ryrie tells us that Lightfoot and Godet both think Phoebe had an official ecclesiastical office; but, although he agrees that *prostates* does imply official ruling, he maintains "there is not a single instance of a woman holding such an office (unless Phoebe herself be the single instance, but such an exception from the Bible would be strange in view of the fact that there is no extra-Biblical exception)." He then rather unconvincingly says, "The writing of 1 Timothy was not many years after that of Romans, which fact (if it be true there were no deaconesses in Romans) does not help the argument that these women were deacons."

In A.D. 112, however, a secular source did speak about women deacons. Pliny the Younger wrote to the Emperor

Trajan, who had recently appointed him governor of the province of Bithynia, and asked for advice about whether he should persecute Christians, since he knew little about them and the "contagious superstition" was spreading in every age, class and sex in city and countryside.

I thought it the more necessary to inquire into the real truth of the matter by subjecting to torture two female slaves who were called "deacons," but I found nothing more than a perverse superstition which went beyond all bounds. Therefore I deferred further enquiry in order to apply to you for a ruling ... because of the number of those who were accused. For many of every age, every class, and of both sexes are being accused.

Why did Pliny choose these female slaves as the ones to torture? Was it because they were least important, hardly regarded as human, or because he thought they could be made to talk more easily? I think it sounds as if Pliny really wanted to know what this Christianity was, and so chose these two because they held some kind of official position and therefore would know most accurately. Ryrie, however, thinks it would be "risky" to use this evidence to prove the existence of a female diaconate: "It would be very difficult to prove that these women acted in any officially designated capacity." It is equally difficult to imagine Pliny using the term if it did not mean anything.

As for women weakly giving way under torture, the opposite was often true. A number of cases are recorded, but one must suffice here. During the severe persecution of Christians in the Rhone valley mention is made of a slave girl called Blandina. F. F. Bruce tells us,

Others feared least her physical frailty might not be equal to the torture. In the event she showed herself such a noble confessor her example strengthened all the others; her tormentors exhausted themselves in their attempts to make her renounce Christ. "I am a Chris-

tian," was her steadfast reply; "and there is no wickedness among us."

Another hint that possibly women held an official position is found in 1 Timothy 5:1-2, which reads, "Rebuke not an elder [literally, *presbyter*] but intreat him as a father, . . . the elder women [presbyteresses] as mothers." W. K. Brown takes the term as indicative of office, Bishop Ellicott and many others as merely referring to age. However, the fact that the office of presbyteress was abolished by the Council of Laodicea in A.D. 363 indicates that at some period prior to that there must have been such a ministry.

There is also the possibility of a special order of widows, as indicated in 1 Timothy 5:9-12. This will be discussed in chapter 18.

Women in Rome   We return now to Romans 16, where after his commendation of Phoebe Paul sends greetings to a list of people evidently well-known to him. No one today knows for certain how the church at Rome was started, but it has been assumed by many that since some of the visitors to Jerusalem at Pentecost were from Rome they returned to the great capital of the empire with the message of the gospel. Obviously there was always much travel to and from Rome by business and civic leaders, and evidently some of Paul's converts and acquaintances from his missionary journeys were now there. Of the twenty-six people listed, eight are women, which is rather surprising.

At the head of the list is Prisca, followed by her husband, Aquila. When this couple is first mentioned in the Scriptures, the husband's name comes first; and some have reasoned that because on four later occasions the order is reversed this indicates Prisca's greater prominence in the work. Paul, by the way, usually refers to her by the more formal Prisca, Luke by the diminutive Priscilla.

The AV's rather weak translation of the word Paul uses to describe them is "helpers" (Rom. 16:3). The same word is applied elsewhere to Timothy (Rom. 16:21 and 1 Thess. 3:2) and to Luke (Philem. 24). It means literally "fellow-workers in Christ Jesus" and "signifies they were professional evangelists and teachers" (Adolf von Harnack). As we have seen in Acts, Luke records how they taught Apollos, leading him into the full Christian truth. Chrysostom, in his paraphrase of Acts 18:26, omits Aquila's name entirely, mentioning Prisca alone as the teacher of Apollos. Even Ryrie admits that "it would be difficult to prove that the 'helping' did not include public teaching, and even possibly missionary work."

Paul says not only that they both risked their necks to save his life, but that "all the Gentile churches owe them a great debt," indicating a wide spiritual ministry. In Rome, as formerly in Ephesus, a church met in their home. This has now been excavated under the ancient Church of St. Prisca, and indicates she came from an aristocratic Roman family.

Tertullian, in spite of his devastating accusation of women, also wrote, "By the holy Prisca the Gospel is preached." There are various scraps of evidence in the early records of the church of Prisca's well-known, acceptable ministry in Rome, and some writings known as *Acts of St. Prisca* were extant until the tenth century.

At least five theologians believe that Prisca wrote the letter to the Hebrews. They offer the following reasons to support this view: (1) The letter is anonymous. The name of a woman might have prejudiced its acceptance. (2) She was known to be an illustrious teacher. Much of what is said in Hebrews might well have been said to Apollos. (3) She had close associations with Paul and Timothy, as the author of

Hebrews obviously had. (4) At the time of its writing Paul seems to be dead, and in his last known letter he had specifically mentioned Timothy, Priscilla and Aquila. (5) The author seems closely identified with the readers of the letter (Ephesians seeming to fit best) and hopes to return to them. (6) In the list of heroes of the faith several women are mentioned. (7) There are a number of practical references to both childhood and parenthood. (8) The letter contains the theme of pilgrimage ("Here have we no continuing city" 13:14) as if the writer had personal experience of this. Four nautical terms are mentioned in the Greek, although these are not all apparent in the English translation, and Prisca made at least four sea voyages. (9) Hebrews shows a great interest in the tabernacle, natural if the author and her husband were tent and leather makers. (10) Sometimes the author's voice is in plural form, which might indicate the inclusion of Aquila. R. Hopper in *Priscilla: Author of the Epistle to the Hebrews* adds further evidence gleaned from Qumran, the excavations in the catacombs at Rome and second- and third-century writings which make this theory seem a strong possibility. Probably, though, we shall have to wait until we get to heaven to know for certain who wrote this letter.

Others in Paul's list at the end of Romans are "Mary who has worked hard for you"; Narcissus, who seems to be the head of a household; Tryphena and Tryphosa, a cute sounding couple whose names mean "Dainty" and "Delicate," who may have been twins and who certainly were "workers in the Lord"; and "the beloved Persis" who had also "worked hard in the Lord" (NASB). Then there is Julia, about whom we are told nothing; and two whose names are not given: the mother of Rufus "and mine," and the sister of Nereus.

One of the most intriguing names is in verse 7: "Salute Andronicus and Junia, my kinsmen, and my fellowprisoners, who are of note among the apostles, who also were in Christ before me." The AV has the name in the feminine with which the majority of ancient commentators agree, but newer versions have put it in the masculine, Junias (perhaps because the translators felt from some of Paul's restrictions on women that it ought to be a man?). The problem is caused by the phrase "who are of note among the apostles." I had always assumed that this meant these two people were known to the twelve. This is not how the early church viewed them, however. Chrysostom wrote, "Oh, how great the devotion of this woman, that she should be accounted worthy of the appelation of 'apostle.' "

The meaning of the word *apostle* is "one sent forth." It was first used by Jesus in sending out the Twelve—"It had reference to the particular mission, not the 12 men." In Acts it is the ordinary name for the Eleven, but denotes not a restricted office but their worldwide missionary service.

The Eleven always regarded Matthias as making up the Twelve, not Paul, we are told, but Paul continually claims to be an apostle. He seems also to apply the term to Apollos, Silvanus, Timothy, Barnabas and the Lord's brother James. He also refers to "false apostles" in 2 Corinthians 11:13, and obviously people would know at once that these were not any of the Twelve. Lambert concludes,

The true differentiation of the New Testament apostleship lay in the missionary calling implied in the name, and all whose lives were devoted to this vocation, and who could prove by the issues of their labors that God's spirit was working through them for the conversion of Jew and Gentile were regarded and described as apostles.

Charles Hodge agrees that the word means "messengers to the churches," but feels the word has a fixed meaning (that is, it is restricted to the Twelve) and is never used in Paul's writings except "in its strict official sense." In the Didache, however, written about A.D. 100-120, the title is applied to the whole class of missionaries who did not settle in any one church; and there obviously is a little tension developing between these and the local church leaders:

But concerning the apostles and prophets, you are to act thus according to the ordinances of the Gospel. Let every apostle, when he comes to you, be received as the Lord; but he shall not remain more than a single day, or (at the most) a second; if he remains three days he is a false prophet. And when he departs, let the apostle receive nothing but bread.

So we must take our choice whether we regard Junia as the wife of Andronicus and a fellow missionary with him (possibly among those who believed at Pentecost since they were believers before Paul) or else as a man.

Women in Other Epistles   Turning to 1 Corinthians, we hear of Chloe. She was probably a wealthy and important member of that church who felt she should send a report to Paul about some of the disturbing things going on there (1 Cor. 1:11). In Philemon Paul addresses Apphia, Philemon's wife. This couple also had a church in their home, as did Lydia and Nympha, the only one of the church at Colossae whom Paul mentions by name in his greeting (Col. 4:15). The AV mistakenly has her name in the masculine. The "true yoke fellow" mentioned in Philippians is thought by many to be Lydia since early in the letter Paul addresses those who fellowshiped with him in the gospel "from the first day"; and of course Lydia and other women at the river were the first converts in Philippi. Euodia and Syntyche (Phil. 4:2) may have done some evangelistic work since Paul describes them as "those women which laboured [strug-

gled] with me in the gospel . . . with other my fellowla-
bourers."

In Paul's second letter to Timothy, written from Rome,
he says, "Eubulus greeteth thee, and Pudens, and Linus,
and Claudia, and all the brethren" (4:21). Who was this
Claudia? No one is certain, but E. M. Blaiklock in *The Century of the New Testament* has this to say:

*Who were Pudens and Claudia whom Paul mentions as prominent
members of the church in Rome? Were they the Pudens and Claudia
mentioned in the epigrams of Martial twenty years later? Martial's
Pudens was a centurian of distinction, Claudia was a British Princess, and Pudens' wife. An inscription in Chichester [England]
tells how a piece of land was presented by one Pudens to the British
chief Claudius Cogidubnus, Aulus Plautius' ally. Was this the
same Pudens, later influenced by his commander's wife?*

Surprisingly, the non-Jewish harlot, Rahab, is mentioned
in two epistles, Hebrews and James, being commended in
the first for her faith and in the second for her action which
demonstrated her faith. The word *harlot* did not necessarily
have the same connotation for the Jew as for us today. The
New Berkeley Version has a footnote on the Levite's concubine saying, "Deserting her bed and board [and returning to her parental home!] was sometimes reason for the
designation 'harlot.' " Jeremias also notes that rabbinic
teaching was that "the harlot of Leviticus 21:7 refers only
to a female proselyte or a freed bondwoman, or to one (Is-
raelite by birth) that suffered connexion of the nature of
fornication." Only a proselyte girl who was converted before the age of three years and one day might marry a
priest, since the Jews assumed that all Gentile women and
girls would practice prostitution and "so on principle assumed that no Gentile knew his own father."

Lastly, there is the second letter of John, which is written to "the elect lady." Many commentators assume that an apostle would hardly bother to write to a woman and that since the church has been called the "bride" of Christ John was actually writing to a local church and its members. But it is the whole church which is the "bride," not each local group. Nowhere else in Scripture is this term "elect lady" used, however, and furthermore the opening sentence here is almost exactly parallel to that in John's third letter addressed to a man named Gaius. (Compare "The elder unto the elect lady [Kuria] and her children, whom I love in the truth," 2 John 1, and "The elder unto the wellbeloved Gaius, whom I love in the truth," 3 John 1.) J. Sidlow Baxter says, "Some would have us believe that this lady and her children were really a church and its members; but verses 5, 10, and 12 convince us such an idea is far-fetched and artificial. We are glad that at least one little epistle in our New Testament is addressed to a Christian *mother*."

All these women, and what is said about them, may seem few and insignificant in comparison to Peter and Paul and their important work. There is no doubt that the majority of full-time Christian workers have been, and probably always will be, men. There is actually more said about a number of these women, however, than about the majority of the Twelve, most of whom are not mentioned by name after the resurrection. Considering the Jewish teaching on women, the prevailing customs of the day and the record of most other religions, these many references are indeed remarkable. These women obviously enjoyed Paul's and John's respect and warm appreciation. They were not merely silent benchwarmers but hard workers for the church, the gospel and the Lord. They have been followed through the centuries by many other sisters in the faith who have heard God's call to Christian service.

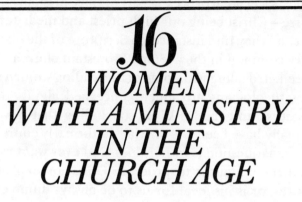

16
WOMEN WITH A MINISTRY IN THE CHURCH AGE

To begin our brief look at women in church history, we will turn first to Father Daniélou, who states,

In considering the question of the part played by women in the ministry of the church we have to take into account two primary pieces of evidence. On the one hand there has never been any mention of women filling strictly sacerdotal offices. . . . On the other hand all Christian history—and particularly in the first centuries—shows that women have played a considerable part in missionary work, in worship and in teaching. The difficulty . . . is that the status of the ministry exercised by women has never been clearly defined. The forms it has taken have varied with the particular time and country concerned. Its characteristics have changed according to different needs. Sometimes it has been integrated into the ordained ministry and sometimes it has been regarded as a lay activity.

I find several points of interest here. Evangelicals do not

consider "sacerdotal offices" a part of the Christian church, of course—Christ being our high priest and mediator. But neither can they find instances in Scripture of the one-man ministry common in the average Protestant church. As we have seen, in dealing with some of the leading women in the Epistles theologians are much concerned about "office" and "status" and the "risk" of concluding that a woman could really have been an "official" in the early church. To me the vital question is rather does God ever want women to open their mouths to proclaim Christ or explain the Scriptures, or is his ideal for us to be always dumb except about trivialities? These "official church services" and many "offices" are purely man-made institutions.

Second, it is interesting that women's Christian activity has varied in different times and in response to different needs, a flexibility which one hopes was due to being available to obey Christ's commands. It seems probable to me that it is in times of great spiritual vitality or revival that women have had the desire and been given opportunity and even encouragement to engage in Christian work. At other times many church leaders have been concerned largely with their own status and privileges or have been toying with theological trifles or the letter of the law.

Daniélou says it was particularly in the first centuries (others have said century) that women played a considerable part in Christian activity. Was the reason for this that at first everyone was full of the joy of the Lord, the power of the Spirit and the expectation of Christ's soon return? Paul's letter to Timothy was personal. His view on woman's not teaching does not appear in any other New Testament document, and in those days of slow communication it perhaps took a number of years before all the churches even heard about it. It is not found at all in the Chester Beatty

Papyri, copied in Egypt in the third century. The beginning and end of this manuscript are missing, and some scholars say there would not have been room for the Pastoral Epistles at the end; others claim, however, that the writing had begun to get smaller in the last half and they could probably have been crowded into the available space.

At any rate, these letters were known to Tertullian (A.D. 155-222), and he thoroughly approved of what Paul said about women. With regard to some of the women Marcion had won over to his church (which claimed to be the sucessor of the Pauline communities) Tertullian wrote, "What effrontery we find among these female heretics! They actually dare to give the church's teaching, to engage in disputations, to practice exorcism, to promise cures, perhaps even to baptize!" (Praescript 41:5; de Baptismo 17:4). Daniélou says the baptizing was probably not found even among the Marcionites but admits there is a "delicate problem" because these things, and much of the part women played according to apocryphal works of gnostic tendency in the second century, were in fact identical with the part played by women in the earliest Christian communities. But two things stand out, he concludes: On the one hand, there is a tendency on the part of these female prophets to magnify their privileges; on the other hand, the heretical leaders exploited them.

I can well imagine that their new freedom, after centuries of being shut in their rooms, might go to the heads of many women. But did they get out of hand and "magnify their privileges" more than many of the men? Was not the whole tendency of the church to magnify the "office" of under-shepherd so that it gradually became one of scholarly superiority or mediating priest, then "lord spiritual," "prince of the Church" and at last infallible pope, none of which can be found in Scripture. Finally, the medieval church was about as contrary as one could get to the way of life and the teachings of Christ or Paul.

Daniélou tells us that apart from sacerdotal functions "each male ministry had a sort of female counterpart of a subordinate character" and implies several times that the instruction of women would be "less important." It is not surprising, therefore, if some of them fell to the persuasions of the male heretics who were astute enough to realize that women can be effective workers, just as Jewish leaders in Acts used women to stir up opposition to Paul. Is it possible, therefore, that if women were thoroughly grounded in the truth (and the dangers of error) they could be as effective for Christ and the church as they seem to have been for the enemy?

If woman's "official" status in the church was uncertain and varied, the changed lives of individual Christian women had a remarkable influence which Tertullian enlarges upon. Clothed with the beauty and simplicity of Christlike character, they no longer needed the former splendor of outward adornment.

They exchanged the temples, theaters, and festivals of paganism for the home, cared for their husbands and children, graciously dispensed Christian hospitality, nourished their spiritual life in the worship, service and sacraments of the church, and in loving ministries to the sick. Their modesty and simplicity were a rebuke to and reaction from the shameless extravagances and immoralities of heathenism. That they were among the most conspicuous examples of the transforming power of Christianity is manifest from the admiration and astonishment of the pagan Libanius who exclaimed, "What women these Christians have!"

Into the Dark Ages and Beyond According to Dwight M.

Pratt in the *International Standard Bible Encyclopaedia,* women's activity in the early church came to its zenith in the fourth century:

The type of feminine character produced in that era is indicated by such noble examples as Emmelia, and Macrina, the mother and sister of Basil; Athusa, Nonna, Monica, respectively mothers of Chrysostom, Gregory and Augustine. Like the mother of Jerome and Ambrose, they gave luster to the womanhood of the early Christian centuries by their accomplishments and eminent piety. As defenders of the faith women stand side by side with Ignatius and Polycarp in their capacity to face death and endure the agonies of persecution. The roll of martyrs is made luminous by the unrivalled purity, undaunted heroism, and unconquerable faith of such maidens as Blandina, Potamiaena, Perpetua, and Felicitas, who, in their loyalty to Christ, shrank not from the most fiendish tortures invented by the diabolical cruelties and hatred of pagan Rome.

So it seems that women were not always easily swayed from the right and, according to Pratt, were even responsible for what little light there was in the Dark Ages. He continues,

In the growing darkness of subsequent centuries women, as mothers, teachers, abbesses, kept the light of Christian faith and intelligence burning in mediaeval Europe. The mothers of St. Bernard and Peter the Venerable witness to the conserving and creative power of their devotion and faith.... The best royalty of Europe was converted through her [woman's] influence. Poland and Russia were added to European Christendom when their rulers accepted the faith of their Christian wives. Clotilda's conversion of Clovis made France Christian. The marriage of Bertha, another Christian princess of France, to Ethelbert introduced Roman Christianity into England, which became the established religion when Edwin, in turn, was converted through the influence of his Christian wife.

We may well question the value of this wholesale "establishment" of Christianity in a country (although it can have beneficial results in humane and biblically based legal systems) but we cannot help wondering whether, had there been some of these godly women in official capacities in the church, it would have sunk to such dark depths.

Supposing many generations could have been mistaken in thinking God forever forebad women to teach or use their voices in a Christian gathering, it might be the church's loss and have deprived women of opportunities of service; but one would think that at least it would prove a great impetus to men to give themselves to the Lord's service, since everything depended on them. Yet there is little evidence of this. During the great persecutions following the early spread of the gospel, both men and women bravely witnessed to their faith in the midst of torture and death. Then gradually women were downgraded, though at first allowed a very limited ministry as official widows and later as deaconesses. Then the more spiritually inclined among them, and the men, were syphoned off into the new nunneries and monasteries, while the main body of the church was increasingly taken up with internal disputes and with manipulating political power.

Once Christianity became respectable and gained political status through the favor of Emperor Constantine, many in the empire wanted, or were even pressured, to join the church. But there seems to have been little evangelism beyond that. The theologically suspect Nestorians (who allowed women "astonishing powers" such as "access to the ambon to read the Gospel, and the right to cense but not to bless the incense," according to Daniélou) did manage to take the gospel as far as China in the seventh century.

Too often, it seems, theologians were more occupied

with saying what women should not do and claiming masculine privilege than in successfully stirring men to their responsibilities. The Eastern church, however, allowed women wider scope of service than the Western.

In the sixteenth century the Jesuits and a few other communities dedicated themselves to spreading their faith throughout the world, but for a long time the Protestant reformers, no doubt occupied with clarifying and establishing their beliefs and practices, apparently didn't feel much responsibility for those beyond their ken. Most of them took seriously Paul's words to Timothy about women, as we have seen in the case of Calvin, but with regard to women not speaking he concludes: "The discerning reader should come to the decision that the things which Paul is dealing with here are indifferent, neither good or bad; and that they are forbidden only because they work against seemliness and edification." Martin Luther, writing to the Bohemian Brethren on the errors of the papal system, said that the "royal priesthood" mentioned in 1 Peter 2:9 applied not only to priests but to every member of the congregation—each man, woman and child—and that therefore women should be allowed to conduct baptisms and communion services. Among Puritan reformers the Congregationalists had an order of deaconesses and the Quakers also recognized a spiritual ministry of women.

Nineteenth-Century Renewal With the great spiritual awakenings and evangelical revivals of the eighteenth and nineteenth centuries the situation changed, however, with regard to both missionary vision and the ministry. In 1739 John Wesley appointed women as "class leaders" in Bristol and by 1787 wrote, "We give the right hand of fellowship to Sarah Mallet, and have no objection to her being a preacher in our connexion so long as she preaches the Methodist doctrines and attends to our discipline."

In America, even before 1800 the Free Will Baptists permitted women to serve as preachers and itinerant evangelists. With the great renewal under Charles G. Finney such preaching "became widespread and developed into the full ordination of women," according to Donald and Lucille Dayton in their article "Women As Preachers: Evangelical Precedents." They point out that this emancipation of women was closely linked with emancipation of slavery. The anti-abolitionists built a "Bible defense of slavery" based on biblical instances of slavery and Paul's admonitions to slaves, while those in opposition who developed a "Bible argument against slavery" discovered that the same questions arose in relation to the "woman question."

The Congregational Church ordained its first woman in 1853, the Wesleyan Methodists in the early 1860s and the Methodist Episcopal in 1869. A. J. Gordon, famous Baptist preacher and major influence behind the founding of Gordon College, was a strong abolitionist and argued for the "Ministry of Women" in an article in 1894. Jonathan Blanchard, founding President of Wheaton College, also an abolitionist, affirmed that "the first alteration which Christianity made in the polity of Judaism was to abrogate this oppressive distinction of sexes" in which "women had almost no rights; they were menials to their husbands and parents." Miss F. Willard, founder of the World's Womens' Christian Temperance Union, served for a while as an assistant to D. L. Moody, speaking on this subject in his crusades. In 1880 she wrote *Woman in the Pulpit,* "a sophisticated and exegetical defense of the ministry of women," the Daytons tell us.

These waves of spiritual renewal awakened the church to

its responsibility for the evangelization of the world, and women again aided in this missionary movement, as they had in the first century. If the Great Commission was literally only for the eleven men who heard it and their ecclesiastical descendents, one can only conclude that God played a cruel trick on thousands of men and women throughout the nineteenth and twentieth centuries who have sacrificially given their lives to take the gospel to every part of the world open to them, sincerely believing that God had specifically and individually called them to do so. For those who may not be familiar with missionary procedures, may I illustrate from my own experience, which is probably typical of the specific call of God received by thousands of others.

On the evening of January 8 of a certain year my husband-to-be and I became engaged. He pulled out his pocket Bible, and in the car we read together the twelfth chapter of Romans. Afterwards in prayer we did what Paul besought the Roman believers to do as their "reasonable service"—presented our bodies a living sacrifice to God.

Right from the time of that prayer we had the feeling that somehow things were going to be different. Bill was a promising young business executive, and there was no financial reason to delay marriage; yet as friends began to ask the date we sensed no liberty to make plans.

Finally we felt we *must know* what God's will was for us and accordingly arranged that the following week, on February 22, we would spend the evening praying for clear guidance. On that morning the verses in the *Daily Light* were on guidance: "What man is he that feareth the LORD? him shall he teach in the way that he shall choose" (Ps. 25:12). "Thy word is a lamp unto my feet, and a light unto my path"

(Ps. 119:105). "Thine ears shall hear a word behind thee, saying, This is the way, walk ye in it" (Is. 30:21). "I will instruct thee and teach thee in the way which thou shalt go: I will guide thee with mine eye" (Ps. 32:8). "O LORD, I know that the way of man is not in himself: it is not in man that walketh to direct his steps" (Jer. 10:23).

On the commuter train to the small Christian hospital for women and children in a slum area of London where I was a medical social worker I met a friend who talked about the Japanese advances into China. At lunch one of the doctors talked about a missionary friend of hers from China. In the late afternoon, as I sat waiting for Bill to come and drive me to his home, a Christian German Jewish nurse, a recent refugee from Hitler whom I had never spoken to before, came in. She sat beside me, held out a little pile of magazines in her hands and said, "Have you read these?" Seeing the unfamiliar title, *China's Millions,* I said no. She put them into my lap and, as I casually leafed through the bundle, right in the middle I saw a smaller sheet headed "For Intending Candidates of the China Inland Mission." God seemed to say at that moment, "This is for you."

My husband's guidance came in quite a different way, fortunately, for we learned later that the China Inland Mission at that time did not accept married candidates, and everyone, man or woman, was required to have a clear personal call to that mission's work and to spend two years in China before marriage. The CIM also required the same Bible courses for both sexes in a concentrated two year program at their own training school for candidates, and there was a strong emphasis on homiletics, our instructor obviously not sharing the view that he was trying to teach fish to live on land.

Three Great Christians Who Encouraged Women's Ministry I had no idea at the time that there was anything unorthodox about this; I did not know that women Christians were supposed to be different from men. In our in-depth study of Corinthians we were taught that the meaning of *laleo* was probably "chatter," and we were told of the prevailing conditions in China. Only recently have I realized that the great missionary movements of the last century, which included women as full members and made the gospel of Christ available to millions of new hearers, were due in large measure to the faith and practice of three great men of God, Hudson Taylor, D. L. Moody and Fredrik Franson.

I do not know if Hudson Taylor ever stated his reasons for using women as missionaries, but since he was a person of such close relationship with God, we can only believe that he felt convinced that God was directing him to include women. His faith in God was so great that when he was finally assured that it was a divine command he arranged to send twenty-six new missionaries to open up inland China without any guaranteed or visible means of support in the conviction that he was "to move men through God by prayer alone," both as proof that it was God himself who had called the mission into being and also so as not to divert money from existing mission agencies.

D. L. Moody's life and gigantic spiritual impact is usually regarded as a result of his yielding his life wholly to God after someone said to him, "Moody, the world has yet to see what God will do with a man fully consecrated to him." Moody silently vowed, "By the Holy Spirit in me, I'll be that man." Here again, it is hard to think that God would allow him to encourage women in Christian service if God did not approve of it.

In the biography of Malla Moe, probably one of the longest serving and most fruitful missionaries in South Africa with a ministry to both men and women, we are told how not long after she emigrated from Norway she attended one of Moody's meetings. At the close he announced, "All Christians get to work, and all sinners come forward." Although already a Christian, Malla wished to hear more of the great evangelist and stayed for the after meeting for new converts. When Moody found she was a Christian, he kindly but firmly put his hand on her shoulder and shoved her out of the room, saying, "Why don't you go to work?"

As Malla slowly began her hour-long walk home she wondered where she could start, and then she saw through an open saloon window two men talking and drinking. She went straight in, told them they should go hear Moody preach and get saved, then fled, terrified. This broke the ice for her, however, and from then on she became active in Christian service. Not long after, she met Fredrik Franson who told her God wanted her in Africa. After much hesitation she became a member of the Scandinavian Alliance Mission he had formed in the United States, originally in response to Hudson Taylor's request for one thousand young volunteers for inland China. Franson had offered to find one hundred from among Scandinavians in America and Europe, and later sent others to Japan and South Africa.

Franson's name may not be familiar to English-speaking people today since much of his work was done among Scandinavians. He was a Swedish immigrant who became Moody Church's first commissioned missionary. He was the human means of revival coming to a number of countries of Europe and of starting various missionary societies there. Also, he personally visited many parts of the world and led individuals to Christ in each, sometimes with little understanding of their language and without an interpreter.

Franson's motto was "constant, conscious communion with Christ." And many have testified to the evidence of this in his life. He felt so strongly that women should be used in the evangelization of the world that he wrote a little book (*Prophesying Daughters*) on the subject, in German, which was later translated into Swedish. E. Torjeson of The Evangelical Alliance Mission (formerly the Scandinavian Alliance) is presently preparing a full biography of this remarkable man whose many-faceted genius was divided among so many countries that few have an adequate idea of all he accomplished. Mr. Torjeson has made available to me the main points of Franson's little book, for which I am extremely grateful.

Much of it we have already covered in this book, but it was from him I learned of Martin Luther's letter to the Bohemian Brethren. Franson carefully notes every reference to any kind of speaking ministry or responsible position of women in both the Old and New Testaments and comes up with nearly one hundred. He considers 1 Timothy 2 and 1 Corinthians 14:33-35 as referring to a wife's relationship to her husband.

He emphasizes that it is very strange that the two verses which appear to be against women's spiritual ministry should be made the basis of a doctrine *which the whole thrust of the rest of Scripture is against*. He warns that this is how heresies usually begin, illustrating the point by telling of a church in California at that time which was filled with toys. Singling out the verse "Except ye become as little children, ye shall in no wise enter the kingdom of God," this group had made a period of child's play compulsory for their members each Sunday!

Franson's constant, conscious communion with Christ had made him very aware of how much the rest of the world was missing not having heard of such a savior and friend. Since two-thirds of the existing church wherever he went was comprised of women, Franson felt the complete evangelization of the world could never take place without their help.

I was interested to learn that he too took the passage in Acts 2 as a clear mandate for the ministry of women, in particular to do evangelistic and missionary work, since those at Pentecost spoke of "the wonderful works of God" to people of many nationalities.

I had been very hesitant to treat the verses in Timothy in any way which might seem to some to "wrest" them from their true meaning and have never voiced such views in any meeting since the missionary's purpose is to proclaim Christ and nurture disciples. But as I came to write on this passage, I heard one of America's finest contemporary pastors preach on the subject of women along some of the lines I was taking, and the same week I learned the gist of Franson's book. So at least I was assured that I, a woman, was not initiating heresy! More recently I have read of many other early evangelical leaders holding similar views.

As I reflected further and prayed about the matter, and remembered the hundreds of thousands in parts of the world known to me, who were saved from a Christless eternity through those they commissioned or the personal ministry of these three great men—Taylor, Moody and Franson—a new thought came. The fact that these men had little formal theological training certainly had its dangers. But one consequence was that instead of studying the traditions of their churches, they went to the Bible itself with hearts and minds willing to do God's will. Each of them seemed to enjoy such a close intimacy with the Lord that he perhaps was able to reveal his wishes to them to an unusual extent. Consequently, though all made some mistakes, they were men of such great character, vision and spiritual maturity that they did not fear their masculine privilege being threatened, nor were they concerned with ecclesiastical status or a comfortable church or medical practice at home. Their one desire was that, by utilizing every believer completely committed to do God's will, Christ might be made known throughout the world in the minimum time.

I believe that was Paul's aim, too. Whether in his words to Timothy he means he does not allow women to act like accredited teachers and in an arrogant attitude to men, or whether he is saying he does not let wives act that way to their husbands in public, I do not know. I am sure that what he wrote must have been right for that time. Very few women were educated or experienced in leadership, and since he believed Christ's return was near he probably never envisaged the need, or opportunity, for women to train as accredited teachers.

Jeremias' description of a wife in *Jerusalem in the Time of Jesus* clearly shows the situation then.

The wife was obliged to obey her husband as she would a master. . . . the husband was called rab*—indeed this obedience was a religious duty*

Like a non-Jewish slave, and a child under age, a woman has over her a man who is her master; and this likewise limits her participation in divine service, which is why from a religious point of view she is inferior to a man.

One famous rabbi is reported to have given his proselyte Gentile slave his freedom on the spot in order to make up the quorum necessary to hold a synagogue meeting. A woman presumably could not be considered free from the bondage of marriage even for so important a matter as that, though she could be divorced for such trifles as burning the dinner. In view of the above idea of married women in religion, it seems probable that Paul had in mind wives and not necessarily all women in his restriction. Now that in many countries wives are no longer legally "under a master" does this make any difference? This is something the theologians must continue to wrestle with.

Two things, at any rate, are certain. One is that God allowed Paul's letter to Timothy to be included in the canon of Scripture. The other is that he has raised women to positions of leadership and teaching in both Old and New Testaments and in the church age, as will be further demonstrated in the following chapter.

17
WOMEN WITH A GOD-GIVEN MINISTRY IN THIS CENTURY

For those whose experience has been limited to reading or writing commentaries in a seminary library and attending a long-established, well-staffed Western church, it may be helpful to hear more of the work of some of the women God has called to a spiritual ministry in various parts of the world.

Marie Monsen   China has been an especially fruitful field for the ministry of women, possibly because of the encouragement given them by Hudson Taylor and Fredrik Franson. Mr. and Mrs. Louis Gaussen of Britain, with whom I traveled to China in 1939, sent home the following report in 1932:

The Lord has been reviving the work during the last few weeks, largely through the visit of Marie Monsen for special meetings.

237

Two men school teachers and one of the two evangelists were brought to real life and blessing. . . . It seems possible to have a strong mental belief in the facts of the gospel, without any conception of the fundamental moral demands of it, and so for church members to be still involved in the toils of the appalling sin in a heathen land without developing a sense of sin. The Lord seems to have given Marie Monsen a special ministry to such.

Leslie Lyall, Candidate Secretary of the mission, in writing the preface to Marie Monsen's *The Awakening*, says,

Among foreigners, Anna Christiansen of Denmark became well known throughout China for her revival and evangelistic ministry . . . and many more [women] were God's instruments in the years of revival, particularly after 1929.

But first of them all, the pioneer of the spiritual "new life movement," the handmaiden upon whom the Spirit was first poured, was Marie Monsen of Norway. Her surgical skill in exposing the sins hidden within the church, and lurking behind the smiling exterior of many a trusted Christian—even many a trusted Christian leader [and these included both Chinese and missionary men]—set the pattern for others to follow.

He goes on to tell us that she began a movement which swept through the churches of China like a cleansing gale of wind. This continued through the 1930s and "gave an impetus to the transference of full authority from the missionaries to the churches." That God was behind this strategic and timely move was soon to become evident when the Japanese invasion occurred shortly thereafter, to be followed later by the communist takeover.

How did Marie Monsen, a faithful, Bible-believing missionary, come to disregard that statement of Paul that he did not allow women to speak or teach men? From this book, *The Awakening*, we learn that her first two terms of service in China were largely unremarkable, except for considerable sickness. Her work among women saw little response. She had an increasing burden that what she was seeing in China was very different from the growth of the churches of the Acts. Gradually the conviction came that only through persistent, believing prayer would God's Spirit begin to work in power. So she began and continued this kind of praying for a number of years, until finally a small breakthrough came in those classes she held for women which we told of earlier. That was the first time in twenty years she heard anyone confess to infanticide, although everyone had said they knew others who did it.

Then word came in 1927 that all missionaries were to evacuate to the coast because of communist uprisings and the murder of a number of Christians and some missionaries. Marie did not stay long in Shanghai, but felt a strong compulsion to go to Manchuria to learn something of the revival which she had heard had been strong in Korea in 1907 and had spread from there to Manchuria. A well-known Danish missionary and his wife, the Emil Jensens, were working there, and on Marie's writing to ask if it would be convenient to visit, they replied with a warm welcome, though she was not personally known to them.

The Jensens had been working there for thirty years, and a large regional conference was just about to begin, with a well-known Chinese Bible teacher as the speaker. The evening before the conference was to start a telegram arrived, saying the speaker was prevented from coming.

Tears streamed down Mr. Jensen's face, and he said, "I *can't* speak at these special meetings. The delegates have heard me over and over again all these years. I have prayed so much for revival and expected it to come.... I had hoped so much from these meetings. I *can't* speak any more, they are tired of hearing me." Then he turned to

Marie and said, "Now you must take the meetings."

The delegates were already gathered, expecting to hear the widely known Pastor Chia, and now it was being suggested that a mere woman, and unknown at that, should speak to them. To Marie the situation seemed impossible.

"I must have this evening alone. I will give you my answer early tomorrow," she finally said.

It was a long night. "He hath chosen the things that are not" was the word from the Lord which finally overcame her hesitation. She also adds that "two of Finney's special Scriptures came back to me, 'Through the law cometh the knowledge of sin,' and again 'The law hath been our tutor to bring us to Christ.' And then I put my faith in the truth that 'the Spirit uses the Word.' On the strength of these words it was possible to speak at the conference."

A deep work was done, many of the delegates coming for personal interviews. Marie notes that she discovered later that the state of mind in which the Jensens and hundreds of other missionaries shared at that time was the work of the Holy Spirit, part of the necessary preparation for revival.

Later, she was able to return inland as far as Peking, was invited to help in various missionary efforts there and saw an even greater work of God. Part of this was at the theological college of a large American mission. The principal, a doctor of divinity, was looking depressed.

"If we cannot have revival here, we may as well close this college and go home. The students are a wild set," he told her.

"Are they all alike?"

"There is only one exception, but even he does not believe that Jesus is the Son of God."

It was not a bright prospect. Only the principal and two

elderly lady missionaries attended that mission's prayer meeting, she found. But she had some Swedish missionary friends also evacuated in Peking, and they agreed to pray for her throughout the week of meetings, all day and into the night, as they were able.

The first evening Marie was, as she describes herself, "like a little laughing stock of a David going out to meet Goliath. The students were proud and condescending, and had been 'ordered to go to the chapel and listen to a woman.' They said afterwards they could not remember ever having seen a woman in the pulpit before."

At the close of the first meeting they were openly supercilious and amused at having to attend such a performance, and stormed out laughing, shouting and bandying between them the texts that had been used, while still within Marie's hearing.

Back she went to report to her prayer helpers, and now they were able to pray for individuals, especially the ringleader, "The Scorner" as they nicknamed him. One, in the depths of agony for his soul, prayed, "Lord, if Thou canst not turn his heart by any other means, hold him over the mouth of the abyss, till he sees it yawning beneath him."

Space does not allow details of the wonderful work God began among those students, of how thefts and many other sins were confessed. But this is "The Scorner's" testimony: "These have been terrible days. What a merciful God we have, he spares himself no labor in order to apprehend the lives he has ransomed. He held me over the very mouth of hell. I saw people I knew there. There is agony there. He wants to save us from that."

Monsen continues,

It was a painful crisis for a proud heart, but he was sincere, and experienced personally that the blood of Christ cleanses from all sin and ungodliness.

I met him again a few years later. He said then that, after his experience of salvation, he had visited all the churches in which he had preached as a student, and asked to be forgiven. "It was an ungodly man who preached to you then," he had said, and added that many had been saved in those places since.

One more incident must suffice, this one connected with Monsen's ministry to missionaries. Hundreds used to gather each summer at Peitaiho, a well-known health resort in northeastern China, where they could escape the desperately sticky heat experienced inland. Meetings were usually arranged with famous speakers from the home countries. Early in 1929, God somehow impressed upon Marie that she was to go to Peitaiho that summer and minister there. She felt utterly unsuitable and said, "Lord, if I am to go there, I leave all the arranging to Thee; I will not take a single step myself in that direction."

A week later a telegram from the organizers of the summer conference arrived, asking her to go there. She did not go joyfully, but clung to the verse that God chooses "the things that are not." Another which had been a particular help to her was the RV wording of Psalm 68:11, "The Lord giveth the word: the women that publish the tidings are a great host."

She was met at the station by a missionary from the Leaders' House:

He was a smartly set-up American and did not take long to size up dowdy me. Before we reached the house, he was through with me, very patently so—as was natural!

One of the great missionary leaders, who had his own reasons for having asked to sit beside me at supper, came to exactly the same conclusion. He, too, had soon finished with me. Again it was perfectly reasonable. I sat there feeling like a sparrow at the heron's dance. This missionary leader was a godly man and a man of prayer. His name was known in missionary circles all over the world. Like everyone else, I had a real reverence for him. He made a deliberate effort to clip the wings of the "sparrow," and he did it very thoroughly. He met with no opposition, nor a single word of self-defense.

However, as in Peking, she had some fellow intercessors. She was given the first of the morning sessions to speak at, and the "clipper of wings" sat right in the front row. Before the first meeting was over, he seemed to turn into a huge mountain over which her message could not reach to the crowd of missionaries behind.

But as prayer was made, the mountain grew smaller, and finally vanished. Only the man remained, and the messages began to sink deep into hearts. One day the "clipper of wings" waited for her and said, "I want to tell you that God is blessing my soul through your messages." He asked her to meet with him for prayer a number of times after that. From then on her days were so filled with personal interviews "there was seldom time to go to supper, and only once for a quick dip in the sea, which lay just below the Leaders' House." She adds that all the missionaries who asked for talks had one thing in common: They felt themselves failures, unfit for the Lord's service. Only the sense of call kept them on the field. And this seems an essential before God can really work in revival. No confidence in mere masculinity, training, modern methods and equipment gives rise to this, only a deep conviction of one's emptiness, of the reality that "without me ye can do nothing" (Jn. 15:5).

After mentioning Anna Christiansen, a Danish missionary of the CIM who did similar work for twenty-three years in nineteen provinces of China at the invitation of missionaries, Marie Monsen tells us, "In time of revival it was not unusual for humble-minded men to say to the women God in His grace was using: 'I thought God would use me in the work you are doing.' One even said with tears: 'We men have failed. Now the Lord is showing us what He can do through women.' "

As time went by, the Lord also called men into the revival ministry, some missionaries but more especially gifted Chinese evangelists: "There was a very blessed fellowship in the great rescue work, and one was continually reminded of the apostolic words: 'There is neither male nor female.' We who saw the Spirit working could say with one voice as never before, 'We believe in the Holy Ghost.' He was great, the rest of us were of little account."

I have given some detail of this woman's ministry so that any who are unacquainted with such a phenomenon may realize both how God may lead, use and bless a woman, and also the opposition from other Christians with which she may be faced.

Contemporary Contributing Women This century has seen other similar great women led of God, for example, Mary Slessor and Malla Moe in Africa, Amy Carmichael, who formed the famed Donavuhr Fellowship in India, and Gladys Aylward of *The Small Woman* fame, an English servant girl whom God led by incredible ways to a ministry among Chinese men, from rough, pack-mule drivers to military officers and even mandarins. In Japan, our well-known Sensei (Teacher) Irene Webster-Smith, after several terms in a children's orphanage, was called back after the war by General MacArthur and had an amazing ministry among the top Japan War Crimes prisoners, leading a number to the Lord before their executions. After that, although long past retirement age, she worked with university students and was a popular speaker at retreats for American servicemen.

In the United States, Henrietta Mears—also affectionately called "Teacher" by the thousands of students in her classes at Hollywood Presbyterian Church—is a woman who has instructed and inspired many outstanding men, among them Bill Bright, founder of Campus Crusade for Christ, and Richard Halverson, pastor of Fourth Presbyterian Church, Washington, D.C. "To challenge young men to enter the ministry was perhaps the greatest of Miss Mears' gifts. In the course of her career in Hollywood over 400 collegians heard God's call and turned their energies to pulpits in America, or to mission stations scattered around the world," her biographer, E. M. Baldwin, tells us.

Mears had 567 officers and teachers in her huge Sunday school, in which she taught the college class herself. (This class sometimes had seventy-five members on its Cabinet alone!) Some of her superintendents—busy professional men and women—managed to spend thirty-five hours a week in the work of their respective departments. She was also the founder of Gospel Light Publications, which has produced high-quality Christian education material of which she originally wrote most of the courses. Harold Ockenga wrote to her:

What a work you have done! There is no young peoples' work in this nation equal to yours. When I think of the tens of thousands who have studied the Bible under your leadership, of the thousands who have faced the claims of Christ and made a commitment to Him, of the hundreds of young men who have gone into the ministry, and other young people into Christian service, I cannot but be struck with amazement. . . . It was one of my fondest hopes to have you as professor of Christian education at Fuller Theological Seminary. Your contribution to ministers would have been the acme of your educational career.

Others who come to mind are Drs. Lois and Mary Le Bar, of Wheaton College, who have also contributed much to the church through their many students now serving in world-wide ministries.

Ryrie states,

Subordination, dependence, and difference of nature are the three reasons the early church assigned for the non-participation of women in public vocal ministry, and this regulation of silence was not grounded in special and temporary conditions in the church, but was related to a far more basic and fundamental reason, that is the difference in position, and nature of male and female. These are the facts whether we like them or not . . . whether this agrees with present-day practice is beside the point.

However, a little later he admits that we do not live in an ideal world and that there are times on both home and foreign fields when there simply are no men to do the work. Then, he feels,

We need to remember Paul not only commanded that things be done decently and in order but also that they be done. In such cases . . . it is better to do the work with qualified women–even though this is not ideal–than to sit back and do nothing because there are no men. However, women must be cautioned against continuing such work after there are men available.

So then, women apparently may undertake difficult and sometimes dangerous pioneer work, with little if any financial return (and always reminding themselves that they are indecent and disorderly?). It would be interesting, too, to know what he considers as "qualified women" since three paragraphs earlier he says that the difference in female position and nature makes her fundamentally unsuited for such work. Actually, since the inferiority of women is so engrained in pagan thinking, it would seem preferable for qualified men to go to those places and for women, if necessary, to take care of the home churches, since members there would be much more mature spiritually after years of listening to sermons and Bible study, and would know that in Christ "there is no male and female." Unfortunately, many of these churches seem to feel they must be fed the very best, and anything will do for overseas.

Remarkably, many women have followed the Lord under unpromising conditions and into the most difficult places, successfully winning to Christ many men, training them for positions of leadership or encouraging and helping them to go to places where they could be trained. We have seen already how some Chinese evangelists were used in the revival movements started by God through women. Little known Margaret E. Barber of England for many years held Bible classes for young men, nearly all of whom later held important places in the church in China. Three even became well-known internationally, namely, Leland Wang, Wilson Wang and Watchman Nee.

At Urbana 67, Akira Hatori, considered by many the best evangelist in Japan today and known to millions as the "Radio Pastor," told how he had both found Christ and begun his training in Christian service under the ministry of an English woman missionary. Takashi Niwa, acting president of Tokyo Christian College, says that when he was a university student, "I went to church with only the desire to learn spoken English from an American missionary working there. As I watched the missionary's life and saw the sincerity and steadfastness of her faith, I realized it was Christ who had changed her life." This led to his own conversion and then to his training for the Christian ministry.

After my husband and I were married in China, we were

appointed to a city where our senior missionary was a single girl, the daughter of China missionaries and just a few years our senior. She had done an excellent job of discipling two male high school teachers, recent converts there, so that they were able to take turns with her at preaching.

It can be seen from these examples that God does indeed use women in the ministry of the gospel, and even in preaching on Sunday with men in the audience. Could the lesson be that we should not be concerned so much with making a list of what is taboo for women, as with putting ourselves completely at the Lord's disposal to take part in his affairs as he directs?

Even in the Old Testament we have examples of women in positions of leadership. Micah has recorded God as saying, "For I brought thee up out of the land of Egypt . . . and sent before thee Moses, Aaron and Miriam," clearly denoting her position as a national leader. In Exodus she is called "the prophetess," and led in singing and praise to God.

Then there is Huldah, also a prophetess. The king of that time, Josiah, actually sent the high priest and other officials "to enquire of the Lord" of her for the whole nation, after they had discovered a copy of the Scriptures which were apparently unknown to most of the people during the wicked reign of his grandfather Manasseh (2 Kings 22:14).

Deborah, an even more curious case, was not only a national political and military leader but was also the human instrument for composing at least a page and a half of the edition of the Bible I have beside me. Ruth and Esther also showed considerable courage and initiative, and are the chief characters of the books of the Bible named for them.

Mention of Deborah's song reminds me that many of the hymns now sung in our Sunday services are written by women. Is that not also a spiritual ministry, and something they could not do if they were really limited only to "learn-ing in silence"?

Some commentators, as already mentioned, suggest that Paul's directions about women were given so as not to prej-udice people of that social milieu against the gospel. If that is a valid reason, then the glib restrictions penned or par-roted by many sincere churchmen against women having any spiritual ministry today, will certainly put a number of women against the church in our own day. Indeed, some are already openly saying that the Christian church has always been the enemy of women.

Virginia Mollenkott, of the Department of English at William Paterson College, wrote in a letter to *His* magazine (June 1973),

At the historical moment when secular society is just beginning to wake up concerning centuries of injustice to women, it is unwise and unjust for evangelical publications to stress biblical passages concerning ancient inequalities between the sexes. By continuing on such a course, evangelicals will only add fuel to the widespread secular concept that the Christian church is an outmoded institution dedicated to the maintenance of the status quo no matter how unjust and inhuman.

She had earlier pointed out that "the whippings, burn-ings, and excruciatingly painful chastity belts of the Middle Ages were all perpetrated under the aegis of the Bible's statements concerning male supremacy."

Certainly the current cultural or social climate can never be a justification for changing or even keeping silent on any of the great doctrines of the Bible. But what if it concerns something about which there seem apparent contradictions at times? I was struck by this observation of F. F. Bruce: "The activity of prophetic women, despite precedents in the Old and New Testaments, has commonly been an embarrassment to settled church officials; they are even more difficult to control than prophetic men." One cannot help feeling that this may be at the bottom of some men's thinking, just as it was the actual cause of the ecclesiastical structure eventually leaving no place for "prophets" of either sex.

I am sure there are many others, however, who honestly feel that 1 Timothy 2 is God's last word about women and that they must therefore shut their eyes to other parts of the Bible that seem to threaten this maxim, or to try to explain them away, as indeed Franson and others have with the words of Timothy. Yet, when we see in the Gospels that Christ never degraded women, but quite the reverse; when we see in other Scriptures that God sometimes put women in places of great responsibility; and when we know of countless women who have since New Testament times experienced God's compelling them into a speaking and teaching ministry, may it not be a little unwise for us to so box God up that he has to seem to break his own rules?

18
THE SINGLE WOMAN AND WIDOW

The reader may have noted that the majority of missionary women mentioned in the last chapter were single, and this no doubt accounts for the great spiritual work many of them were able to accomplish. Having completed our study of woman in general in the Epistles, we come now to those references dealing with virgins and widows. Three main subjects emerge from these verses: (1) the basic reason for marriage, (2) the desirability of remaining single and (3) the scope of Christian service possible to the unmarried.

In only three Epistles do we find specific references to young women. In Titus 2 it is assumed that all the younger women are married and should therefore be taught "to love their husbands, to love their children" (v. 4). Again, in 1 Timothy 5:14, Paul writes, "I will therefore that the younger [widowed] women marry, bear children...." Yet

251

in 1 Corinthians 7:8 he states, "I say therefore to the unmarried and widows, It is good for them to abide even as I [that is, unmarried]"; and in verse 38, "So then, he that giveth her in marriage doeth well; but he that giveth her not in marriage doeth better." He then adds that in his opinion and, he believes, in God's, a widow will be happier not married again. Given the almost slave-like condition of many wives in those days, it may well have been true that most would be happier unmarried; but not many appear to agree with him today.

What is the reason for Paul's apparent change of opinion? Many consider that the Pastoral Epistles were written at least ten years later than those to the Corinthians. It is possible, therefore, that whereas Paul thought when writing to the latter that Christ would return very soon, ten years later, with his own death approaching, he was more concerned with building stable churches whose members would have a good reputation amid the heathen society in which they lived.

Another possible explanation results from the Corinthian environment with its rampant sexual impurity connected with its obscene goddess worship. The Corinthian believers had written to Paul with specific questions about marriage, especially to unbelievers, and also about celibacy. In the midst of the general moral morass of those times there had been a swing to the opposite extreme of asceticism, some couples even living together in a kind of "spiritual marriage," priding themselves on having no sexual intercourse. It was in such circumstances, and in answer to the above questions, that Paul's words in 1 Corinthians 7 were written.

The Basic Reason for Marriage   One commentator states

that there is no contradiction in what is written in that chapter and in 1 Timothy 5 since in the latter case Paul regarded all those widows as incontinent! That seems rather too sweeping, but it is obviously based on the first principle of marriage Paul states in 1 Corinthians 7:2, namely, that marriage is a provision to meet a strong physical need: "Nevertheless, to avoid fornication, let every man have his own wife, and let every woman have her own husband."

Many have accused Paul of expressing a low view of marriage here, but he was just answering some of the questions sent by the Corinthian church, not giving a full discourse on the marriage relationship.

He also states with brutal frankness in verse 9, "If they cannot contain, let them marry: for it is better to marry than to burn." Contrary to what has often been taught in the past, this "burning" is not of itself immoral but is only the intense desire for the fulfillment of a God-given instinct of the human body. In some people it appears to be stronger than in others; and Paul does not call the control of it only a matter of the will (v. 37) but also one of God's gifts given to some in greater degree than to others: "every man hath his proper gift of God, one after this manner, and another after that" (v. 7).

So then, Paul is saying that any single person—man or woman—who has a strong urge with which his or her mind might be obsessed *should* get married. It is noteworthy, and revolutionary, that he recognizes an equal need, and right, for the woman as well as the man: "Let every woman have her own husband" (v. 2). This raises an interesting and important question. Is there not something drastically wrong with Western civilization's system wherein a girl can marry only if she attracts some man's attention sufficiently to arouse within him romantic feelings strong enough to make him "pop the question," while at the same time the more she appears to be "man-hunting" the less likely her appeal usually is to the male?

A Chinese writer and philosopher, Lin Yu-tang, has pointed out the "cruelty" of the Western system compared to the Orient, where parents consider it their most important duty to find a suitable mate for their sons and daughters. He considers that with their lifelong knowledge of their children, parents can judge far better the most suitable temperament needed in a match, rather than leaving it to the child's chance emotional "falling in love."

This no doubt would be true of ideal parents, but in the East they are quite likely to depend blindly on the dictates of the horoscope, rather than the actual character of the children, while the history of nearly every country, East or West, reveals that too often the wealth and position of the prospective bridegroom are the criteria carrying most weight with the parents. A Greek maiden of marriageable age in Paul's era lamented,

Faces strange, and tongues unknown
Make us, by a bid, their own.

Jane Austen showed in her books that conditions were not much better in the England of her day, and the well-known Japanese novel, *The Makioaka Sisters*, reveals that the same conditions hold there, where arranged marriages are still in the majority.

Surely a Christian-influenced society should be able to devise some better method of obtaining a husband for a girl who desperately feels the need for one; or else its members should stop preaching that that is all a girl is made for. Many Japanese pastors do now take some initiative as middlemen for Christian girls in their churches (perhaps the same is true in some other countries), but they are often faced with a seemingly insoluble problem: There are more Christian girls than fellows.

This problem did not seem to occur to Paul, yet the New Testament mentions so many widows one wonders if they could automatically follow his advice to "marry and bear children." Certainly lack of men has been a problem in Europe for decades. In spite of the male's superb ability in "the management of affairs" and his skill in bringing them to a successful conclusion, men still manage to slaughter hundreds of thousands of each other in various wars in every generation.

It is fortunate that with higher education for women there are now many interesting and satisfying jobs open to them, so that some prefer to remain single; but for a non-Christian girl who has a strong desire for marriage but cannot find a man, this must be bitter and frustrating. A Christian single woman, however, has the privilege of committing her life to God and the confidence that he will lead in the way he knows is best for her; and if she is to remain unmarried, then he will assuredly give her the accompanying gift mentioned in verse 7. *every man has his proper gift of god, one after this manner and another after that.*

She can also gain comfort from Paul's second principle about marriage—a surprising one for a Jew—namely, that it is best avoided! All through their history the Jews have considered marriage and reproduction a command of God. Rebekah's blessing from her family when going off to marry the unknown Isaac was, "May you be the mother of millions!" (Something that to today's thinking sounds almost like a curse!) The Greeks of Paul's day, too, as do most Japanese families today, considered it socially discreditable to keep daughters at home for any long period after adolescence.

Possibly it was this which Paul had in mind when he wrote

verses 36-38:

But if any man think that he behaveth himself uncomely toward his virgin, if she pass the flower of her age, and need so require, let him do what he will, he sinneth not; let them marry. Nevertheless he that standeth steadfast in his heart, having no necessity, but hath power over his own will, and hath so decreed in his heart that he will keep his virgin, doeth well. So then he that giveth her in marriage doeth well; but he that giveth her not in marriage doeth better.

Commentators and translators have varying views about the meaning of these verses. Some believe they refer to young men wanting to marry virgins; others, to Corinthian fathers having daughters of marriageable age. Some say the Greek word can only mean "to give in marriage," others that it can also mean "to marry." No doubt since that interpretation is more understandable to Westerners today, most modern English paraphrases take it in the sense of a young man wanting to marry.

The Amplified New Testament starts with the young man and changes to the father, while the ASV takes the text to be speaking of the father all through. To anyone who has lived in the Orient, the most natural explanation is that the words were addressed to Greek fathers concerned about whether they should marry their daughters off in view of the strong social pressure to do so. This interpretation would appear to give more consideration to the girl's feelings, too. If the man Paul refers to is the prospective husband, then *his* self-control appears the only consideration.

The NEB takes the text to refer to ascetic celibate couples, who historians tell us were a common feature of those days. At any rate, whomever Paul was referring to, he asserts that marriage is certainly not wrong. If their sex urge is strong, then let them marry, but, for the Christian, to refrain from marriage at that time would be even better.

The Desirability of Remaining Single What are the main reasons Paul gives for the desirability of remaining unmarried?

First, he claims it will be easier because of "the present distress" (v. 26) and also because the married will have "trouble in the flesh, but I would spare you. . . . The time is short . . . the fashion of this world passeth away" (v. 28-31).

Most modern commentators regard these words as a reference to strong persecution at that time and to Paul's belief in the imminent return of Christ. Calvin, however, living in a generation just emerging from the centuries-old domination of Roman Catholic teaching, believes they are speaking of the normal difficulties of marriage: "Marriage brings with it hindrances from which I should wish you to be free and exempt." He continues that some people expect "unmixed honey" in marriage and are disappointed. Among the particular "troubles" of marriage in his day Calvin includes the loss of children, widowhood, conjugal quarrels, faults of children, and the rather intriguing "marriage fooleries, jests, and other things with which married persons are taken up." He considered marriage "a burden by which the mind of a pious man is weighed down, so that he does not move Godward with so much alacrity." Evidently he did not quite agree with God's view that it is not good for man to be alone.

However, he does add that these evils do not belong to marriage per se but "proceed from the depravity of man." This universal characteristic not only spoils the partners of a marriage, of course, but also the lives of those who plan to be celibate for religious reasons. Calvin speaks of the conditions in his day with a bluntness which must surely shock some modern ecumenical ears: "See what kind of devotement to the Lord there commonly is on the part of the monks and nuns, and the whole scum of the papistical clergy, than whose celibacy nothing can be imagined that is more obscene, infamous, and abominable."

Calvin was here referring to Paul's second argument, namely, that there is an important difference between a wife and a virgin: "The unmarried woman careth for the things of the Lord, that she may be holy both in body and spirit; but she that is married careth for the things of the world, how she may please her husband" (v. 34).

This strangely unqualified statement makes it sound as if every single woman is automatically devoted to the Lord, and all married women are not. Yet every church, at home and abroad, has surely known single women in their midst who were sometimes self-centered and as concerned about housing and kitchen sinks as married women, and, conversely, some married women who appear to neglect husband and children because they are so busy in "the Lord's work." Perhaps Paul was thinking here about girls who were still in their parents' home possibly run by slaves, and who therefore had few domestic chores. Or else he was speaking of what he regarded as the ideal.

There is, of course, a general truth in what he says, as every married woman finds on occasion, particularly throughout the child-rearing years. A single woman, with no one dependent on her, can be wonderfully free from many distractions; she can set her own times for meals, sleep, washing, ironing and so on, and thus can give first place unreservedly to serving the Lord.

So, while Paul's first argument about the "present distress" and the "fashion of this world passing away" may not have much weight today (although in the atomic age it could be very relevant indeed), his second reason remains to a large extent true. Therefore, the woman who remains unmarried, from choice or circumstance, can rejoice that she is spared some difficulties and that God has given her the opportunity of serving him more freely.

The Scope of Christian Service for a Single Woman Just how is a single girl to serve God? What precisely did Paul have in mind when he wrote: "The unmarried woman careth for the things of the Lord, that she may be holy both in body and in spirit: but she that is married careth for the things of the world, how she may please her husband. And this I speak for your own profit . . . that ye may attend upon the Lord without distraction" (vv. 34-35)?

In what way is she to "attend upon the Lord"? And what exactly are these "things of the Lord"? These are important questions for women, yet in the dozen Bible commentaries I consulted not one even mentioned the subject of a single woman's service, let alone suggested what it might consist of. Most modern translations merely substitute "affairs" or "business" for "things of the Lord," although *Living Letters* gets around the problem by saying an unmarried girl is "anxious to please the Lord in everything she is or does." But surely many of us Christian wives want that, too. So the problem remains: What exactly *should* the unmarried woman be or do, and what *could* she do in Paul's day?

I once asked a group of single girl missionaries what they thought Paul had in mind and, evidently not wanting to stick their necks out or appear too "lib" at first, their suggestions were caring for the sick or orphans. James put a high priority on such people (see Jas. 1:27 and 5:14, though in the latter it is the elders' job), and Christ certainly was concerned about them. Yet in Paul's day there were many widows available, probably with more experience in these areas than the young virgins, and it seems doubtful there would have been enough sick and orphans in the churches to occupy all the Christian women, especially if most stopped getting married. However, we must not forget that the church began to take in exposed pagan babies, too. Nevertheless, this would be much the same kind of work the wives were doing in their homes. It is hard to see how looking after a houseful of orphans could be much less "distracting" than having a few children of one's own, especially with no husband to help control them!

Since he is to silence and subject women (or wives) in the latter part of this letter, what else could Paul have in mind here? Does he expect a good part of a girl's time should be spent in prayer, especially if there are slaves to do the housework? Many of the girls of that time probably were not able to read the Hebrew Scriptures, although the Greeks did have the Septuagint.

Further, can these verses give an average girl today any guidance? With so many high-school marriages, not many women even have time to be a "single girl" professionally. And the professional is usually in full employment after completing her education. Even on some mission fields, the most welcomed woman candidate often is one with teaching, nursing or secretarial skills, in addition to compulsory Bible training. If, as some do in the Tokyo area, she clocks in at 8:30 after struggling an hour in densely packed bus and subway, works a full day, returns home through the same crowds, deals with house chores, prayer letters, family and supporters' letters, quarterly and annual reports, income tax returns, language study, a Bible or Sunday school class and guests, she has little more time and energy left for prolonged personal devotions than a busy housewife.

Possibly Paul has in mind a deeper unrivaled devotion to the person of Christ. I remember so well, after receiving a letter from my fiancé saying he thought the Lord's return might be very near, my feeling of guilt on realizing that my first reaction had been to hope the Lord would at least delay until we were married! (In self-defense I might add that the marriage was then only a few months away, after a four-year engagement, no meeting for over a year, and having between us first two continents and oceans and then over two-thousand miles of war-torn China.) Does Paul mean that for a single girl it is better not to have one eye on "dates" and the other on the Lord? Such teaching is almost unheard of in North America, though there are some evangelical orders in Germany with something of the same conception of being "married to the Lord" as is found in the Roman Catholic church.

Nor is this idea entirely limited to ecclesiastical orders. While in missionary candidate school I heard the testimony of Jessie Gregg. She told us she had not been long out of language school when the Lord spoke to her from Ezekiel 16:8: "I entered into a covenant with the . . . and thou becamest mine." She felt this was meant for her in a very personal sense—that she was not to marry and that the Lord would give her many spiritual children. When she told her senior missionaries of her experience, with understanding and imagination they prepared a little wedding feast to mark the occasion of her becoming wholly the Lord's. Though she later received several proposals of marriage, she turned them down, and was eventually used to bring more than ten-thousand women to Christ in cities across north China. This suggests that complete devotion to the Lord does not necessarily limit a single woman just to private prayer at home, and we have already seen that in New Testament times some women who appeared to be single were active in the church and were approved by Paul.

A few weeks ago at our mission's annual conference I met a single girl who had the overall responsibility for the translation of the whole of the New Testament into the Amis language in Taiwan. Most of us know, too, of the painstaking work, in the most primitive conditions, of the many single girl members of Wycliffe Bible Translators. It is not likely that such possibilities occurred to Paul, but God has certainly given these gifts to many devoted women.

Of particular interest in this regard is the report in Wycliffe's *Who Brought the Word* about Tariri, a Peruvian Indian chief who told one mission official, "If you had sent men, we would have killed them on sight. Or if a couple, I'd have killed the man and taken the woman for myself. But what could a great chief do with two harmless girls who insisted on calling him 'brother'?" (Tribal law of the Shapra Indians was that men must always defend their sisters.)

A somewhat similar situation can be cited in Japan. Since the entry of Protestantism just over one hundred years ago, the northwest part of the main island has been particularly resistant to the gospel. One city especially, Daishoji, had kept any missionary or Japanese evangelist from settling there. The first missionary who rented a house for a few days in 1879 had to withdraw and witness the owner of the house driven out of town with bamboo spears, banished for ten years. One time a church building was begun but was destroyed before it got much beyond the foundations. A Japanese evangelist later tried to live there, but a fence was put around the house, and no one was allowed in or out.

After the war, when our mission began work again in Japan with many new missionaries, they made a careful survey to find out the areas most needing churches. Daishoji was discovered, of course, but the family who planned to go there could not find anyone willing to rent them a house.

Finally, two young single girls volunteered to try. Through a contact with a Daishoji girl studying in another city and attending an English Bible class held by another of our missionaries, they were at last able to rent a house, and eventually a church was established. The opposition had evidently felt that two young women posed no threat!

Other mission fields, I am sure, could give abundant evidence of the way God has called and used single girls whose lives were truly devoted to him.

Service for Widows Only one other Scripture passage refers to the service of unmarried women, this time widows. The meaning of this text also is obscure; but unlike the above passage about virgins, it has rated much attention from the commentators. The passage is 1 Timothy 5:9-12: "Let not a widow be taken into the number [enrolled] under threescore years old, having been the wife of one man, well reported of for good works; if she have brought up children, if she have lodged strangers, if she have washed the saints' feet, if she have relieved the afflicted, if she have diligently followed every good work."

Being neither a widow nor a church administrator, I had never given serious thought to this passage. And not until I read it in *Living Letters* did I fully realize what it might be saying:

A widow who wants to become one of the special church workers should be at least sixty years old and have been married only once. She must be well thought of by everyone because of the good she has done. Has she brought up her children well? Has she been kind to strangers. . . ? Has she helped those who are sick and hurt? Is she always ready to show kindness? The younger widows should not become members of this special group because after awhile they are likely to disregard their vow to Christ and marry again. And so they will stand condemned because they broke their first promise.

What a surprise! Why hadn't I noticed this before? Why doesn't the evangelical church follow this today? Why should it be so terrible to marry again after becoming a church worker? These were my first reactions. I now have gathered literally pages of notes from numerous commentaries, but must limit myself to the essentials about these "respectable elderly females."

The "number" means an official list, or enrollment; but opinion is divided about whether it is the list of those who are to receive church support, of those who are chosen for some kind of church office or "order," or of those just given special jobs to do without having any official status. Each view presents some difficulties.

If it is merely a list of widows needing material help, there must surely have been some who needed it earlier than sixty, before their children became independent. The qualifications seem severe, too, and a far cry from the generosity of Christ or the church of the Acts. Who could conscientiously claim to have "diligently followed every good work"? Jerome even went so far as to demand they "demean themselves as becometh holiness, that their very walk, motions, countenance, language, and silence shall present a certain decorous and sacred dignity." This seems rather much to require of someone whose main problem is destitution.

Another difficulty is that if these widows were just in need of some material support, and one qualification was that they had only had one husband, why does Paul later in the chapter say that younger widows *should* marry again, for they would thus cut themselves off from any possibility of later getting on the "roll"? And if they had indeed "brought up their children well," it would seem strange that all of these children had died and not one was left to support his mother.

A second view is that these "exemplary Christian matrons" formed a definite church order which demanded a vow of celibacy and devotion to Christ (as the *Living Letters* translates). One man states that being the wife of only one husband "implies a measure of sacerdotal dignity." Apparently the Romans thought ceremonies performed by such a person were more auspicious and acceptable to the gods.

It is hard for us today to understand Paul's horror at the thought of these women marrying again. "Do not put on your list widows younger than 60. . . . For such, when they chafe and fret against the restrictions which their alliance to Christ involves, wish to marry, and so expose themselves to censure as being untrue to their first devotion to Him," as one person paraphrased it. In this regard another commentator says, "Her qualifications must be carefully investigated. It would be far better to reject some, who *might* have proved useful, than to run the risk of admitting any who would exhibit the scandal of having been supported by the church, and specially devoted to acts of mercy, and having after all returned to society as married women with ordinary pleasures and cares." This makes one wonder just how unholy "holy matrimony" is, but this must be left to our chapter on wives in the Epistles.

Other commentators prefer to think that these women performed "certain ministrations [of a material and physical nature] for the good of the church," without being a formal order. Yet it seems rather hard to expect a widow to start some new form of active work at that age. Possibly longevity was greater then than subsequently, however, for Plato also considered sixty to be the ideal age for priests and priestesses.

If the widows were something like a deaconess order (although most evangelical commentators seem loathe to give them such status), the question still remains, What exactly was their function? And why does the church not follow Paul's directions today? It could be partly because the average longevity decreased considerably in the Middle Ages so that by 1891 in Europe it was only forty-one years. A special function for widows of sixty would therefore long ago have become irrelevant.

According to Father Daniélou, both the Eastern and Roman churches took these words of Paul seriously, and there are many references to these special widows in early ecclesiastical literature. Polycarp called them "the altar of God" and said their main work was prayer, although their functions and status seem to have varied and fluctuated during the first three centuries, and they died out in the late fourth century. Clement of Alexandria lists them among "persons of distinction" following bishops, priests and deacons. Origen states that if the role of widow consisted solely of footwashing, which could be done by servants, "there would be no reason for ranking them with those enjoying a definite ecclesiastical status." Tertullian included the four groups—bishops, priests, deacons, widows—as constituting church order. Other literature places them after or between readers and subdeacons, and one text specifies that they are not to be ordained because "ordination is for the clergy, because they perform the liturgical services, while the widow is instituted for prayer, which is a function of all Christians." The Canons of Hippolytus, on the other hand, specifically include widows as part of the ordained ministry, their special duties being "constancy in prayer, care of the sick, and frequent fastings."

In *Didasculia Apostolorum*, which appeared in Syria about

mid-third century, the mission of the Order of Widows was said to exist merely to pray for benefactors and the whole church:

If asked questions she will not reply immediately, unless the question is concerned with justice or faith in God. She will refer questions to those in charge. . . . If non-Christians hear those who proclaim the Word of God failing to do so rightly, especially where the Incarnation and Redemption are concerned, they will jest and mock instead of praising God's Word. And the Widow will incur severe penalties for having been the occasion of this blasphemy. Also they may not lay hands on or pray over anyone [sick] except by direction of the bishop and deacon.

While appreciating the concern for the right proclamation of God's Word, one would think it a fairly simple matter to instruct these women in the truths of the incarnation and redemption. And it seems a pity that severe penalties were not also imposed on ecclesiastics who departed considerably from the scriptural version of these two great truths.

Chrysostom attests to the existence of the Widows Order in Antioch up to the end of the fourth century, but Daniélou tells us that decay was beginning to set in during the second half of the third century: "It died of its own ambiguities. Up to the end, however, it kept the various aspects which it had had in St. Paul's time."

One of the reasons for the Order's end was the distinguished place the ideal of virginity began to attain in the third century. Also a new institution, that of Deaconesses, gradually took its place. Both widows and virgins could join this, and the age of eligibility was changed from sixty to forty by the Council of Chalcedon. Ryrie has an interesting observation on the subject of virgins. After mentioning the example of Christ's own dealings with women he continues, "The secondary force in promoting the activity of women was the developing strain of asceticism which tended to give priority to the unmarried woman and her service. . . . One must recognize, too, that this ascetic spirit and prominence of virgins had an exalting effect on the status of women." Evidently most men, who before had always thought of women merely as sex objects or secondary creatures with "an inordinate sexual desire for a husband," at last began to realize that there were some of whom this was not true or that at least they had the capacity to think and live beyond these confines.

We can only conclude, from the lack of any more definite instructions in the Scriptures about the kind of service meant for virgins and widows, that God has chosen to retain his sovereignty in directing his children individually, to meet the needs of each generation. While not necessarily God's ideal for all womankind, it is clear that single women and widows are important to him, have more opportunity to be wholly devoted to him, and are more easily available than is a wife for all kinds of service—whether this involves caring for orphans, delinquents, missionary children, travelers, the sick or the aged, or working in secretarial positions, bookstores, tract distribution, music, writing, teaching or even preaching. While not all unmarried women make themselves as fully available for the Lord's work as they could, I am thankful that I have met many who have. Fortunate are the missions or other Christian organizations which have some of these in their ranks.

WOMAN AS WIFE

As I have mentioned in earlier chapters, no one is quite sure when the references to "women" in the Epistles are largely meant for wives since all women in Jewish culture were expected to marry, and at a very early age. However, the AV does use "wives" in some places and understandably so, since most of these references also deal with husbands. These passages are usually instructive, and some are quite surprising.

An Unholy Christian? While attempting to find the scope of service for a single woman, we noted two verses which appear to cast some doubt on the accuracy of the common term *holy matrimony.* The first of these, 1 Corinthians 7:34, tells us, "The unmarried woman careth for the things of the Lord, that she may be holy both in body and in spirit." This

269

seems to carry the unpleasant implication that these things cannot *both* be true of a married woman. I am not aware of a grammatical rule which would indicate with certainty which of the two is the "extra" quality possessed by a single woman, but since every believer has the Holy Spirit, are we to assume that it is in *body* that the wife is not holy? Interestingly, the same does not seem to be implied of a married man in this passage; of a single man Paul just says that he will care "how he may please the Lord." Does Paul intend to make any important distinction?

The explanation in Lange's Commentary does not make the matter any clearer: "The marriage state obligates the body in an earthly and worldly relation, and involves the power of the man over the body of his wife and easily occasions a defilement of the physical life." I am not quite sure what this means, but in any case there seems no adequate scriptural ground elsewhere for such a view. And this commentator apparently forgot that Paul also said the wife had power over her husband's body.

Still with the thought of something "unholy" about marriage, 1 Timothy 5:11 suggests that a desire to marry, after being put on the church list of widows, *follows* "waxing wanton against Christ." Yet for us today the thought of a missionary or any other widowed Christian worker wanting to marry again seems perfectly legitimate and consistent with a devoted love for the Lord and his service.

In spite of God's clear plan of sexuality given in Genesis, a few Old Testament texts seem to suggest that sex may be dirty or unholy for both man and woman. Before the giving of the Ten Commandments Moses told the people to wash their clothes "and come not at your wives" (a rather unpleasant euphemism) for three days (Ex. 19:15). The RV substitutes "a woman" which might limit the prohibition to extramarital relations, but that seems unlikely since one of the Commandments was to forbid adultery at *any* time. Perhaps that did not include fornication, however. Later, Levitical rules made a man unclean for a day after any emission of semen, a woman after the birth of a child and also during her menstrual period, rules common among pagan peoples also. The Christian church, without any specific inspired written instructions, has by and large come to regard these things as abrogated by the gospel, with the exception of the view that women are unclean following childbirth, a view which in some churches has been eliminated only in the last century.

Then we have David's poetic statement in the midst of his contrition for his sin with Bathsheba: "Behold, I was shapen in iniquity; and in sin did my mother conceive me" (Ps. 51:5). Many preachers seem eager to identify themselves and their congregations with this confession, and it has caused many people to regard even sexual activity in marriage, or at least the woman's part in it, as sin. Obviously, however, procreation was God's plan and purpose from the beginning; and if David's statement were universally true, then Mary would have contaminated Jesus in the process of bearing him. We can only conclude that there was something irregular about David's birth, perhaps confirmed by the fact that his father did not call him at first when Samuel asked to see his sons. Or perhaps David was trying to attribute the cause of his sin to his parents—a favorite place to lay the blame these days. And it is true, of course, that the inherent tendency to sin is passed on by human parents. The New Berkeley Version's "Behold, in sinful state was I born" conveys this idea better, I think.

Finally in Revelation 14 is the strange case of the 144,000 redeemed "which were not defiled with women: for they are virgins." One commentator suggests these had died in infancy, but most either ignore the statement or say it is only meant in a "spiritual sense."

All these passages probably account for the idea often prevalent in the church throughout its history that sex is "unholy" and its only legitimate purpose the procreation of children. Clement of Alexandria and Tertullian even went so far as to assure continent widows that they were in God's sight as maidens—that is, put back on God's official list of virgins for a second time! So, whereas the author of the footnotes of the Amplified Old Testament claims the busy matron of Proverbs 31 as "God's ideal woman," Paul in places (for example, 1 Corinthians 7:1: "It is good for a man not to touch a woman") seems to imply that the virgin woman (and man) is God's ideal, and the Roman church, especially, has largely endorsed this. The NEB, however, has as a footnote alternative Paul's quoting from the Corinthian church's letter to him: "You say, 'It is a good thing for a man to have nothing to do with women'; but. . . ."

Paul then tells the Corinthian Christians that it is better to marry than burn with lust, a phrase which the Living Bible surprisingly retains. Phillips' translation certainly sounds preferable, "than to be tortured by unsatisfied desire." The word *lust* has taken on a rather worse connotation since King James' time, and in any case one cannot always tell where natural instinct ends and lust, in the more limited modern sense, begins. Paul had clearly stated early in chapter 7 that marriage is the right and proper provision for those with strong sexual impulses, "that Satan tempt you not." And again, "If thou marry, thou hast not sinned. . . . If her husband be dead, she is at liberty to be married to whom she will; only in the Lord." But he does add that he thinks widows will be happier if they stay unmarried. Thus Paul is not suggesting that marriage is the lesser of two evils, but the lesser of two goods: "He that giveth her in marriage doeth well, but he that giveth her not in marriage doeth better."

For those of us who are already wives, what instruction or encouragement can be found in the Epistles? The fact that Paul in other letters uses marriage as an illustration of Christ's relationship to the church surely suggests that marriage is not automatically a "second-best" for a Christian woman. The Bible as a whole, too, clearly indicates that marriage was planned by God at creation. According to the AV, Hebrews 13:4 says sexual intercourse in marriage is honorable (the RSV and other recent translations, that it *should* be held in honor) while outside of marriage it displeases God. 1 Thessalonians 4:4 also has the possible meaning of marriage's being "in sanctification and honor," although no one is quite sure about what the "vessel" is which one is supposed to possess in this way. The RSV has "that each one of you know how to take a wife for himself in holiness and honor," and the NEB "each of you must learn to gain mastery over his body, to hallow and honour it."

The need for information on this subject is great among people in the West these days, as it also was for many Japanese Christians. We knew one young man there who had been a student in seminary several months before discovering, to his surprise, that adultery was wrong for a Christian. Another university graduate, converted in our church and planning to get married, asked if marriage was adultery. Soon afterward I saw in a newspaper that as the result of a series of particularly erotic films the young Japanese were getting the idea that "sex is dirty." So there was obvious need for clear Christian teaching, emphasizing that the God-ordained method by which two become "one flesh" is both holy and beautiful for those married in the Lord.

I had no idea then that the need would be just as great at home in a few years as a result of situation ethics and a lack of moral standards in almost every educational institution. One cannot help wondering if, after the long succession of sick films constantly advertised today and the growing practice of jumping into bed with a succession of partners, it may become impossible, even for those who are later converted, really to appreciate sex. Rather, like Augustine, they may be inclined to repudiate it entirely.

It is important that people today do not fall into the error so common in other generations of going to the opposite extreme of asceticism after a period of sexual licentiousness. As S. B. Babbage points out,

A careful distinction is made in the N.T. between "the flesh" and "the body." . . . *It is the flesh, in Biblical usage the unsanctified nature of fallen man, which is sinful. The body is holy, a "temple" for God, not an impediment and hindrance to the life of man [and presumably woman], but an indispensable instrument for the expression of the personality.*

A Paradox: Status Yet Submission   Probably the most obvious instruction in the Epistles, appearing three times, is that a wife should be submissive to her husband. "Wives, submit yourselves unto your own husbands, as unto the Lord. For the husband is the head of the wife" (Eph. 5:22-23). "Wives, submit yourselves unto your own husbands, as it is fit in the Lord" (Col. 3:18). These are Paul's contributions. Peter also admonishes, "Likewise ye wives, be in subjection to your own husbands. . . . Even as Sarah obeyed Abraham, calling him lord: whose daughters ye are, as long as ye do well, and are not afraid with any amazement" (1 Pet. 3:1, 6). In view of this clearly stated principle, how do we account for the paradox that Christianity is usually credited with raising the status of women and bringing equality and democracy to the world?

Undoubtedly what has most influenced those people who have studied the Bible is the example of how Christ himself acted toward women. And when women began attending Christian services, how could they help applying to themselves what was preached, unless told it was only for men? As in country after country women learned to read—primarily to study the Bible, as was the case in China when we were there—their vision, mental powers and other abilities could not help but increase, with the Holy Spirit indwelling them. If a woman is completely limited to cooking and cleaning, it is no wonder she in desperation seeks an outlet in gossip. How much better to have something more challenging to do and to think about!

Since our present study is concerned with the Epistles, however, what grounds can we find in them for the uplift of women? The most remarkable, I think, is the revolutionary things Paul and Peter have to say about the responsibilities of the husband, and this is so important I have made it the subject of a separate section.

In addition, we can say that the rising status of women was probably the logical outcome of Paul's statement that in Christ there is neither male nor female, although in the West it did take some additional hard work on the part of abolitionists and suffragettes to turn this obvious logic into legal fact. While I doubt it is the work of God's ideal woman to be fighting for rights for herself, the cruelty and degradation to which women have habitually been subjected in many non-Christian countries and even sometimes in so-called Christendom have certainly called for some action on the part of God's people; and we women in the West should

275

be thankful for what has been accomplished for us through the outworking of the gospel in some godly men's hearts.

Incidentally, there is still an Anti-Slavery Society for the Protection of Human Rights, based in England, which claims that slavery, serfdom, the sale of children and servile forms of marriage exist in thirty-eight countries of Africa, Asia and Latin America. Just recently it reported that two young girls, their wrists chained, were seen being dragged behind camels on their way to their purchasers. A foreigner, riding by with some officials, tried to intervene, even offering to buy the girls, but without success. The government officials merely looked embarrassed. Such things most often happen in Moslem countries, but even they, perhaps from outside pressure, are gradually beginning to institute some reforms.

Probably Paul had no idea that what the Spirit inspired him to write would one day accomplish the abolition of slavery in so-called Christian countries, and the raising of women above the chattel class on an almost worldwide scale.

Now, in fact, the pendulum seems in some respects to have gone too far the other way, particularly in the United States where divorce laws unequally favor the wife, and where a woman too often is the head of the house. An additional reason, however, could be that in the New World, until very recently, the male population outnumbered the female, placing the latter at a premium.

In Germany, for centuries a "man's world," women over forty now outnumber men by two million. But post-war male babies have far exceeded female births so that marriageable girls of between twenty and thirty are at a premium. Thus one of them could boldly advertise in the newspaper, "I am a woman who has decided to marry. My interests are art, literature, sports, politics, etc. Who wants to be my husband? He must respect my inclinations. He can be up to 40 years old, and about 5 ft. 11 ins." This certainly seems a reversal of the role of the *frau* of previous generations, which was evident even among German missionaries in China.

Christianity having led the way, is it now for agnostic democracy or even the law of supply and demand to determine the nature of the husband and wife relationship? Are Paul and Peter's words an anachronism which we can now ignore, inconsistent with the main teachings of Christianity? Such has been the view of many people in recent decades. Yet the drastic breakdown in marriage and family life in recent years, and in the United States particularly, has made some take a fresh look at what the Bible has to say on the subject. Although in Christ there is no "male and female," obviously the marriage relationship is the one sphere where the difference is of supreme importance, and planned so by God.

Before we examine the three passages I quoted earlier, perhaps it will be helpful to see exactly what the position of a Jewish wife was in New Testament times. Joachim Jeremias gives us considerable detail in *Jerusalem in the Time of Jesus.* Up to the age of twelve-and-a-half years a girl's father had full power over her. She had no rights of possession; the proceeds of her work, and anything she found, belonged to her father, and she had no right to refuse a marriage he arranged. He could also sell her into slavery, but only to a Jewish family. "This very extensive paternal power naturally led to daughters, and especially minors, being considered mainly as cheap labor and a source of profit." Even when a girl was over twelve and a half, the marriage money her future husband had to pay at the betrothal belonged to her father. The marriage customarily took place a year later, so, since the usual age for a bridegroom was eighteen to twenty, she would obviously seem rather like a child to her husband.

When asked "Is there any difference between the acquisition of a wife and the acquisition of a Gentile slave?" the scribes' answer was no. "She is acquired by money, or by writ or by intercourse.... A Canaanitish bondman is acquired by money or by writ or by usucaption." Legally the wife did actually differ from the slave in two ways. First, she kept the right of possession (but not disposition) of the goods she brought as a marriage portion. Second, her marriage contract fixed the sum to be paid her in case of divorce or the death of her husband.

After marriage, a husband was required to support his wife, and she could demand this before a court. He had to provide her with food, clothing and shelter, and "fulfill his connubial duty." He also had to redeem her from captivity, give her medicines if ill and provide a funeral if she died—with at least two flute players and one woman mourner.

The wife's duties were also outlined. She had to grind meal, bake, wash, cook, suckle the children, prepare her husband's bed and, as repayment for her keep, she had to spin and weave wool and sell it. Other duties were preparing her husband's cup and washing his face, hands and feet. These expressed her servile relationship to her husband, for a Jewish male slave was never required to do these things. The husband also had the right to claim anything his wife found or earned. "The wife was obliged to obey her husband as she would a master—the husband was called *rab*—indeed this obedience was a religious duty." Relationships between children and parents were also determined by a woman's duty of obedience to her husband; the children had to put respect for their father before that for their mother. In case of danger to life, the husband had to be saved first unless the wife's chastity was threatened.

Religiously, this was important: "Like a non-Jewish slave and a child under age a woman has over her a man who is her master, and this likewise limits her participation in divine service, which is why from a religious point of view she is inferior to a man." Jeremias points out that in neither the Old Testament nor the Mishnah is there found the feminine form of the Hebrew adjectives *pious, just, holy*. But we certainly know of some women to whom these words could apply (1 Pet. 3:5). For a scribe, however, "The woman, says the Law, is in all things inferior to a man." Even in her home, a wife was not reckoned among the number of persons summoned to pronounce benediction after a meal.

A woman also had no right to bear witness because the rabbis concluded from Genesis 18:15 that she was a liar. ("Then Sarah denied, saying, I laughed not.") They ignored the fact that Cain was the first recorded liar and that Abraham himself had begged Sarah to lie to save his skin. They also said, "Let not the testimony of women be admitted because of the levity and boldness of their sex." Perhaps Christ chose to give to woman the privilege of being the first witness to the resurrection to counteract such a view.

Obviously women at that time were legally obliged to obey their husbands. And although Jewish women were better treated than the rest of the world and had some provision in case of divorce, society in general would hardly be ready for a sudden throwing overboard of restrictions on wives, any more than on slaves.

It is generally believed that the three letters containing these passages on submission of wives were written within a short time of each other, and the similarities are so great that some commentators think they were taken from a kind of catechism current in the churches. J. N. D. Kelly says, *We have plenty of evidence that the arrangement of ethical instruction in classified lists [e.g., one's duty to gods, country, parents, etc.] had become conventional practice in popular stoic morality, and that a closely similar pattern of duties had been taken over by Hellenist Judaism. The Christian scheme is broadly the same in structure and content, so it appears that when the apostolic church set about working out its practical catechesis, it freely plundered existing models, modifying them in details in the light of its own theology, and supplying the appropriate Christian motivation.*

In our verses the latter, of course, would be "in the Lord," "as is fit in the Lord" and Peter's reference to ancient practice in the person of Sarah, wife of the Jews' most revered patriarch.

Some think that Paul and Peter's main concern was the favorable reception of the gospel by the lost, and "If the observed effect of the gospel were to make women worse wives, it would not commend it to the heathen." It is also pointed out that Nero stated that the reason for the persecution he began in Rome was that Christians were upsetting the current social institutions, which would include marriage.

In line with this idea Alexander McLaren states,

If Christianity in the early days had once generated into the mere instrument of social revolution, its development would have been thrown back centuries, . . . so Paul never said a word to encourage any precipitate attempt to change externals. He let slavery alone–he let war alone, he let the tyranny of the Roman Empire alone–not because he was a coward, not because he thought these not worth meddling with, but because he believed in the defusion of the principles he proclaimed, and the mighty name he served. . . . "Do not trouble about external conditions. . . . Art thou a slave? Seek not to be freed." ... *Get hold of the central, vivifying, transmuting influence, and all the rest is a question of time.*

John Stuart Mill defends Paul on much the same lines: *Paul said "Wives obey your husbands," but he also said "Slaves obey your masters." It was not his business to incite to rebellion against existing laws, ...* [*It was propagating the Gospel.*] *The apostle's acceptance of all social institutions as he found them did not mean he would disapprove of attempts to improve them at the proper time. His declaration "The powers that be are ordained of God" did not mean he regarded a military despotism as the only form of political government. To pretend that Christianity was intended to stereotype existing forms of government and society, and protect them against change is to reduce it to the level of Islam or Brahmanism. It is precisely because Christianity has not done this, that it has been the religion of the progressive portion of mankind.*

Since Nero's time, some things in Western countries have certainly changed for the better, often as a direct result of Christianity. Now that many of these countries are repudiating any belief in God or Christ, however, conditions are changing for the worse in many respects, and particularly in the home. It is this which ultimately influences every other area of life, and so there is a great need to examine again what the Bible has to say about this vital area.

A Second-class Christian? In 1 Corinthians 11:3 Paul writes that "the head of every man is Christ; and the head of the woman is the man," and in Ephesians 5:23, "For the husband is the head of the wife, even as Christ is head of the church." We have already reached the conclusion elsewhere that there is no ground for believing that all men are the heads of all women, and so we assume that Paul was thinking of the marriage relationship in both the above cases.

James Hurley in his recent article quoted previously and Larry Christenson in *The Christian Family* both make a good case for the husband's being head because of God's planned hierarchy at creation (or divine order and chain of command), and it seems likely this is what Paul had in mind. But I cannot see it spelled out clearly in Genesis—only in the Jewish oral law, as we have also seen. This said children were to show more respect for their father than mother, and Christenson says a wife's authority is only derived from her husband; yet that first commandment with promise said "Honor thy father and mother" without any qualification, and Christ repeatedly stressed this, as we noted in the first section of this book. Further, it is a curious fact that pagan peoples have usually subjected their women more than have Jews and Christians. If this divine hierarchy idea is really true, it is strange that the heathen should observe it best and that Jewish women have had lowest status at times in Israel's history when foreign influence was strongest.

I have no desire to evade this issue, but really want to know God's will. I can see the hierarchy idea as a real possibility, yet, if it is so essential, one wonders why Christ never gave any indication of this. All he said about marriage, apart from its being limited to this earth, was that a husband should not divorce his wife (as was commonly done) but cleave to her for life.

J. S. Mill, plus many commentators and liturgical prayer books, quote Paul as saying in the passages about submitting, "Wives, obey your husbands." Paul Bayne, a Puritan theologian and master of homiletics, went so far as to divide this "obedience" of Ephesians 5 into four parts, with some quaint illustrations. A wife must (1) heed her husband's rebukes, (2) obey his commands, (3) fulfill his desires ("The

man hath a negative vote, if he say no, all must be dashed.
... Though she be never so set upon this or that, if he be
otherwise minded, he must carry it. This is God's yoke upon
you, though the devil in your husbands may put it on.") and
(4) follow his calling (for example, as Sarah left Ur with
Abraham). There was one small exception to the latter,
however: "If men in a jetting, inconsistent humour wander
hither and thither, they [wives] may let them go alone."

Actually, and rather amazingly since the obedience of
wives was a legal requirement of that day, the husbands
having paid good money for them, Paul did not use the
word *obey* but said *submit yourselves* or *be subject to,* or as Phillips paraphrases it, "Adapt yourselves to your husbands."
As we shall see later in a more detailed study of the passage
in Ephesians, Paul first tells *all* Christians to "submit yourselves one to another in the fear of God." Obviously that
does not mean in the strict sense of obeying—every believer
having his turn to issue orders that all the others must legally obey—but rather a gracious yielding and adapting to one
another.

Similarly, he goes on, "As the church is subject unto
Christ, so let the wives be to their own husbands in everything." How is the church subject to Christ? Voluntarily,
it seems, although Christ has purchased us with his blood
and has absolute right over us. In some centuries the
church hardly noticed him in its leaders' strivings for power
and riches. When did Christ tell the church its bishops were
"princes" who should live in "palaces"? Or that black suits
and white collars were what he wanted ministers to wear?
Once a church gets highly organized, it rarely subjects itself
to Christ to the same extent that many husbands have
thought they should control their wives. And ministers are
more apt to think of the Archbishop, President, Secretary

General or whatever as their boss rather than Christ himself.

Every fallible institution of fallen man seems to need a human head (at least it has people striving to be the head), whether it is a government, business firm or school. Whether Christian institutions were meant to be the same is not so clear, since Christ steadfastly refused to appoint any of the disciples as head. The Epistles continue with the Jewish system of elders, however, and the customary headship of the husband in the family. Woman by her very constitution seems the more adaptable generally and probably in the majority of cases is glad to have the security of someone else as leader. It is interesting that in a secular survey of families in Hamilton, Ontario, the happiest families were generally those where the husband was regarded as head of the home.

A wife usually has her own special creative joy and responsibility in the bearing and upbringing of children, which can be accomplished in a variety of locations. Obviously then, the husband's work should be of main consideration; he should function as creatively and be as satisfied as possible. Since marriage I have not only changed my name, but gradually my denomination, nationality, field of service, mission and, yet again, country. Being the timid, stick-in-the-mud type by nature, few of these moves would have been my own choice. But I did not resist any of the changes, for I believed that the decision for such things was my husband's although sometimes I did ask a confirming sign from the Lord.

J. McNally says, "Headship appears to be a matter of the stronger caring for the weaker, and would make it encumbant upon the woman to maintain the subordinate position necessary for the one being cherished, nourished and protected." But she also adds this warning: "Headship is a matter concerning the social relations between the sexes. In spiritual matters a woman may have to go against the wishes of the men in her family." In support of this, we have the example of Sapphira, whom Peter felt should not have agreed with her husband's scheme. Many men, however, feel headship goes beyond mere social relations and is divinely planned by God to cover every area of marriage.

Some have thought a wife should not, or even cannot, have direct communion with God. A friend of mine actually heard a speaker at a summer conference a few years ago say a wife can only approach God through her husband. Even K. Gangel, in his book *The Family First,* includes as one of a husband's biblical roles that of priest. Because Ephesians says the relation of husbands to wives is "parallel to the relationship between Christ and the church" and because Christ was a priest, therefore "the intermediary function of the priest in representing man to God and God to man carries over to the husband's role in the home." But is not the *love* required of a husband the main quality Paul is talking about when referring to Christ's relationship to the church? "Husbands, love your wives, even as Christ also loved the church, and gave himself for it. . . . So ought husbands to love their wives as their own bodies." Christ's work for the church is greater than anything a human husband could accomplish, but a husband can love and give himself.

Hebrews states that Christ is the great high priest of all believers forever, and yet Peter says too that *all* believers are kings and priests. Certainly it is lovely to have a husband home to lead family devotions, share God-given thoughts on the Word and bear the family up in prayer to God. But for missionary wives or any others whose husbands have to be away for extended periods, it would be a wretched existence indeed if we were not only separated from them but also from communion with God and would indeed imply that women are second-class Christians. Surely every believer needs to experience his or her own private devotional time with God as well as the joys of family worship.

Self-Submitting for the Lord's Sake We will now examine in detail the three passages on wives submitting. The first is Colossians 3:18-19. Paul addresses this letter to all who are "risen with Christ" (3:1), and after exhorting them to be merciful, kind, humble in mind, forgiving and truly loving, he continues, "Wives, submit yourselves to your own husbands, as is fit in the Lord." J. B. Phillips has the rather free paraphrase: "Wives, adapt yourselves to your own husbands, that your marriage may be a Christian unity."

It is important to note that the verb *submit* is in the Greek middle voice, meaning literally "place yourselves in submission." It indicates a voluntary act of will rather than a legal requirement, as we shall see further in the Ephesians passage. The reason Paul gives for this act is that it is "befitting" or "convenient" rather than that it is divinely commanded.

Peter, who must have enjoyed his wife's company or else been rather dependent on her since Paul speaks of him taking her around on his travels (1 Cor. 9:5), has a little more to say. He did not write his letter in chapters, of course, and someone has pointed out that in 1 Peter 2:13 he is speaking to all believers, "Submit yourselves for the Lord's sake to every human *creature*." J. N. D. Kelly says the verse should be translated using *creature*, not *human institution* or *ordinance*, since neither of these renderings is possible in the Greek. He points out that Peter continues, "Do honour to *all*" (v. 17)—pagans, Jews, as well as Christian brothers—

then "slaves be submissive" (v. 18) and finally "in the same way wives" (3:1).

Peter especially has a word for wives with unbelieving husbands. He says these men may even be won without words, but just by the pure and reverent attitude of the wives in their desire to do as the husbands wish. It is certainly encouraging to hear of this very thing happening today as women testify at various groups such as Christian Women's Clubs and Winning Women.

Peter continues, "Even as Sara obeyed Abraham, calling him lord: whose daughters ye are, as long as ye do well, and are not afraid with any amazement." This last is a difficult expression, and perhaps refers to Proverbs 3:25. Other translations are "as long as you live good lives and do not give way to hysterical fears" (Phillips) and "if you do good and show no fear" (NEB), something that must certainly have been difficult to do in view of the cruelty and thoughtlessness with which many wives were treated in those days.

The reference to Sarah's obeying Abraham and calling him lord has given rise to markedly different comments. Larry Christenson quotes André Bustanoby as pointing out that both Peter and Paul "state the command for a wife to be submissive without qualification" (evidently not believing or understanding it is a voluntary self-submitting). "Peter's use of Sarah as an illustration of obedience is notable," he says, "since Abraham twice in order to protect his own life denied that Sarah was his wife and allowed her to be taken into a ruler's harem.... By stating the case absolutely, both Peter and Paul forestall capriciousness in the matter of submission." Another commentator says "the lesson to be gleaned involves Sarah's consistent attitude of reverence, even when jesting, that showed her regarding him as more important than herself." That is certainly the attitude that all Christians are asked to have toward one another.

J. N. D. Kelly, however, tells us,

The reference is to the story of Sarah's amused incredulity at the promise that, despite her barrenness, and Abraham's advanced age, she would bear him a son. (Gen: XVIII:12: After I have waxed old, shall I have pleasure, my lord being old also?).... In fact, this manner of speaking of her husband conformed to conventional practice, but the Rabbis expounded the text as demonstrating Sarah's "obedience" to Abraham.

So once again the oral law may have been incorporated into church teaching. It is odd that the Rabbis put so much stock in Sarah's inaudible comment, yet her lie has been cited by them as the reason for never allowing a woman to act as witness!

Cohen in his introduction to *Everyman's Talmud* tells us,

The significance of the Biblical characters and the hold they were able to obtain upon the Jews for more than a thousand years, is primarily due to the Jewish preachers of the Talmud era.... They made bold to depict the lives of the Biblical heroes as immaculate, Scriptural narrative notwithstanding, and idealized the celebrated incidents in Israel's history... stirring the heart and mind of the Jews for countless generations.

Is this the explanation for Peter's use of Sarah as an example to follow; surely she is the Bible character the women would most like to resemble as the great cofounder of their nation?

If we turn to the actual Genesis account of Sarah's life, it hardly seems to merit such a role as the rabbis ascribed to her. The one place the word *lord* is used is when the writer, Moses, put these inaudible words into her mind when he recounted the incident hundreds of years later. Nowhere in Sarah's conversations with Abraham recorded in Scripture does she use this term. In one, in fact, she sounds more querulous than reverent: "My wrong be upon thee: I have given my maid into thy bosom; and when she saw that she conceived, I was despised in her eyes: the LORD judge between me and thee" (Gen. 16:5). The other two times she is telling him what to do. After the first (Gen. 16:2) the text says, "Abraham hearkened to the voice of Sarai," and after the second (Gen. 21:10-12) God said to Abraham, "In all that Sarah hath said unto thee, hearken unto her voice." Yet neither of the things Sarah suggested seem admirable.

That it was a common practice to call people *lord* seems obvious from the fact that Rachel addressed her father, Laban, as lord, as Rebecca did Abraham's servant; so also the sons of Heth, Abraham's neighbors, called him lord. Yet no lesson seems to have been drawn from this for present day usage among Christians, nor for the Jews to address others with that title.

Gangel, however, from this verse in Peter concludes that one of a husband's roles is that of "ruler." Helen B. Andelin, the author of *Fascinating Womanhood*, also points out the deep need of men to be considered "king" of their castle and assures us that this is one of the best recipes for a happy home.

Ephesians 5 is the passage in the Bible which most exalts the marriage relationship. It begins in much the same way as the section in Peter. In verse 21 Paul tells all Christians, "Be subject to one another" (RSV) and then in verse 22, "Wives to your own husbands," without repeating the verb. Yet all the translations I have seen which use paragraphs, with the exception of the RSV, Berkeley and NIV, have started a new paragraph with "Wives be subject. . . ." This hardly seems honest. Most commentators consider it a legal requirement that the wife obey the husband, but, if so, then it equally must be required for all Christians to obey each other since both groups are the subject of the one verb.

This verb is also in the Greek middle voice, meaning "subject yourselves." The *Augsburg Commentary* has one of the most helpful explanations. Beginning with verse 21, it states that submitting was asked of each member to every other member, irrespective of sex. From there, Paul goes on to the special case of the wife in Christian marriage. "Paul was not proving the inferiority of women, or subjecting all women to all men. In the case of the wife it is not a subjugation by the husband, but voluntary self-subjection by the wife, 'as unto the Lord,' that is, in order to please the Lord."

This commentary goes on to point out that Christianity has elevated woman and wifehood from their pagan degradation and made male and female one in the church, but some women have refused self-subjection to husbands because of a false view of emancipation. This seems true, especially today when so much stress is placed on individual rights. Some forget that true emancipation comes only from Christ and that his desire is that all his followers live in a spirit of meekness, "submitting themselves to one another." How much more, therefore, should a Christian wife submit to the man she has chosen in love.

The *Augsburg Commentary* concludes by suggesting that if a man will love and treat his wife with all the care and consideration he gives himself, the wife will be delighted to subject herself to that love. Human nature being as corrupt as it is, one cannot guarantee that even this will be one hundred per cent successful with all women, but I am sure it will be the most effective.

Larry Christenson has some stimulating views which he claims have been successful in revolutionizing family life for those who have tried it, and we will consider these later. Here we will conclude with one of his thoughts on a wife's submission:

God has given wives the opportunity to choose freely the submissive role, even as Jesus chose to be submissive to the Father. . . . When a wife's submission becomes a harsh demand from the husband, God's order has been overthrown, and a mere human authority remains. But when a husband fulfills his role in God's order–which is to "love his wife, and not be harsh with her" (Col. 3:19) then a wife's submission to him becomes a fountain of mutual love and devotion, a thing of surpassing moral and spiritual beauty.

Revolutionary Instructions to Husbands In the New Testament period, there was nothing new in the idea of wives being submissive to their husbands, for, after all, that was a legal requirement; but it was a great departure from custom to request it voluntarily. What was utterly revolutionary, however, were the instructions to *husbands*. Both Peter and Paul have some amazing things to say about the *mutual* responsibilities of husband and wife.

In 1 Corinthians 7:3-4 we read, "Let the husband render unto the wife due benevolence: and likewise also the wife unto her husband. The wife hath not power of her own body, but the husband; and likewise also the husband hath not power of his own body, but the wife." These words would surely have been a shock to Solomon, or even David. Paul's concluding advice not to withhold sexual intercourse from each other, except by mutual consent for the purpose of prayer, seems a little strange to modern Christian ears, for prayer can be a very suitable prelude to this sexual unity planned by God. Charles Shedd puts it well in his *Letters to Karen* when he tells her that this part of life is not a duet, "it is a trinity. . . . A wise creator made your bodies different for His purposes. So begin your sex life together on the premise this is God's life you are sharing. This is beautiful. This is holy. This is sacred."

Larry Christenson cautions us to remember it is *fun*, too, and not to constantly over-spiritualize it. M. N. Beck, past president of the Canadian Psychiatric Association, in an address to that body in 1973 entitled "Christ and Psychiatry," pointed out that "both Old and New Testaments... place the full enjoyment of sex at the core of the marital relationship. They portray the expression of sexuality, on the basis of full equality between the partners, with a warm-hearted openness, and in the Bible anticipated by at least 2,000 years the findings of Masters and Johnson."

In speaking of the single woman we have already considered part of a second pertinent passage: "He that is married careth for the things that are of the world, how he may please his wife,... she that is married... how she may please her husband" (1 Cor. 7:34). So surprising to some is the idea that a man should think about pleasing his wife that one commentator suggests this was just a "touch of humor" on Paul's part, not to be taken seriously. To me, a desire to please one's partner sounds like an important principle for an ideal marriage.

It is also noteworthy that Paul did *not* say married people ought to spend more time on the Lord's work and less on each other, but rather that if one does marry, then it is normal to have a mutual desire to please each other, and this hardly seems limited to sexual needs. Even the Old Testament has that curious verse in Deuteronomy 24:5, "When a man hath taken a new wife, he shall not go out to war, neither shall he be charged with any business: but he shall be free at home one year, and shall cheer up his wife which he hath taken." This is a practice long discontinued, but worth reviving.

In Colossians 3:19 Paul tells husbands, "Love your wives, and be not bitter against them." One commentator says this literally means, "Stop being cross"—letting things build up to the point where everything is looked at with a bitter, harsh spirit. Another observes, "One easily becomes bitter towards an inferior. A husband is not to treat the wife as an inferior person in the home, as his subject." The Boldreys add that nowhere is a husband told how to rule his wife. The only time this phrase is used is as a qualification for bishop and deacon, "One that ruleth well his own house, having his *children* in subjection" (1 Tim. 3:4). This "ruling" literally means to preside, govern, lead. It is the same word used in the feminine of Phoebe, as we noted earlier.

Peter also has an idea quite foreign to his world when he tells husbands to give honor to the wife as "unto the weaker vessel, and as being heirs together [on an equal basis in God's sight] of the grace of life" (1 Pet. 3:7). To the Jewish rabbis, and in most oriental societies, honor and respect went one way only—up—while those beneath one socially were regarded with disdain. One cannot help wondering if Peter received this insight into the marriage relationship directly from Christ, as he lived among and taught the disciples.

Commentators disagree about what Peter means by "weaker vessel." Some are sure he only means weaker in a physical sense; others that he is referring to status, or even moral or spiritual weakness. The word *vessel* is another puzzle. Some take it in the sense of "jar," evidently picturing the woman as the receptacle of the male's semen. But the fact that Peter uses the comparative, indicating the male is the stronger, makes "jar" seem inappropriate. Kelly suggests the meaning "body" or "being" with the idea of "the vessel containing the soul." He refers back to 2:13 where Peter had enjoined believers to "respect every human creature" and says that "husbands in the same way should exercise their leadership with proper deference, and show understanding and Christian insight and tact." Peter considered this so important that he tells husbands their prayers will be hindered if they do not heed what he says. So obviously this honoring and understanding of the wife by the husband is something which God regards as of considerable importance.

Gangel lists the results of a survey taken in Belgium on what wives considered the most common failings of husbands. At the top were lack of tenderness, politeness and sociability; failure to understand a woman's temperament and peculiarities; unfairness in financial matters; and frequency of snide remarks and sneers at the wife in company or before the children. These are all things that the exercise of understanding, honoring and love would eliminate.

Finally in Ephesians 5 we have the most detailed and beautiful account of the husband's part:

Husbands, love your wives, even as Christ also loved the church, and gave himself for it; . . . that he might present it to himself a glorious church. . . . So ought men to love their wives as their own bodies. He that loveth his wife loveth himself. For no man ever yet hated his own flesh; but nourisheth and cherisheth it, even as the Lord the church: for we are members of his body, of his flesh, and of his bones. For this cause shall a man leave his father and mother, and shall be joined unto his wife, and they two shall be one flesh. This is a great mystery, but I speak concerning Christ and the church. Nevertheless let every one of you in particular so love his wife even as himself; and the wife see that she reverence her husband. (vv. 25-33)

Typical of some commentators is the Amplified New

Testament which gives no clarification of the "love" the husbands are to give but amplifies tenfold the meaning of the "reverence" required of wives: "that she notices him, regards him, honors him, prefers him, venerates and esteems him; and that she defers to him, praises him, and loves and admires him exceedingly." (It is careful to add a footnote that Webster includes the word *adore* in the meaning of reverence—"but in the sense not applied to Deity"!

In this case, however, the male commentators have a woman author to back them up. Helen Andelin in *Fascinating Womanhood* heartily encourages wives to do all these things, saying they will then receive the kind of love they desire from their satisfied husbands. She quotes many witnesses who have tried it and found it works. Somehow the message seems to come better from a woman than a man. Perhaps that is why Paul later said that the older wives should teach the younger how to love their husbands.

Ephesians is a favorite book with ministers for the midweek service, but in spite of the greater length of the passage addressed to husbands I have actually heard a few pastors spend a whole evening driving home their duty to the wives of the congregation and the following week do little more than read the passage about husbands and pass on to the next! Some might justify this on the ground that it might make their fellow men vulnerable to attack from their wives, saying they were not doing what the preacher said. But when is this truth to be taught? Is this the usual subject at a Men's Night?

Others may say that love is not something that can be commanded or legislated; it is an emotion. Apparently the verb used by Paul to the husbands, however, is in the present imperative—keep right on loving with no end to it. Few commentators I have read point out, as does Larry Christenson, that this is *agape* love which Paul is speaking of—love which is measured by sacrifice, not feeling or emotion. It is much more subject to the will than is generally supposed. Romantic love is not the only basis for marriage. "Much of the real joy of marriage comes from *giving*, not *getting*. For marriage is modeled on the relationship between Christ and His Church. In every Christian marriage the world should be able to see that mutual giving and self-giving which characterizes the relationship between Christ and the Church."

I have no doubt that such passages in the Bible have helped to raise the status of women in countries which have accepted Christian standards. It is interesting, however, to note the variety of comments on these verses. Chrysostom said, "Wouldst thou that thy wife should obey thee as the church obeys Christ? Do thou then care for her as Christ the church, even if thou must lay down thy life for her—her that is the partner of thy life, and the mother of thy children, the spring of all thy joy." As he was one of the early church bishops and celibate, however, he perhaps did not realize that wives unfortunately can often be a source of irritation and are not "all joy."

Most prefer to stress the superiority of men. Woman is "the ivy which clasps itself so lovingly around the oak, pines and withers when the tree is fallen; and there is only one head. This marital headship is man's prerogative in virtue of his prior creation, for he was first formed in sole and original dignity." Pining and withering hardly seems the right reaction today for a missionary or military wife whose husband is often away, but this constant switching back and forth of roles requires an agility of mind and mood which not all wives can achieve or are willing to continue. Some wish to remain head of the house, hence some marriages break down. Unfortunately, too, the pining, withering ivy is still expected to support the family if the oak should fall, and the more children she has the less likely she is to find a new oak willing to be clung to!

Another commentator continues in a similar vein, saying, "Man carries in himself a likeness to the greatness and majesty of God in so far as he rules in his own sphere with God-like power and freedom." One, with rare humility, admits (what most wives discover sooner or later) that "the husband, unlike Christ, is a sinful and fallible human being like herself." That seemed to be something which escaped the notice of the rabbis and of most commentators. One, however, suggests that what was enjoined on the wives "is a matter of practical adjustment, rather than an ethical principle." Most would not agree with this, however, considering it God's basic order for all time.

Gangel, in his usually helpful book *The Family First,* has a rather odd comparison of what he calls "The Biblical Roles of the Husband" and "The Biblical Roles of the Wife." Those of the husband are a fine sounding list. He is to be Lover, Provider and Protector, Teacher, Ruler and Priest. For the wife, however, what he terms her "biblical roles" are not roles at all, but merely a string of adjectives. She is to be Encouraging (taken from the obscure verse about Isaac's finding in his new wife a good mother-substitute, although her later life was not too exemplary). She is to be Loving (her love is to be so strong it deserves the term *reverent* in Eph. 5). She is to be Submissive (which he calls a command, although the verses he gives in support are those discussed in this chapter). She is to be Consistent and Stable (his personal selections from the many attributes of the lady of Prov. 31). Finally, she is to be Attractive. On this latter point his reasoning seems a little curious, at least to a woman. He begins with the statement, "The Bible makes it clear that spiritual beauty is an internal, and not an external quality," but neither quotes the verse which says this nor discusses spiritual beauty, and instead continues, "Yet one is impressed in looking at Gen. 12:11 that Abraham was able to consider Sarah's attractiveness in his decisions and plans." (But Abraham's decision there was both cowardly and immoral!) And he concludes, "One imagines that the overwhelming majority of men desire their women to look, smell and act feminine."

There is no disputing his last statement, but is there really much difference between his picture of a "biblical wife" and that of Esther and the other beautiful young women rounded up and groomed for Ahasuerus' oriental harem? Is this all that *God* wants in a woman who is a wife?

He indicates no spiritual quality in his "biblical role" of the wife, although it is true in a previous chapter he has said that a Christian must not marry an unbeliever. He completely ignores Priscilla, certainly a biblical wife, and makes a quite arbitrary choice among the many possibilities in the Bible. I believe the majority of men would approve his list of attributes, however. It makes a cozy picture, with no thought for anyone outside the husband, apparently; but this may be quite legitimate since he is dealing with woman as wife only.

I can understand his difficulty in not finding any roles for a wife; I can't either. Is the reason that "wife" is just one of the roles of woman? Other possible concurrent ones, if we limit ourselves to examples in the Bible, are (in addition to "sex partner" if she does not rate the term "lover") daughter, daughter-in-law, mother, neighbor, hostess, nursemaid, teacher, cook, laundress, cleaning woman, interior decorator, weaver, seamstress, girdle maker, consumer and marketing expert, and so forth.

Jean Jacques Rousseau had a view similar to Gangel's, although he includes all women, not merely wives:

The whole education of women ought to be relative to men. To please them, to be useful to them, to make themselves loved and honored by them, to educate them when young, to care for them when grown, to counsel them, to make life sweet and agreeable to them—these are the duties of women at all times, and what should be taught them from infancy.

This is obviously what most men want, and if a woman chooses to be a wife she should bear it in mind. But is it necessarily God's ideal for every woman to limit her ministrations to her husband? There are many lonely elderly women and orphaned children in the world who also need someone to care for them and "make life sweet." These things that men want are, in fact, desired by every member of the human race.

The publishers of *The Family First* tell us on the cover that "God's preventive and corrective purpose in the roles of individuals as well as the collective roles of the family and the church are seen reinforcing each other in the clear teaching of the Word of God." As noted already, *role* is not a scriptural term. The woman of Proverbs 31, with her many irons in the fire, is very different from the Greek lady hiding away in her quarters or the Palestinian women wandering the countryside with their children listening to Christ's teaching. Are we in danger of going role crazy?

Perhaps I am a little prejudiced because I did some social work among the physically handicapped, some of them men who became paraplegics through car or industrial accidents. This is an extremely traumatic experience for anyone, but I noticed that those least able to face it were men of European background where only the man was supposed to work and the wife be dependent. Often the wife of a paraplegic not only had to work but also had to suffer from her husband's resentment being turned against her for doing what he could not do! What seems most needed is the development of maturity of outlook, rather than obsession with traditional roles.

Christ never legislated men's and women's roles. He is more interested in what we are, and what our heart attitude is, than the role we are playing. True, he suggested that a woman mixing yeast in dough is an illustration of the kingdom of heaven, but does that mean a Christian woman must always bake her own bread and never buy from a bakery, where the work was probably done by men?

To the religious leaders of his day Christ must have seemed a dangerous scrambler of roles when he, a Master and Teacher, spoke to women, held children, took a towel and washed feet (a Gentile slave or housewife's duty) or cooked breakfast by the lake. The latter in many times and places has been considered women's work. No Victorian gentleman would think it anything he should do; yet many men today regard barbecuing on the patio "their thing." Abraham, Jacob and Esau also did some cooking.

Some would say a wife's role is eternally determined by God's words to Eve, that she was henceforth to have a succession of painful pregnancies and be ruled by her husband. But did that mean that this is to be true of every woman? If so, then it would seem that the role of every man is meant to be that of Adam: a sorrowful, sweating farmer (Gen. 3:17-19).

On this subject of roles, Christenson quotes a noted psychologist, Bruno Bettelheim, on the danger of a husband's becoming "mother's little helper" by taking part in household chores: "Male physiology and psychology aren't geared to it. Not that there's anything wrong with a father occasionally giving a baby a bottle if the situation requires it, or he enjoys it. What's wrong is thinking that it adds to his parenthood. When a father tries to be a 'better' father by acting like a mother he is not only less fulfilled as a father, but as a man, too." Then he speaks of the danger of children's having a blurring of mother/father roles. "Because many fathers wash dishes and perform other traditional female tasks their sons often don't know what it means to be a man. If father and mother do the same chores a child doesn't have a clear father or mother image."

No doubt there is considerable truth in this. On the other hand, we remember that John Money said males also have the "mothering" circuit in their brains. It may be that they are not intrinsically unfit psychologically, but rather have been the victims of tradition. Doesn't motive come into it, too? Is a man doing these things to "add to his parenthood," or is he in self-giving love trying to help his wife out in a specially busy time? If, as Bernard Ramm says, every cell of his body is coded masculine, surely this cannot drain away with washing a few dishes, nor can his son's by seeing him at the sink. In most modern houses and apartments few "masculine" chores are left, and doing nothing while at home but reading newspapers and gazing at television hardly provides an inspiring father image either. Throughout the history of mankind, fighting for his clan or country has been regarded as one of man's traditional roles, and David in Psalm 144:1 declared it was the Lord "which teacheth my hands to war, and my fingers to fight." Yet some clergy and many other people today claim that war is "obscene" and "sinful." How binding is tradition and who is to say when it is to be changed?

If a wife is always *telling* her husband to do this or that of "her" chores, then this would be a dangerous and unchristian situation, I believe. The other night, however, I was among some dinner guests at the home of a big, ex-football player, British Army chaplain. After we had been there a short time, he excused himself, saying he would like to see if he could give his wife a hand. I do not know what the male guests thought, but to me this seemed a nice example of agape love in action.

Charles Shedd's books *Letters to Karen* and *Letters to Philip* show an amazing understanding of the natures of both man and woman. Shedd gained this through many years of counseling plus, it appears, real success in his own marriage. One of his suggestions is that each partner come to the marriage not with the thought of a 50-50 relationship, so common today, but rather 60-40, the biblical principle of "let each esteem other better than themselves."

Larry Christenson has a different way of figuring, namely, for the wife to be 100 percent wife and the husband 100 percent husband. This has much to commend it, and his book is certainly one which should be read by anyone concerned by the present widespread breakdown of marriage.

Christenson bases his view of the marriage relationship on the ground not of the natural superiority of man but of merely divine order. He gives credit for much of his thinking to a small book by a German author of the last century, H. W. J. Thiersch, called *Christian Family Life*. Although the latter does refer to "man being formed first" as part of the reason for his headship, his argument rests mainly on God's dictate at the Fall as the result of the sin of both Adam and Eve:

Upon man is laid the authority to rule. But with it comes heavy care and hard labor upon a cursed earth. . . . Gladly would the man allow the rule to pass out of his hands–if at the same time he were released from the care and the responsibility. The number of men who have abdicated their position as heads of their households bears testimony to this in our own day.

The woman is not afraid of the toil, but desires the rule. The continual self-denial of her own will is her heaviest trial.

Thus the burden of both man and woman is chosen for them so as to fall most heavily upon the natural inclinations of each. In the natural state, man and woman find the burden to be truly a curse. . . . The yoke should be so heavy to them that they cannot bear it without God's help. . . . [With his help] then a hidden blessing opens up in the curse. The burden becomes only half as heavy. It serves as a purification. It shows itself as the ordering of Divine wisdom and love. It is a preparation and education for the kingdom of God.

I am not sure that woman wants her own way any more than man does. This seems a general human weakness. And throughout history it would appear that, rather than abdicating their position, even more men have clung to their rule and dispensed with the care and love demanded by the New Testament. Apart from these small points, however, Thiersch's theory does seem a good explanation for the difficulties of marriage and the common idea that man "can't live with woman and can't live without her," and vice versa.

This view about men's shrinking from responsibility was brought out recently in a secular source, also, under the heading "The Cost of Swinging" by Jenkin Lloyd Jones of the Tulsa *Tribune*. Jones refers to an article in *Harper's* by George Gilder, entitled "The Suicide of the Sexes":

Gilder's thesis is that males must be enticed into family responsibilities, and without such responsibilities they have a hard time standing tall in their own eyes. When no longer compelled by the institution of marriage to assume responsibilities, Gilder contends, men are robbed of the self-esteem that comes to the protector, the teacher and provider. They are only itinerant studs—a career that may look alluring for the moment, but after 35, what?

Two months later the *Readers Digest* gave a long condensation of Gilder's article, and, since it may have far-reaching influence in these desperate days of family disintegration, it bears further examination.

The differences between men and women are the single most important fact of human society, Gilder feels, and the present drive to deny them threatens society as never before. Sex is really the life force and cohesive impulse of a people, he maintains, not merely the act of copulation with which many equate it today. When true sex is devalued, the quality of life declines and the whole social fabric begins to unravel. (This is certainly an accurate description of present conditions, although I believe it is due to ignoring all God's laws, not just ideas about sex.) According to Gilder, in this larger context of sex the husband's role is trivial and subordinate—it is the wife who conceives, bears and suckles the child, and is the only one who is necessarily present at its arrival. Therefore the man has somehow to be given a way to make himself equal by cultural mores. Gilder sees this as the origin of various tribal ceremonies through which by some specific action, a male officially enters manhood. In America this is usually the getting of a job.

Female identification, on the other hand,

is affirmed and demonstrated monthly in menstruation. Even if she does not bear a child, she is continually reminded that she can, that she is capable of performing the crucial act in the perpetuation of her family and the species. Regardless of any other anxieties in relation to her sexual role, she at least knows that she has *a role. Her knowledge is stamped on her very being.*

This was a new thought to me. Perhaps that is how it appears to a man, but for many women menstruation is a quite painful and embarrassing inconvenience during which they are hardly likely to have great thoughts about perpetuating the species; and for a single woman it must be very frustrating indeed. Even for a wife today it cannot be a very consoling thought since the emphasis is so strongly on *limiting* the population. Not many women these days bear children during more than about a twelve-year span, so if they live to be seventy that means for the greater part of their life they are not filling this role.

Perhaps there should be more education for girls along this line, but then they might be inclined to get too proud and overbearing at the thought of being so indispensable to the human race! Such would be quite unjustified, of course, for the male is equally necessary. Does *he*, by the way, have these great thoughts about perpetuating the species with every emission of semen? If so, one would think it must be frustrating for him, too, to realize he should limit his vast potential to one woman partner.

According to Gilder, however, the institution of marriage is necessary to transform individuals into voluntary participants in the social order. "Throughout history societies have recognized the great price to be paid in securing family commitments from men. Women have had to use all their ingenuity, all their powers of sexual attraction to induce men to create and support families. And the culture has had to invest marriage with all the ceremonial sanctity of religion and law." Here he has the order reversed, of course, but it is interesting to find a secular voice now recognizing the vital importance of a divinely planned institution, though his picture of the male is a little different from the average commentator's!

Gilder then explains the importance of a job for the male in Western society: "A man's job is a central part of the sexual constitution. It can affirm the masculine identity of its holder; it can make it possible for him to court women in a spirit of commitment; it can make it possible for him to be married and thereby integrated into a continuing community." So, like most theologians, he recognizes the man's role as provider, though not on the ground that he is a superior creature, but rather the reverse:

Crucial to the sexual constitution of employment is that . . . it assures that over the whole society most men will make more money than most women. For a man who does not make as much money as the significant women in his life–his girlfriend, wife, and closest co-workers–will often abandon his job and will pursue women in the plundering masculine spirit that the women's movement so condemns. . . . The man is paid more, not because of his special virtue, but because of the key importance of taming his naturally disruptive energies. . . . If all the usual job stresses are intensified by sexual competition, men will retaliate through bureaucratic sabotage or viciousness on the job, or they will desperately try to escape–either to the street or higher levels of bureaucracy.

This is a sad picture indeed, and rather different from the commentator's sturdy oak with clinging vine. Or was that just a cover-up for basic insecurity? If Gilder's remarks were true, it would make it seem impossible for a woman honestly to "reverence" a man. Certainly there are some men who continually make snide remarks about women to make themselves feel big. And it was disheartening to hear recently of some male students who had married, let their wives put them through school, and then when they were established in good jobs divorced their wives and married again, apparently not being able to stomach the thought of having been dependent on a wife. But I certainly do not believe this is true of all men. There are mature people even among the unregenerate, and one who has been made a

new creation in Christ, a son of God, has no need to feel in-
secure, imprisoned in tradition or uncertain of his purpose
in life. Christ can meet his particular need, just as he has for
countless single and widowed women who have been
denied their natural "role" in life. Later in this chapter we
will consider examples of some highly mature and successful Christian men who have acknowledged receiving some
help from their wives without apparently going all to pieces
afterward.

I must admit I found the comments about the attitude
to "closest co-workers" a little disturbing. One can understand a man's wanting to be the provider for girlfriend or
wife, since that is his normal God-given responsibility. But
is he meant always to appear better than any woman? Is it
really God's intention that all women be economically dependent? Or is it that because the wife is usually occupied
with bearing and rearing children the husband should have
the responsibility of providing for them? In any case, I am
still not certain that God does not want a woman to be paid
what her work is worth. In the United States in 1970, 3.2
million wives were earning more than their husbands and
the latter who were interviewed did not seem to object. No
doubt a good number were working wives of students or of
the unskilled or unemployed, but one was earning
$38,000 to her husband's $27,000 and another $419,248 to
his $336,000. Perhaps beyond a certain point the ego is not
so sensitive.

It is hard for a woman to understand this supposed need
to feel superior by making others inferior, but at least for a
wife who loves her husband the obvious thing seems to be
to enable him to feel "tall in his own eyes" and as comfortable and happy as possible.

Gilder's main thrust appears to be not against women's

liberation per se, however, but against that part of it which encourages promiscuity, sex which "loses contact with its procreative sources" and then becomes increasingly "undifferentiated, homosexual, and pornographic." He sees the most important step in restoring a sense of order and purpose to be in reestablishing "the social pressures and cultural biases in favor of durable monogamous love and marriage. It is women who will most benefit in the beginning, for their discomfort in the toils of male sexuality is already inducing a revulsion toward sex altogether. But ultimately the whole society will gain."

As already intimated, it is interesting to find a purely secular source recognizing the desperate state society has come to and advocating the plan which God initiated at the dawn of human history. If we do not acknowledge God, however, or seek his design for the marriage relationship, it seems that in a possible backlash there may be danger of woman's being pushed back into the old pagan bondage.

If "social pressures" are to be put in effect, then I would think the most effective for making an average woman who has had an interesting job and adequate income content to become a wife and mother and remain at home would be for the husband, and society, to acknowledge openly that she is doing a vital service both to himself, the family and society, instead of regarding it as a "nothing" job which any moron could cope with. This would be scriptural, too, for the woman in Proverbs was highly praised by her husband, even though she seemed to be quite a provider herself. There are still many wives who never receive any word of appreciation, and some in Canada and Europe who receive not a cent of recompense apart from their food, shelter and some clothing. I read recently of a Canadian high-school teacher who married a fellow teacher. He was so annoyed when the babies began to come and they lost her salary that he did all the grocery shopping himself, and she had to beg him repeatedly to get money even to buy a pair of pantyhose. On the other hand, the American matriarchal boss is also an unpleasant picture. How is the husband to be returned to his proper position as head and provider, without becoming the dictator tyrant he has so often turned out to be?

From Thiersch's basic theory, Larry Christenson does an excellent job of detailing the "burden" of responsibility for the husband instead of leaving the onus largely on the wife to be submissive, as so many do. In fact, he makes it so hard he wisely leaves the chapter "God's Order for Husbands" until the very last, after those on God's order for wives, for children and for parents, because without first being hooked by those probably most men would not take the one on husbands seriously. If they do, they will most likely revolutionize not only their homes but also their churches.

We have already quoted Christenson on the voluntary submission of the wife, and he certainly has no half measures for her. But he does make a distinction between *submission* and *servility*. The husband, too, has to be one hundred percent the authority ordained by God.

At first glance . . . this seems like a fine perch for the man: "I'm king of my castle." . . . But one must look deeper. For the divine authority vested in a husband is modeled upon Christ. And Christ's authority was rooted in the sacrifice of himself. . . . The authority of Christ, and therefore of a husband . . . is not a human "fleshly" authority. It is not one person lording it over others. It is a divine and spiritual authority which is rooted in the sacrifice of oneself.

As an illustration of its outworking, he cites the case of a family argument flaring up. It is the husband's place first to humble himself and ask forgiveness:

This is death to the ego. It may be the wife's guilt is great or greater. No matter. His call is to love his wife as Christ loved the church. Jesus humbled himself under the guilt of sin "while we were yet sinners" (Romans 5:8). . . . . A husband who falls to lecturing his wife on her duty to be submissive to his authority has already yielded up the ground of his authority. His call under God is to fulfil his role in the family.

He suggests that if a wife is unsubmissive to her husband it may well be because the man is secretly or openly rebellious against Christ, and points out that only those who are under his authority are fit to wield authority. If a husband goes through the humbling experience of putting himself right with God, a new spirit of gentleness and meekness will probably appear in his family "and, amazingly, a new measure of authority—authority which he must no longer strive for, but which is yielded gladly, for he has 'died to self' and therefore God has been able to establish his authority in the family." It would certainly be hard to find a more revolutionary view of the "headship of man" than this.

Christian Marriage as Witness I was encouraged to hear of a good example of a loving husband in a new missionary couple in Japan a few years ago. After a little language study, the pair took an exploratory trip through Japan with an interpreter, looking for a suitable place for future service. At the end of the tour the middle-aged interpreter remarked that he could see that a loving husband made a submissive wife, and he must try and show more love to his own wife. How different this is from another couple we heard of where the husband was the big boss: After the two left, their Japanese helper said that if that was what a Christian husband was like, she did not want one.

Gangel points out that there are two sides to Paul's anal-

ogy of the husband's relationship to his wife being like that
of Christ to the church. On the one, the husband looks to
the example of Christ's love for the church to see how to
love his wife. It can have a much wider impact, however.
The world may also learn something about Christ's relationship to the church by seeing a Christian husband's love
and sacrifice for his wife. Without ever being in a church,
unsaved neighbors may learn something of God's truth by
observing the behavior of a Christian family.

Nowhere is this more true than on the foreign mission
field. While often, as evangelical missionaries, our greatest
concern is to stuff as much sound doctrine as possible into
our contacts, actually what usually impresses the oriental
first may be the price and style of our clothes or our tone of
voice and gestures. There is probably no area in which we as
Christians and foreigners are more closely watched and
judged than in the husband-wife relationship. Our older
daughter once attended a small flower-arrangement class
with the wife of an Indian diplomatic official and a young
Japanese lady, and the favorite topic of conversation of the
other two was how husbands behaved to wives in their respective countries. That is probably why Paul wrote to Titus
that the older women were to teach the younger wives how
to behave "so that the word of God be not blasphemed."
The early pagan world was gradually impressed with the
character of Christian wives, as well as virgins and widows.
They were not crushed, ignorant, gossiping chattels, but
they willingly and helpfully submitted to their husbands for
the Lord's sake.

Japan for centuries has been known as a "man's world,"
with baby girls taught from earliest years to submit smiling-
ly (sometimes with tragic moral results). Many foreigners
have been deceived by the women's outward docility, think-

ing them the ideal submissive wives Christians are supposed to be. But subjection without love easily leads to hatred. The results of a poll taken in Japan to find out what people would like to be if reincarnated in this world showed that many women wanted to reverse roles with their husbands so they could treat them as they had been treated.

A review of one of Pearl Buck's books spoke of her "God-drunk" father who ignored his wife in the name of the Lord so that her love gradually turned to silent hatred. Fortunately, not all foreigners were like that in China. An English woman lecturer, a widow, visiting some Chinese universities in the '30s, when winds of reform were sweeping the country, was amazed at the frequency with which students would ask questions about the Christian relationship of husband and wife or else say that when they married they "wanted to behave like an English Christian gentleman" to their wives. (Now, unfortunately, most oriental countries think they know what a western man is like from seeing American movies.)

It is not always easy to know exactly how much to conform to the standards of the country one is living in and where to draw the line to demonstrate a Christian relationship. When missionaries first penetrated into China and for long afterwards, it was the custom for a wife always to walk respectfully a few steps behind the husband. Missionaries were therefore advised to do the same, especially those who had adopted Chinese dress. But, I have heard, a few American couples refused to do this, out of a desire to show the Christian teaching of the equal worth of women. In Japan, for the same reason, I have heard of an occasional missionary referring to his own wife by the honorific title reserved for the wife of another, one's own wife being referred to merely as "the inside person." I have no idea what impression these departures from custom made on the respective local people, since no explanation was given, but perhaps the desired effect could have been obtained by tone of voice or facial expression, which seem to convey much more to the oriental person than the occidental.

A Japanese pastor friend told me that when, as a young Christian, he went to a Canadian Bible college the hardest culture shock to absorb was the "ladies first" pattern of life. So if we are living in a "man's world," it surely does not matter if we women do not go through a door first or receive the first cup of tea or coffee. And I doubt it does any good to the Christian cause by pushing the equality of women for its own sake. We want to win the men, and their families, to Christ, not put them off with superficial things. Maybe that was Paul's thought, too, in some of his restrictive instructions.

On the other hand, if there is a real need to be met, people may see the meaning behind the unusual act. I remember an old elder in China once escorted me on a three-hour walk to a village where two single girls were already holding some women's meetings, and he insisted on carrying my overnight bag. This was unheard of for a man to do (except for the professional coolies). But he had seen J. O. Fraser—of Lisuland fame—and mission superintendent for that province help women missionaries in this way, and it was evidence of a high degree of Christian grace that this Chinese gentleman was willing to follow his example.

I think of a Chinese servant woman, too, who nearly worshiped the husband of the missionary couple she worked for, because when the wife was still in bed after the arrival of a baby and the servant needed to hurry off to market, the husband hung the washing out and did similar acts whenever there was a need. I have read of at least one Japanese woman accepting Christ because a missionary gave her his seat in a streetcar. In contrast, I once saw someone stand up to give a seat to a woman in an advanced stage of pregnancy, but before she could maneuver herself into it a Japanese man ducked beneath her bulge and triumphantly dropped into the seat first!

All these examples have been the acts of men, and, of course, it is the Bible's instructions for men which made Christianity so revolutionary. Nowhere does the Bible teach that a woman should push herself forward to demonstrate her equality. So we may conclude that the most important thing for a missionary couple is to show real concern and love for each other within the framework of the scriptural pattern rather than to try to change outward social customs. On the home front, however, where there is now legal recognition of equality, it is not likely a man will win converts if he loudly demands "obedience" from his wife "in the name of the Lord." But I believe the whole world wistfully longs to see a couple married some years who are really loving to and considerate of each other.

Because of this, Christenson sees the present breakdown of family life as an unparalleled opportunity for the Christian family to be a witness for Christ:

The most hardened pagan will sit up and take notice of a family which has learned to live well together—a family where husband and wife show mutual love and respect, and the children are polite and well behaved. Those whose families are barren of love and laughter . . . look with undisguised envy at the family up the street which has such a good time together. . . . This is the opportunity . . . to so experience the reality and power of Christ in our homes, to so live according to his Divine Order, that those around us can see that something has happened.

Older Wives as Teachers Two verses in the Epistles refer to older wives. The first is 1 Timothy 4:7, which in the AV reads, "Refuse profane and old wives' fables." But some modern versions have changed it to myths and fables "fit only for old women." This does not seem a kind or even sensible thing to say; if the things were really untrue or profane, they were surely not fit for anyone! At least it can be a reminder that God wants us to love and serve him with all our heart and *mind*, whatever our age.

The other, more important passage, is Titus 2:3-5:

The aged women . . . be in behaviour as becometh holiness, not false accusers, not given to much wine, teachers of good things; that they may teach the young women to be sober, to love their husbands, to love their children, to be discreet, chaste, keepers at home, good, obedient to their own husbands, that the word of God be not blasphemed.

Who were these "aged," actually "older" women? I have sometimes asked my students what age range they would give for "younger women" and they usually say up to about thirty. It seems likely, therefore, that these "older" ones were all those over thirty. On the other hand, they could have been real grannies or even some of the widows on the church roll.

Another interesting problem is where these older women were to do their teaching. Some of the modern translations, as well as some commentators who are sure women are not meant to teach anything, suggest the "teaching" was just that of the example of their lives. But if they were the grannies, then their husbands were likely dead and their children grown and away, so they could hardly demonstrate these things by life only. The Amplified New Testament makes it much more than this. "They are to give good counsel, be teachers . . . wisely train. . . ." But was this to be done as a mother-in-law in a family situation, as a wider house-to-house visitation course or as teaching at a kind of women's fellowship meeting?

Few evangelical churches until recently seem to have had any idea of the value or need for such teaching. In fact recently a young male expert on Christian education came to give us helpful hints on improving or streamlining church life, and his first suggestion was to cut out the Women's Missionary Fellowship. As a missionary, I knew that this group was most helpful to the missionaries and planned good programs for the women themselves. When two-thirds of the church membership are women and they are denied any voice in ordinary church services or administration, it seems heartless, and indeed conceited, to suggest that their only meeting is a worthless part of church life!

There may well be some Dorcas Guild-type meetings in older churches which are really only make-work affairs with little purpose, but in most evangelical churches they have a real ministry. The tremendous response to such organizations as Christian Women's Club, Christian Business and Professional Women and Winning Women indicates that the personal needs of women, and opportunities for outreach, have not been adequately met in many churches. Talks on self-submitting to husbands are received better from another woman than from a male preacher who obviously stands to benefit from such teaching.

The subjects these older women were to teach may have seemed a little strange, and unnecessary, at least a generation ago. Then mothers were thought to love their children by instinct, yet we have already seen that child exposure was common in Paul's day. Our own newspapers today reveal an obvious need for this teaching, too. Three to five children are battered to death by their parents each week in the United States, and many others are hospitalized every day. Also, I believe, much of the present permissiveness is due more to laziness and misjudgment than real love.

It may seem strange to some that wives might need to be taught to love their husbands since most western marriages begin with a romantic courtship. However, our lawcourts are full of cases of women who evidently have not been able to accomplish this feat for long. In spite of the many books written on the subject today, usually by ministers or male psychologists, young people are not prepared for the tests of marriage, especially since most have been brought up to have their own way and "stand up for their rights." The women in Paul's day had little or no rights, the marriages were usually arranged, the spouses were possibly unknown to each other beforehand, so that love was something which needed to be taught, particularly in the churches so that "the word of God be not blasphemed" by ugly conduct.

There is a desperate need today for instruction on Christian marriage a good while *before* the event, so that when girls really know what self-submitting means they will not be in such a hurry to marry but will make sure they have found someone they can "reverence." And boys should be taught that it is not enough to drive a car, use the right deodorant and know how to make love or even have a job; they must be worthy of a girl's reverence (which is not likely if they engage in premarital sex) and be willing to practice that giving love Paul commanded. Unfortunately, Paul did not say who was to give this instruction, and the church has not done a very good job.

May a Wife Never Teach Her Husband Anything? We have already seen that many men regard Adam's sin as "hearkening unto the voice of thy wife," while others think that when Paul said he did not allow a woman to teach or domineer "the man," he was referring to a husband and wife. Thiersch is emphatic on this point. If a wife should become a Christian first, "Let her beg him to go with her to hear the preaching of the Gospel, but let her not teach him herself. SUCH AN ATTEMPT WILL AND SHOULD FAIL. From one evil springs a second which is greater: her persuasions change into complaints and lecturings. Displeasure, coldness, and estrangement follow, and the foundation of a lasting mischief is laid." Like Peter, he believes the husband will be won by her submissive conduct, not words.

We certainly find few examples in Scripture of wives even giving advice to their husbands. Sarah did, and Abraham followed it at God's command. Manoah's wife and Hannah come near the mark. Abigail and her husband Nabal are an interesting case: "She was a woman of good understanding, and of a beautiful countenance, but the man was churlish and evil . . . and David said to Abigail, . . . blessed be thy advice, and blessed be thou, which hast kept me this day from coming to shed blood" (1 Sam. 25: 3, 33). But that was *before* he married her.

Many modern marriage counseling manuals also suggest leaving anything in the way of criticism to the husband's boss, the wife concentrating on building up her husband, admiring and accepting him as he is. Even for a wife to *appear* competent, intelligent or able "to kill her own snakes," is usually disastrous, according to Helen Andelin: "The average red-blooded man" when he meets a capable looking woman then feels like "a futile, ineffectual imitation of a man." Previously I had had no idea masculinity was so fragile, having been told that men saw things objectively while women take things too personally. But it helps in understanding reactions noted in some men.

Both that author and many men declare it is a woman's dependency which men find so charming and which makes them feel masculine. This no doubt is true. Unfortunately, in fallen human nature, power usually corrupts. Chivalry has not been the universal response to the enforced dependency of women, and there is little evidence of chivalry in the Bible. Abraham twice left Sarah to the probability of rape by heathen strangers, in the hope of saving his own skin. Lot offered his virgin daughters to the lecherous Sodomites rather than have his male guests molested by the homosexuals attacking his house; likewise the Levite his concubine in the hideous story in Judges. Many in Christ's day (and every other day) found the dependency of widows a great opportunity to defraud them. So it is not the dependency of the wife alone which will ensure a happy marriage, but the willing self-subjection on her part and Christlike love on the husband's.

But to return to the question of the possibility or permissibility of a Christian wife's ever offering helpful advice or even criticism to her husband, it would seem that, perhaps fortunately, not all men are "average." It is remarkable to find in recent years some of the men most used by God giving a good deal of credit to their wives as critics, helpers or teachers. In the prefaces of books written by two men who have been outstanding preachers in England and America during the last twenty years, we find similar words. (By "outstanding" I mean those whom other evangelicals would gladly take the time to go and hear if opportunity occurred.) These are men very different in style, but men whom God has used greatly: I refer to Martyn Lloyd-Jones and Billy Graham.

Lloyd-Jones states, "Like many of my fellow preachers I

acknowledge that my best and severest critic is my wife."
In one of his books, Billy Graham expresses appreciation
to "My wife, Ruth, my most valued critic." I have also read
that from her own private devotions she sometimes gives
him ideas he uses in his preaching. J. B. Phillips also dedi-
cates his New Testament paraphrase to "My wife and finest
critic."

Going back a little farther, I once heard Ethel Barratt
read a letter from D. L. Moody's son which mentioned the
gracious way Mrs. Moody added a little "couth" and grammar instruction to her less educated husband, and how he
never let a day go by without telling her he loved her and
publicly thanking God for her in family devotions.

It would be interesting to know the secret of the greatness of these different men. Some have declared that the
sum of a husband and wife as a unit should ideally be
greater than the sum of the parts, and in line with this it is
probable that the success of these men as preachers may be
partly due to help from their wives in understanding the
feelings, needs and reactions of the people in the pew. But
I think they must have been men of great character to begin with (indicated in a wise choice of wives)—men who
were not afraid to listen to and give credit to even a woman
lest it should detract from their masculinity or reputation.
Their words of appreciation for their wives are undoubted
proof of real Christian humility and maturity, and this
probably accounts for the fact that God has been able to use
them so outstandingly.

Howard Hendricks, one of the most popular speakers in
North America at the present time, with a wide ministry
richly blessed by God, writes in *Say It with Love*, "The secret
of my own life and ministry is the one flesh relationship
with my wife which God brought into being and is nurtur-

ing. It is my greatest satisfaction in life, and it's all of Him."
(By one flesh relationship he does not merely mean sex, but
intimacy, openness and honesty.) In another place he
states, "My wife taught me that a relationship is far more
important than a clean home. We can have a *Better Homes
and Gardens* layout, and a *Mad* family life. The floor can be
cleaned after little feet have muddied it, but bruised relationships are not so easily restored." This reminds us again
of Tournier's saying, "It is from woman, and under her influence, that man can acquire a feeling for persons."

Larry Christenson, in distinguishing between submissiveness and servility, says that when a wife sees her husband's judgment is wrong or unwise she should tell him
so—with all respect, but freely and honestly:

*The judgment, wisdom and opinion of a loving wife is one of man's
greatest assets. It saves him from many a foolish mistake, and it is
his privilege and responsibility as a husband to receive the wise
counsel of his wife. . . . She must tell him her thoughts fully and
make her case as strongly as she can, never laying aside her respect,
but never concealing her honest doubts. . . . When she has done
this, then she may let the decision rest with her husband, trusting
God to give him good judgment.*

*In spiritual things, especially, a wise husband will welcome the
counsel and opinion of his wife. Women often have a more direct
grasp of spiritual realities than men. . . . The spiritual health and
direction of the family is fully as dependent upon the insight and
concern of the wife as upon the authority and protection of the husband. Submission . . . to authority means that you put yourself
wholly at the disposal of the person who is set over you. This is the
meaning of "Yield yourselves to God . . . and your members as instruments of righteousness" (Romans 6:13). It is on this kind of
submission the husband/wife relationship is modeled. If a wife with-
holds her understanding and feelings on the matter, she is being less*

than submissive for she is not putting these things at her husband's disposal.

He does add a warning against spiritual pride, however, and quotes Thiersch as saying a wife who allows others to remark that her husband is less enlightened than herself is a "disgusting creature."

A wife also is not to try to force her opinion through at any cost, but must fully express her feelings if the family is not to

be denied the blessings God intends to channel through her. Thus the subordinate role of the wife does not stifle her personality. On the contrary, it provides the best environment for her creativity and individuality to express itself in a wholesome way. It is God's way of drawing upon her gifts of intelligence, insight and judgment, without at the same time burdening her with the authority and responsibility of decision.

Christenson also quotes from *A Man Called Peter* where Catherine Marshall recounts what her husband had once said about the responsibilities of a wife:

The average woman, if she gives her full time to her home, her husband, her children. . . . If she tries to understand her husband's work . . . to curb his egotism while . . . building up his self esteem, to kill his masculine conceit while encouraging all his hopes, to establish around the family a circle of true friends. . . . If she provides in the home a proper atmosphere of culture . . . she will be engaged in a life work that will demand every ounce of her strength, every bit of her patience, every talent God has given her, the utmost sacrifice of her love.

It would certainly seem so, and not every husband will be prepared to receive these things women are asked to give. The killing of conceit or even the giving of advice may seem to some more like a bee sting than a blessing, and a man may clam up or else leave everything to his wife. Charles Shedd, while he seems to state the case fairly for the man and the woman's side in earlier books, in a recent interview said he thinks the feminist movement is an indictment of the way many men treat women: "Many husbands are clods who won't relate. The problem with women is not women, but men." It seems, too, that men are less willing to seek help for an unhappy marriage relationship, either because of guilt or because they think it is the wife's job to adjust and change.

It is good to know that this is not true of all men, however, as these various quotations have abundantly shown. Even a few rabbis occasionally admitted that a woman's influence or advice could be for the good of her husband. They cited the case of a fine, good-living couple who unfortunately had no children. So after ten years, as was the custom, they divorced, each marrying again. The husband married an evil wife, and became bad himself. The woman married an evil man, and before long he had become good!

One of the heroines of the Talmud is the wife of Rabbi Meir. Some lawless men were living in their neighborhood, and they used to vex the rabbi sorely. Once he prayed that they should die. His wife, Beruriah, exclaimed, "What is on your mind? Is it because it is written, 'Let sinners cease out of the earth' (Psalm civ.35)? But the text can be read so as to mean, 'Let sins cease out of the earth.' [The same consonants can be vocalized to give the word for "sins" instead of "sinners" explains the footnote.] Glance also at the end of the verse, 'and let the wicked be no more'—i.e., when 'sins shall cease' then 'the wicked will be no more.' Rather should you pray that they repent and be no more wicked." Rabbi Meir offered prayer on their behalf and they repented (Ber. 10a).

So there is evidence that a woman may be able to offer

some helpful advice or even teaching both for the home and even sometimes in the area of a husband's work and that a godly man will not necessarily be out of the Lord's will to listen to her.

Aquila and Priscilla: Ideal Couple or Exception? Can we find in the New Testament any examples of actual husband and wife situations? We know that Peter and some of the other apostles took their wives around on their preaching trips, but we are given no details (1 Cor. 9:5). Among the people Paul greets at the end of his letters are very few couples. In his letter to the Roman Christians, of the eight women mentioned only two appear to be married, and that is assuming Junia is feminine and was married to Andronicus.

The only couples we know much about are Aquila and Priscilla, and Ananias and Sapphira. Some people might consider the latter the ideal wife, since she submitted to her husband's scheme, but the Holy Spirit evidently thought otherwise.

What about Aquila and Priscilla? Paul called them "my helpers in Christ Jesus: who for my life laid down their own necks: unto whom not only I give thanks, but also all the churches of the Gentiles. Likewise greet the church that is in their house" (Rom. 16:3-5).

It would be interesting to know if these two are "God's ideal couple," working together as a team both in their tent (leather) making, and also in their spiritual ministry. "Aquila and Priscilla . . . took [Apollos] and expounded unto him the way of God more perfectly." Or was it that they had no children, and are thus the exception that proves the rule that it is usually the husband only who has a spiritual ministry?

Most evangelical missions today do regard their couples as both being "in the work," yet there are exceptions. According to Joy Turner Tuggy's helpful book *The Missionary Wife and Her Work*, at least one husband felt it must only be considered "his work" and the wife merely the "homekeeper." There are no doubt some men who feel a deep, innate need to establish their superiority, and others who sincerely feel, still, that God could never be glorified by a woman speaking about him.

When I was still a new Christian, I remember reading a book by one of the well-known evangelical preachers of the early twentieth century (I forget which) which stated that a minister's wife should never be a better speaker than her husband. This shocked me, since I naively assumed at the time that most ministers were pretty well perfect creatures. Also, if a woman was a good speaker, it must be the Spirit which enabled her to be so, and wouldn't it be hypocritical to pretend she was worse than she actually was? Since then I have learned a good deal more about human nature, and it is noteworthy that in fact it is usually only single women and widows whom God is able to use in a remarkable public way.

Some of the greatest missionaries of all time, however, have given their wives credit for help in their ministry. For instance John B. Myers in his biography of William Carey tells us of this high tribute Carey paid to his wife:

She lived very close to God. The Bible was her daily delight, and next to God she lived only for me. Her solicitude for my happiness was incessant. . . . It was her constant habit to compare every verse she read in the various German, French, Italian and English versions, and never pass by a difficulty until it was cleared up. In this respect she was of eminent use to me in the translation of the Word of God. She was full of compassion for the poor and needy. . . . She entered most heartily into all the concerns of the Mission.

J. C. Pollock, in his biography of Hudson Taylor and his wife, seems to consider Maria the making of Hudson: "She served to steady his faith while he deepened hers. Maria tempered without quenching his zeal, was largely responsible for the common sense and balance characteristic of Taylor at the height of his powers."

Nor was she devoid of the usually desired qualities of a wife: "Her passionate nature fulfilled his warm-blooded yearning to love and be loved. She gave him full response, fostering and feeding affection so that together they had such a reservoir of love that it splashed over to refresh all, Chinese and European, who came near them" as well as producing a series of children.

She helped him in very practical ways, too. "She improved his cumberous style, teaching him to write good English though she never cured him of split infinitives. She brushed up his Greek . . . imperceptibly she polished him. . . . Undoubtedly the overriding factor of their marriage was an equal, uninhibited loyalty to their vocation. But without Maria, Taylor could never have embarked on his life's work."

By the latter, of course, Pollock is referring to the founding of a new mission on then unorthodox lines, and Taylor needed to get other Christians to trust and follow him. He had already had missionary experience and amazing personal faith in God's ability to meet his every need. The above is Pollock's assessment of the situation after studying all the private papers, but Hudson's trust in Maria is obvious from the fact that he made her his administrative deputy when he had to take frequent trips. "Maria had been left in charge at Hangchow. She had every right to be. Despite her 'fragile body and sweet expressive face' she was no insipid Victorian mamma. Indeed, some members thought she was the backbone of the mission at that time. Hudson had so learned to value her judgment and prayerfulness that he never took a step without consulting her."

How did this affect the young masculine members of the mission?

But she did not obtrude.... At thirty years of age Maria had reached her prime.... The younger missionaries were slightly in awe of her. She was so obviously a lady, and she had sharp intellect and powers of concentration. They admired her skill in the language, literary and colloquial, and the way she got close to the Chinese. They admired her strength of will... but awe was tempered by affection, she always sympathized with everyone—it showed often in little things.

These were remarkable tributes indeed for Victorian wives!

God is continuing to use wives alongside their husbands. In *Daktar/Diplomat of Bangladesh*, probably the greatest missionary epic of this decade, the author, Viggo Olsen, tells us he owes a particular debt of gratitude "to my wife Joan who spent hundreds of hours wisely advising and helping me" in the writing of the book. Within it he gives another detailed insight into the way she had helped:

For the first several months of the year I functioned as [mission] Field Council chairman, which increased my administrative work load [including the Hospital administration]. In our March annual meeting Joan was re-elected Field Council secretary for the third consecutive year, keeping her administratively involved as well. The night school training in secretarial work, which Joan had taken years ago [while he was in medical school] was paying off. Her minutes [of the meetings] were detailed and lucid. She distilled the nuggets from Roberts' Rules of Order *and other such books to produce a practical parliamentary rule book which was at once understandable, workable, and geared to our Field Council approach.*

I am particularly delighted with that last piece of information since on our own mission field at annual conference we, a Christian organization, were required to follow rigidly every jot and tittle of *Roberts' Rules*, planned originally, I believe, for procedure at West Point. This irked me a little, and often wasted precious time. The rules did not always accomplish their intended purpose either, since certain people with an axe to grind could usually introduce some astutely worded amendment to a motion, the real drift of which the more naive among us did not always distinguish, and we could be left for the year with something quite different from what the majority felt to be God's will. I hope Mrs. Olsen's rule book becomes available to other organizations, though there no doubt are some who would be horrified even to think of a woman being on an administrative council!

Olsen continues in praise of his wife:

She culled the Field Council minutes from day one, and produced a booklet with an organized listing of all the Field Council's official actions, and home board regulations. She greatly assisted the constitutions committee . . . to finalize our Field Council constitution. In addition she taught school, visited in the Women's ward, kept our home functioning, and helped me in a hundred different ways. What a wife and helpmate! Thank you, Father.

Not all women have the opportunity or capacity to be so helpful in their husband's particular work. It does seem, however, that every couple should recognize personal counseling and visitation work among women and children as part of a Christian ministry.

During my time in Japan, the women of our mission began to have a yearly ladies' retreat. It was run completely by themselves, with no outside speakers, and put together by a different committee each year, and I was impressed with its consistently good organization and with the fact that there were always speakers with deeply helpful messages as well as detailed testimonies of the Lord's having worked in wonderful ways to bring each to himself. Many of these were wives of whom we in Tokyo normally heard little, but one could not help feeling that many of the husbands were fortunate to have them as fellow workers in difficult places.

When children are in the home, they are the wife's primary reponsibility. But if God chose to use Aquila and Priscilla as a team, and Paul praised them so highly, who are we to say they were out of the Lord's will? I would like to go a little further and think of them as God's ideal couple, functioning like Adam and Eve in the beginning of creation. Yet obviously the ideal for every couple may vary at different stages in their lives and circumstances, and some husbands' employment will be impossible to share.

So we can only conclude that the most important thing for a wife is her day-to-day obedience to Christ himself which can inspire a willing submissiveness to a husband and such a sensitivity to Christ's character and example that it will make it easier to "esteem others better than ourselves" and live "in honor preferring one another"—things which do not come naturally to any "red-blooded" human beings, including wives.

20
WOMAN AS MOTHER

We finally come to a study of woman as the Epistles depict her in her unique and most obvious role. Though so many commentators tell us that the scriptural emphasis is all that a woman's place is in the home as a producer of children, the New Testament has surprisingly little instruction on how to be a mother. At first this seems a strange omission, since the role of Christian mother is presumably an important one—in fact the *only* God-appointed one, according to some. Even the secular press has a seemingly inexhaustible flow of print from the experts, dealing with motherhood and child-training, much of it contradicting itself from decade to decade.

From a human point of view, one might assume that having no wife and children himself Paul was not interested, or experienced enough, to write on the subject. Perhaps he assumed mothers knew by instinct how to function. More probably his belief in Christ's near return made it seem an unnecessary subject. Even Peter, who was married, has nothing to say about women as mothers, and, as we saw earlier, Christ himself gave no specific instructions for them. Yet when one looks at such books as the *Encyclopedia of Psychological Problems* and sees so many ills and aberrations attributed to faulty parental behavior, one is tempted to wish the New Testament had a handy list of all of a Christian mother's duties, plus guaranteed methods of child-rearing.

One reason there is not more instruction in the New Testament may be that the Old Testament did give some guidance to the Jews which made them normally a strong family unit. Between this and the few references in the New Testament we can discern some principles to apply, and perhaps a diligent search there may be more helpful in meeting the needs of each generation and culture than if a more detailed list of specific instructions had been made in the first century. In addition, we have the opportunity and encouragement to seek wisdom from the Lord for each situation as it arises: "If any of you lacks wisdom, let him ask of God, that giveth to all men liberally . . . and it shall be given" (Jas. 1:5).

In just a few places the Epistles do give us some constructive insight or advice about the role of a Christian mother. Let us look at these closely.

To Love Her Children In his first letter to Timothy, Paul advises that "the younger widows marry, bear children" (5:14), so presumably he would say the same for young wives. His reason is to ensure that they might not otherwise "learn to be idle . . . tattlers . . . busybodies" (5:13). With our population explosion today this may not seem to some people an adequate or worthy motive for the procreation of children. But evidently in that less literate and highly immoral age and circumstance there was real wisdom in Paul's instruction, since earlier he had advised that it was better not to marry but devote oneself wholly to the Lord's service.

In a verse we considered in the last chapter, dealing with the teaching to be done by the older wives, Paul tells them to teach the younger ones "to love their husbands, to love their children" (Tit. 2:4).

As we said then, to most people in the West in recent generations this may have seemed an unnecessary suggestion, since they regarded the love of a mother for her child as a natural instinct. In the typical, rather matriarchal American family, the mother even seemed for a time to gain a quasi-sacred status, and derogatory references to her were taboo in most journalism until comparatively recently.

But not any more. The rush for abortions as soon as they became legal and the mounting total of battered babies tell a different story. A few years ago, even before the legalizing of abortions, the Canadian women's monthly magazine *Chatelaine* carried an article entitled "Do Canadians Really Love Their Children?"; while at about the same time an American Christian magazine contained a letter from a mother wondering if she really loved her child plus an answer from a psychologist giving reasons why some parents do not.

More recently the Canadian Press, in an article headed "Not All Parents Like Their Children," dealt with a report for the Ontario government on physically abused children. It quoted one male social worker as saying "There are a whole number of people who don't have this beautiful feeling of maternity. We have to be more sensitive to other people's values." He contended that people must be given a choice whether to become parents or not, adding that contraceptives were not available everywhere. On the other hand, the Chief Coroner for Ontario felt there was a real need for "excessive concern over child abuse. To me, these deaths are not overstrict discipline [as apparently the social worker's report had suggested] but outright torture—long slow deaths and the worst form of murder I know."

Not all lack of love leads to physical damage, of course, but its effect can be harmful in other ways. One of our church members now working in a big city among juveniles as a policewoman shared some of her experience with our women's fellowship. She said it was hard to believe some of the things parents do in neglecting their children, and not only in the poorer districts. She mentioned a fifteen-year-old boy who was given a considerable sum of money by his father to get a room in a motel for the weekend while his parents had a big party at home. This boy started snatching handbags—in the hope that it might "make his parents notice he existed."

This reminded me of something that occasionally used to occur in Japan. When our children were small and we first started going to one of the three summer vacation spots available to missionaries, we spent most of our time with the children on the beach—playing with sand, teaching them to swim, going for Sunday afternoon walks in the woods, reading aloud or playing endless games of Cap-it-and cop-it or Chinese checkers. These activities cemented a real sense of family unity which continued as interests widened through the years. Many families, however, demanded that we hire a lifeguard so that parents no longer had to be with their children on the beach. In a large family, with children of varying ages and needs, I can see how helpful this would be to a mother whose husband was away preaching. But if it was just to "get rid of the kids" in order to play Rook with other adults or even to spend time in preparation for "The Work," it probably revealed a real lack of love for the children. Most of us were deeply involved with our work the rest of the year and surely should have been prepared to give ourselves to our children during a brief vacation.

I am afraid most people will find that if they have not done much with their children in the young and often rather tiresome stage, they will lose communication with them in the teen years. Gangel, for example, comments, *"Family vacations may make a significant dent in the budget, but the constant togetherness away from telephone and television may produce benefits far in excess of the cost. Family counselor Alma Jones reminds us that "scientific studies show that maladjustments of children decrease as family recreation increases; also that understanding and confidence between parents and children increase as shared activities and good times together increase." Many times it is the parents who have begun digging the ditch producing the communication gap.*

Love needs to be expressed to the ones loved, by word, action and choosing their company, and nowhere is this more essential than with children. Paul himself often set a good example of this in his greetings to those whom he regarded as his children in the Lord.

To Nurse, Cherish, Share   In 1 Thessalonians 2:7-8, Paul gives an even clearer picture of his view of motherhood when he states, "We behaved gently among you like a devoted mother nursing and cherishing her own children. So, being thus tenderly and affectionately desirous of you, we continued to share with you not only God's good news, but also our very own selves as well, for you had become so very dear to us" (Amplified). The picture is of a mother or wet-nurse, lovingly breast-feeding the babies the only source of food available to them in Paul's time.

Breast-feeding is a subject deserving some attention today. One occasionally sees in doctors' columns in newspapers or in women's magazines the pros and cons of breast- and bottle-feeding. Two of the most common reasons given for not breast-feeding are that husbands think it will spoil the shape of their wives' bosoms or else that one or both of them feel it is "animal-like" and disgusting. Occasionally in the English language newspapers in China and Japan one used to read outraged letters from visiting American businessmen, not against the easy availability of prostitutes or sick movies, but against the fact that they had actually seen some woman feeding her baby while on a public train! This unobtrusive performance of an act which God had obviously created her to do seemed to be worse than adultery. To what depth of degradation were these savages sunk, was the obvious implication.

With regard to the first objection, quite the reverse is true, and those women who have nursed their babies also appear far less liable to develop breast cancer. These men are the victims of our perverted culture with its commercialized sex symbols. The second objection is equally ridiculous. It seems that many people feel that breast-feeding is a trait left over from their ape ancestors and think that now man, through science, has produced a far superior method —a view constantly strengthened by the advertising expertise of the manufacturers of such products.

Actually the best that these baby formula manufacturers can claim about their product is that it is the nearest thing to mother's milk. And what could be more "animal-like" than drinking the fluid intended for the offspring of cows, goats, waterbuffalo, camels or whatever is the particular culture's customary source of milk? Far from being "unscientific" the female breast is an amazing organ still puzzling the best scientists. No one yet knows, for instance, by what chemical reaction the normal body fluid is transformed into milk. Nor is the latter of a constant composition. The first four days it is the most easily digested form of nourishment, specially constituted to clean out a baby's system; after that, the amount of calcium it contains increases in proportion to the rapidly growing skeletal needs of the baby.

It is not only the perfect type of nourishment, but it comes at a perfect and constant temperature, and with no cost! It is not only a marvel of chemistry, but also of engineering. No manmade machinery has ever been able to produce so intricate a product in so small and aesthetically satisfying a container. It also is of great psychological value to the child, too, as we shall see shortly. The breast-fed baby will also not have a "blurred" mother and father image.

The most frequent real reason for mothers not breast-feeding today is that it ties them down too much. Someone else can always give the baby a bottle, or it can even be propped up and left with the baby alone in the crib. But scientific experiments are beginning to show that babies need regular, loving, *physical* contact. It was long ago recognized that orphans, who usually lacked this, had resultant personality problems; some even died. Now similar symptoms can be found in many children growing up in their own families.

A few years ago I was struck by a comment of friends of mine who had had five children, two of whom brought considerable sorrow to the family while the other three enjoyed real communication with their parents. The parents said they were beginning to wonder if the reason might be that the three were breast-fed while the two were not. This idea interested me greatly, since our own two children were breast-fed and we have always enjoyed a close feeling of family unity.

Since then I have seen in J. C. Moloney's book, *Understanding the Japanese Mind*, some views which encourage such a belief. Moloney, a psychiatrist working with the American occupation forces after the war, was amazed to find how few cases of schizophrenia there were among the Japanese, as compared to Americans. For example, in 1948 in the United States every fourth or fifth bed available for mental patients had a schizophrenic, and the percentage was growing. Through research, Moloney concluded that because Japanese women breast-fed and demand-fed their babies there was no early mouth-conflict-with-the-mother memory patterns, which are a necessary predecessor of schizophrenia. Not only does such a baby not suffer this frustration, but he also does not need to turn to self for gratifications, for example, thumb sucking, masturbation or tongue sucking.

For an American baby, Moloney points out, the mother is usually a thing apart—seen, heard, maybe smelt, but in constantly changing clothes, with and without make-up (and now wigs), so that her baby does not always know who she is. The ultimate in contact, he says, is skin-to-skin, and this is fully available with breast-feeding. I then remembered so well my own first baby's little hand constantly feeling all the skin surface within reach though I was quite unaware of any particular reason for it.

Moloney continues,

Skin contact with the mother, particularly with a motherly mother, advances the development of the skin ego. An accurate and objectively correct memorable picture of the skin surfaces promote a sense of reality. . . . The very young baby should be held against the mother's bare skin; for there is perhaps no other way in which the realness of the mother's body is so accurately and consistently registered upon the child.

With regard to a child who is bottle-fed, and thus may have little skin contact with the mother, he goes on,

As a result of this separation of the child from the mother, I postulate that self-identity is blurred, because without excitation of the skin areas of the child, the sense of body boundary is not memorially recorded as being different from the memorial picture of the mother's boundaries. This neglect of feeling influences, or actually encourages, the infant to set up part of his own body as a plastic representative of the absent mother. . . . In brief, I theorize that the consistently good physical relationship between the Japanese baby and mother reduces to a minimum the danger of the child ever developing a psychosis.

(And this, even though Japanese children are later subject to much stronger authoritarian pressures than usual in the United States. In the last two decades, however, the "scientific" baby bottle is also everywhere in Japan.)

While we should be thankful that a chemical formula and bottle have been perfected for the few mothers who through sickness are unable to feed their baby, we cannot be sure that there is not some yet undiscovered "human essence" about a mother's natural milk, the lack of which could conceivably account for this strange sense of "not knowing who they are" among today's youth in the West.

Another suggested advantage is that a breast-fed baby can more easily hear the mother's heartbeat, a sound with which it was familiar in the womb and which thus tends to reduce anxiety amid all the strange and frightening experiences following the baby's first propulsion into the outside world.

It is true that it is sometimes a little difficult to start breast-feeding, but most mothers give up far too easily and many hospitals hardly bother to teach or encourage them, believing they will not continue after they get home. It took nearly six weeks to get my second child fully on breast-feeding, and I would never have dreamed of trying so long if the first baby had not been such a joy. John Money, quoted earlier, stated that there are three biological imperatives for the female: menstruating, gestating and lactating. The first most of us would prefer to do without; the second may involve considerable discomfort and even danger; but the third becomes pure joy—the essence of self-giving—especially after several months when the child greets the mother with such anticipatory pleasure for something which no one else can supply. This, I think, is what Paul had in mind when he spoke of behaving like a devoted mother —nursing, cherishing, sharing her very own self with her children.

To Be a "Keeper at Home"   In addition to loving their husbands and children, younger wives are to learn to be "keepers at home" (Tit. 2:5). To Timothy Paul recommends that younger widows marry, bear children and "guide [lit: *be masters of*] the house" (1 Tim. 5:14). The first instruction implies that women in New Testament times were not quite so confined to the house as some historians claim. So also does the fact that some wives were converted before their husbands (as is evident in Peter's letter). It would seem that there was quite a lot of visiting back and forth, perhaps especially by the widows, but if slaves were kept there probably was not a great deal of work that a wife herself had to do.

However, in view of the importance of early child-rearing, it is obvious that a mother cannot normally give such care if she is not at home much of the day. Communist China is the only country I know of where there are nurseries attached to factories so that working mothers can go and breast-feed their babies during the day.

Even when that first stage is passed, the preschool years are especially formative, when character is being built and attitudes formed. Anyone prepared to hand her child over to someone else to supervise for that period of life is running a considerable risk, I believe, and missing out on much herself. Admittedly, mothers benefit from occasional brief separations for a few hours and will probably appreciate the children even more after them, but frequent attempts to push them off on other people, however capable, hardly indicates a true love for them.

Although my own children when of school age might spend nights with friends or at camp, I remember going away from them only twice, once to the hospital with pneumonia and later, when they were in high school, to visit some of the places where the early pioneer work of our mission had been done in order to write a book on its history. I am not a very demonstrative person, and it was a real surprise to have both girls give a warm welcome back and say "It just wasn't the same" not having me to see them off and greet them on their return from school.

Since they had to leave soon after 7 A.M. to get to the school for missionaries' children and did not return until 5 or 6 P.M., I was fortunate that I could do my missionary work, mainly teaching, and be home before they were. Except for one year, I kept the weekends free for them, not even taking a Sunday school class, so that my mind would not be preoccupied with the upcoming class but would be free to really listen to them or so that they could invite friends over to our small apartment without any feeling of strain.

A recent study of sex among teenagers showed that sexual intercourse between teenagers does not usually take place in a parked car but comfortably in either the girl's or boy's home, both parents being away working or seeking entertainment. It is fashionable for most teens who live at home to say their parents do not understand them, and the parents mistakenly often think they should keep out of their children's way as much as possible. But a young missionary in Japan, whose parents had been missionaries in China, told me that he was interned by the Japanese during his four years at high school and that he and the others in the prison camp felt they needed their parents even more in those years than when they were younger.

The working wife is a fact of life now, but, as a member of a faith mission with few luxuries, I would like to suggest that the "extras" are just not worth losing your children for. It is true there usually is not enough to keep most women busy all day in modern homes with labor-saving appliances, but one can at least try to find some occupation that can be done in the home or while children are at school. Since women in the North American work force number many millions more than the unemployed men, our national economies would suffer severely if all women quit. Therefore why not demand that their work schedules be made to fit in with their more important work as mothers?

To Exercise Christian Discipline Gangel gives a helpful clarification of the concept of discipline, often misunderstood to imply punishment. *Discipline* is the establishment of boundaries while *punishment* is what must be used if discipline fails and a child deliberately transgresses the boundaries.

While we have just seen that it is not usually a sign of real love to be always pushing your child off on someone else, the same is equally true of spoiling a child and letting him do whatever he likes all the time. This had been clearly stated in the Old Testament and was probably so well-known and practiced that the New Testament writers felt no need to repeat the instructions, but rather considered them a fact of life. "If ye be without chastisement, whereof all are partakers, then are ye bastards, and not sons" (Heb. 12:8). Unfortunately today, even in Christian families, this applies to many children, so strong has been the impact of Dewey permissiveness at all levels of education.

I was interested to see that James Dobson, in his excellent book *Dare to Discipline*, recommends spanking only for disobedience and defiance, a principle which had guided me. Larry Christenson has a forthright and detailed chapter on spanking and also about forgiveness afterward. He also says spanking is the father's job. I had always thought it would be rather mean to take the "wait till your father comes home" approach. With many people now being alerted to the possibility of battered children in their neighborhood, a Christian parent's spanking may be apt to be misunderstood and he or she certainly needs to exercise wisdom more than ever.

The most important emphasis needs to be on consistency rather than method of enforcement, I believe. After thirty years experience of families in home churches and on the mission field, I would say the one Scripture more applicable than any other is "Let your 'No' be No!" (Mt. 5:37). If a child learns this from his earliest years, it will save the parents endless trouble and arguments and give the child a sense of great security.

A parent should not even *say* "No" until he is sure he really means it and has the ability and stamina to enforce it. It is far better for a parent to say "I must think about it first" than to say "No" and then let the children importune him to change his mind. Of course there should be areas where gradually children are encouraged to make their own choices, and perhaps some where they are allowed to exercise the art of persuasion. But not on something about which a parent has first said "No."

Further instruction in child-rearing is given in Ephesians 6:4: "Fathers, provoke not your children to wrath." Maybe fathers are more prone to this, but I am sure mothers are sometimes guilty, too; and *Living Letters* has it paraphrased, "And now a word to you parents. Don't keep on scolding and nagging your children, making them angry and resentful. Rather, bring them up with the loving discipline the Lord Himself approves." I do not know if the original Greek allows for the inclusion of both parents, but certainly the pattern of the modern urban home where the father is usually away until evening seems to warrant the inclusion of the mother.

Other modern translations throw light on the word *provoke*. "Don't overcorrect your children or make it difficult for them to obey" (Phillips). The NEB has, "You must not goad your children to resentment, but give them the instruction and correction which belong to a Christian upbringing." Children are forgetful and do need reminders; but if a firm line has been established in the early years and they know parents mean what they say, this will eliminate the need for a lot of repetition and nagging.

Among the major causes of children's being provoked

may be inconsistency, unjust treatment, such as undeserved punishment or one child's being favored more than another, and hypocrisy, which we will touch on a little later.

We must not dwell only on the negative side of this text, however, but also the positive: "Bring them up in the nurture and admonition of the Lord." This takes time, thought, hard work and an understanding of what we are trying to produce. One of the most important parts is bringing our children to the place of forming their own Christian values and standards. Gangel puts it well when he says, "Christian nurture in the home requires a consistent day by day inculcation of Biblical values which lead the child to the place at which he volitionally makes genuine Christian choices on the basis of what he has learned."

While thinking of values, I will add a note on materialism, since that appears to be a hang-up of many young people today as they note its effect on parents. The most appropriate text would be "For the love of money is the root of all evil" (1 Tim. 6:10). I remember being concerned at a missionary PTA meeting in Japan when the subject of finding part-time summer jobs for the students was discussed. While I can see that anyone with a large family of boys might be thankful to find, during a long vacation, some outlet for their energies plus a little income, some of the things a few students had already done must have deprived some Japanese students of a job. Only one person voiced the idea of encouraging the students to give their services freely for others, for which there were opportunities. The emphasis seemed to be to teach our children the time-honored American maxim, "Money doesn't grow on trees." This was a phrase I had been unfamiliar with and certainly our girls never had learned such a concept. They early learned that in a faith mission money comes from the Lord through his people, and the elder one was able to prove this right through college graduation, while the younger had more part-time jobs available.

Since coming home I have learned to be thankful that children on the mission field can escape some of the extreme pressures of our excessively mercenary age. In many of the churches here, most of the women work, the teenagers have part-time jobs and few people have much time for Christian service. Even parents who could put their children through college seem to want them to earn all through vacations, either because they are not prepared to make any sacrifice or so that the children "will value it more." Meanwhile most Christian camps are chronically short of staff, yet more lives are influenced for Christ there than in almost any other situation.

Paul's principle was rather, "The children ought not to lay up for the parents, but the parents for the children. And I will gladly spend and be spent for you" (2 Cor. 12:14). Of course those in early American pioneer families all had to pull their weight, and more, but from sheer necessity. Furthermore, they were in a rural setting free from many forms of temptation. At the missionary briefing for Urbana 67, we were reminded that the coming-of-age symbol now is not the presentation of the door key at twenty-one, but the family car key at sixteen. With pockets full of self-earned money, plus motorized transportation, adolescents are quickly and easily beyond supervision, and this early independence often leads to delinquency. Isn't it better to keep them dependent as long as we can without frustrating them? An allowance given graciously, at personal sacrifice, can be used to teach tithing, and may produce gratitude. If a child has to earn all his money by work he has been pushed into by his parents, he may justifiably resent attempts by them to control how it is spent and question their real concern and love for him. Also getting a permanent job may lose much of the significance of symbolizing entrance to manhood which Gilder regards as so important if the children have been earning money from an early age and freely spending it on luxuries.

To Be Honored "Honor thy father and thy mother" is an oft-repeated command, both in Old and New Testament, which would be a little surprising if the female were really the inferior and more wicked sex. The best way to ensure this respect is for a father to set the example, and instruct the children, rather than for a mother to demand it. That is why the last cause of complaint listed in the Brussels survey, "frequency of snide remarks and sneers at the wife in the presence of the children," is legitimate. On the other hand, the wife, by word and example, should teach the children to honor the father.

Children can hardly honor for long those whom they do not respect. Those who abdicate their parental authority for an aimless permissiveness will soon have children who secretly feel their parents are not doing their job and therefore do not really love them. They really want to know what the acceptable boundaries are. After our older daughter had left Japan for college, I, together with other selected parents who "seemed to have produced some pretty good specimens," was asked to take part in a PTA panel on how to try to communicate with our children. I wrote to my daughter, asking if she had any helpful advice. It was a joy to receive as part of her reply: "We don't try to communicate, we *do* communicate. Tell them that what kids are looking for in them is parents, not pals."

Another way parents forfeit respect these days is by constantly harping on how much more children know today than they did when in school. Hiding behind the recent, much-touted explosion of knowledge, they do not even try to understand what their children are learning. It is true they are taught more scientific facts and theories today, but they generally know less history, literature and languages. Parents should make a point of looking at what their child is being taught and study some of it so that they can discuss it together rather than having the child constantly thinking he is smarter than his parents. My husband learned the New Math largely for the purpose of understanding and helping the children.

I well remember one evening when our second daughter said she could not understand one of her biology questions. I was tempted to say I had three classes to prepare for next day and in any case had never studied biology (only some lady-like botany and physiology). However, I glanced at her book. I think the chapter was on genetics and was full of diagrams of mysterious specks with impossible names, only a few of which I could guess the meaning of from a knowledge of Latin. I looked at the question she couldn't understand, and hadn't a clue to its answer. There were unknown verbs as well as nouns. I asked if she remembered reading these terms in the long chapter. She thought so, and finally found the pages. Then I read them through, and, though I did not know what the answer was, I could at least tell that it was within two particular paragraphs and that the question had been worded in rather poor English! Having reworded the question a little, she was then able to find the answer. It had taken nearly thirty minutes, but such time and thought goes a long way in keeping communication open with teenagers, and also in maintaining their respect.

Similarly, it helps to teach them all you know about sports (or whatever); keep on beating them as long as possible at tennis or pingpong, and don't early develop into a lazy, overweight slob.

To Set an Example   While the Epistles do not say it in so many words, there is a truth in the Old Testament which I have always found frightening. In the lists of the kings of Israel and Judah the Old Testament often states, "His mother's name was------- and he did that which was right in the sight of the Lord"; or else, "and he did that which was evil in the sight of the Lord." Whether a child grows up pleasing to the Lord or not may depend a great deal on the mother, and the Lord will hold her responsible. Can we say "Be ye followers of me" (1 Cor. 11:1) as Paul did, and be sure our example will be only for good?

Children will soon discover our hypocrisy if we tell them to do one thing, such as speaking the truth, yet ourselves say what are really lies as we give excuses over the phone. Again, some parents may be gracious and flattering to guests while they are in the home and then criticize them unmercifully when they are gone.

I heard a good illustration of this principle once from the aunt of a girl of three. On a visit to her grandparents' house, the child's father asked the little girl for something and she replied, "Here you are, fathead." This did not go over too well in that family of German background, and then the mother suddenly remembered she herself had used the same expression to one of the older children a few days before. I am constantly amazed at the language even some Christian parents use with their children, telling them to "Shut up" and using other similar expressions. We treated our girls with courtesy and respect, and have always received the same from them. There is no doubt that the things which make the most lasting impression on children are the things which are taken for granted in their home as well as those which are constantly taught verbally.

To Teach a Living Faith   The verse in Ephesians about not "provoking" children ends with the exhortation to instruct them in Christian teaching, and while it is there addressed to fathers another passage points to a mother's undertaking this work. In his second letter to Timothy, Paul writes, "From a child thou hast known the holy Scriptures" (3:15). He also says, "I call to remembrance the unfeigned faith that is in thee, which dwelt first in thy grandmother Lois, and thy mother, Eunice; and I am persuaded that in thee also" (1:5). Since his Greek father was not a Christian, it seems likely Timothy got his faith from his mother. It was not just a head knowledge of the Scriptures and a statement of faith which he learned, either. The NEB expresses it as "a faith which was *alive* in Lois your grandmother and Eunice your mother before you, and which, I am confident, *lives* in you also." We need to teach our children not only to have faith that Christ can deal with our future destiny but to have a living, vital trust in his love and power in our lives day by day.

At a ladies' tea held during a Leighton Ford Crusade, I asked him the best way to avoid having children brought up in a Christian home, with no experience of life entirely without Christ, getting overfed and bored with a secondhand faith. After a moment's reflection, he said he thought the best thing was for the children to be able to see Christ actually at work in their parents' lives, enabling them to apologize when necessary, conquer some weakness and so on, as well as teaching the children to look to Christ for similar help in their own situations.

Sometimes we do not trust the Lord enough ourselves and fear to put him to the test before our children, lest it weaken their faith. I remember once hesitating to tell one of our children to pray to find a lost item since I thought I had already searched everywhere!

What a joy it was, however, to overhear this daughter talking with a friend who had brought up the subject of dreams. My daughter related that when she was very small she began to have a certain bad dream every night so that finally she was afraid to go to sleep. She had told me about it then, and I had suggested we both pray about it; after that the dream never came back. This had been her first vivid answer to prayer, she said, and it had made a lasting impression on her. In the press of language study I had soon forgotten the incident and had no idea of the deep and permanent impact it had made on her. How thankful I was I had resisted the temptation not to put God to the test then!

This is not the place to go into detail about the conflict and tension a missionary mother may feel about how much time she should spend on "The Work" and how much on the children. Much depends on the mother's capacity, and the age and disposition of each child. Suffice it to say that a well-loved, controlled and courteous family, who know and live what they believe, is a great asset to the witness for Christ on the mission field, and equally at home.

There is much hard work, responsibility and even considerable anxiety to being a parent these days, and many are opting out by way of contraception and abortion. I recently completed the preparations for our second daughter's wedding and can at last feel unmixed joy at the privilege of being a mother, with no heartaches, and the addition of two sons-in-law both in Christ's service.

Some sophisticates have suggested that missionary children have lived such narrow, sheltered lives "away off there" that they do not know anything else to do than follow in their parents' footsteps. Neither of our girls, however, married until they were twenty-four, having completed their desired education and formed their own sense of values. It was not that nothing else was open to them in choosing their life mates, but rather they knew from experience that letting God direct one's life is really the most satisfying way to live.

While in graduate school the younger girl wrote an article for a youth publication which was in the form of a letter to us. Had it been private, I would never have thought of including it here. But since it has already appeared in print I will include extracts in the hope that it may give other parents ideas.

Dear Mom and Dad:

I just wanted to take this opportunity to thank you for being such wonderful parents. I'm grateful for the atmosphere you created at home—an atmosphere of love and acceptance. I did not have my sister's beauty, nor did I have her talents. But you loved us equally and that meant a lot to me.

Thank you, too, for the example you were, especially in your daily time with God. Do you remember that summer I came home from camp, Mom, and for the first time shared with you what Quiet Time meant to me? I'll never forget that. As cabins filled quickly with campers, suitcases, sleeping bags, hairdryers, even a few stuffed animals, . . . our counsellor told us everyone was to go outside, weather permitting, from 7:30 to 8:00 A.M. for Quiet Time. I gulped. What would I do for thirty minutes? . . . Then I thought of you two. You usually spent at least an hour each day in quiet time, and then you had devotions together at night. And you seemed to even enjoy it; it made a difference in your day. This made me think that half an hour might not be so bad after all. At least it was worth a try. Others felt the same; but God's word came alive, and by the third morning we were going out at 6:30! I began to understand your love for God's word, and I couldn't wait to get home and tell you how much I now enjoyed quiet time.

You never forced me to have a quiet time; never needled me by asking "Did you have it today?" It was my decision whether I wanted to spend time with God or not. But Mom and Dad, you set an example that appealed to me. Since you enjoyed meeting with God, I thought maybe I would, too. . . .

You made prayer a vital part of your everyday experiences. Mom, do you remember how I used to have nightmares about snakes, and how you suggested we pray about it before going to bed one night? We did, and I didn't dream about snakes any more. You led me to experience my first answer to prayer. In fact, you and Dad prayed about everything. . . . If I had a Latin test at 10 o'clock, I knew you'd be praying, whatever else you were doing. And after I accepted Christ and began to grow the harder you prayed.

I have talked to many parents who were most relieved when their kids were saved, and they somehow felt they could "ease up" on praying. But you never did. When I went off to counsel at camp, you prayed continually. You seemed to realize that opposition increases when service to God increases. Again, it was your example that made me want to experience a vital prayer life. I've often thought of the words "Train up a child in the way he should go." You trained primarily by being an example; you let me observe your lives, and that's just what Jesus did in training His disciples.

I appreciate the fact you were not jealous in your love for me. You did all you possibly could as parents, but you also recognized that there were teachers and youth leaders who were able to counsel in some areas more capably. . . . Do you remember how I used to phone and say I'd be late for supper because I was talking with Johnny [the youth leader]? You were glad there was someone like that. . . . You never "questioned" me when I came home. . . . I'm sure you longed for me to share with you, but at the same time you respected my silence. As long as you sensed I was happy and getting answers to my questions, you were happy, too.

Thank you for being interested in every part of my life. Remember how we'd go through my school calendar together, and you'd mark down special dates so you wouldn't plan anything that conflicted? That meant a lot. You came to basketball games, choir concerts and plays. You helped write articles for the high school newspaper when I couldn't get anyone else to do them. Yet you were not possessive. You let me plan how I would use my time, and even when I let myself get involved in too many activities, you didn't rebuke, instead you helped me out.

Thank you, too, for trusting me, and for allowing me to make my own decisions. At times it meant you had to watch me stumble . . . but you were willing to go through the hurt with me as you guided in my search for independence.

Finally I want to thank you for your honesty in sharing your frustrations, as well as your joys. You showed a real willingness to learn. I remember sharing with you some questions I had on guidance, and Dad, you said that you had been struggling with the very same questions. Together, then, we were able to look to God's word for help, and that was exciting.

With love,

J.

We don't deserve all that, and I know she could have written about some points where we failed, too. But such a letter is what makes parenthood really rewarding. Some of the things she mentions I had definitely aimed for, but others God in his grace had brought about without full awareness on our part.

So it is wonderful to be a mother in the Lord's will and with his guidance. But I think I could not have been as much help to the children if I had not already had some wider interests than my own housekeeping. And if my whole purpose in life were just to bring them successfully to maturity, what a bleak prospect would await me now, with both of them in another country and my husband away so much. It is when we are really seeking first the kingdom of God and his righteousness that he adds the other blessings. We must not be possessive and value our children more than the Lord himself, yet there is no doubt he regards them as our first responsibility; and gradually he will provide increasing opportunity for wider service once they are all in school and finally away from home.

Perhaps we can conclude then that the ideal mother, like the ideal woman, may not necessarily be one who fences herself in with various taboos or rigidly limits herself to a few traditional "roles"; rather, she will be one who represents Christ most clearly to those around her as she seeks day by day to obey him in the varying circumstances he may bring into her life.

21

DOES GOD HAVE AN IDEAL WOMAN?

As we have traced woman through the New Testament, we have not found that a mother or even a wife is necessarily God's ideal, nor indeed that he has given any detailed blueprint of such. Paul several times suggests that the unmarried state is the best. Woman is not all mother, although this is a wonderful capacity given her by God with potential for tremendous joy and also great sorrow.

We saw that Christ repudiated the view of women as mere walking wombs and breasts, but rather regarded them as individual human beings to whom he showed great courtesy and concern, revealed deep spiritual truths and assigned important responsibilities. We found the fulfillment of God's promise that in the last days he would pour out his spirit on all flesh, irrespective of seniority, sex or social status; and that in Christ there is no longer the distinction of Jew and Gentile, slave and free, male and female. Women were full members and played an active part in the churches of the Acts, many being highly recommended by Paul as fellow workers in the gospel.

We examined in great detail the few restrictions which later appeared to be placed upon women's (or was it wives'?) activity in the church. We found uncertainties about the meaning of the original language in some passages relating to woman, hence the varying and sometimes contradictory views of Christian commentators, some being hampered in their interpretation through having only experienced the long traditions of Western church life.

We looked at the supposed reason for some restrictions, namely, that the female is the second and therefore inferior creation, weaker and more sinful than the male, but did not find this theory supported in the Genesis account of the creation. Eve later, however, was the first to be deceived by Satan and to disobey God. Yet a Savior who would vanquish Satan was promised through her. And we found grounds to suggest that Satan's reaction to this is a possible reason for the phenomenon that woman's subjection seems to be "engrained in the conviction of mankind." We found no evidence that all women are inferior to or supposed to be subject to all men, but ample proof of God's promoting some women to positions of spiritual responsibility and usefulness, both in the Bible and in the history of the great missionary movements.

This book certainly is not meant as an authoritative statement on doctrine, but as useful data for those who are wrestling with the problem of the position of woman in the church in these days when she is no longer legally merely the "property" of a man nor considered ceremonially unclean. We hope that real experts in the original languages of the Bible will study afresh the earliest manuscripts available and without prejudice or preconceived ideas state all the possible meanings of the texts and that theologians will evaluate isolated principles in the light of God's known practices.

Christianity Today (Sept. 27, 1974) published the results of a survey of two-hundred-fifty church leaders, college presidents and deans, magazine editors and signers of the Chicago Declaration of Evangelical Social Concern, to find out if attitudes toward women are changing in evangelical circles. The results revealed the great uncertainty felt by many about this matter. Only 64 out of the 220 men polled responded, and 23 out of 30 women. The answer of one anonymous magazine editor to the question of whether he would welcome a woman pastor probably reflects the thinking of many who were afraid to give an opinion: "Mentally my mind says yes. Emotionally I hesitate, and theologically I don't know."

This is a very understandable position, and I hope this book has helped to at least clarify all three areas. Those whose emotions are negatively involved can take courage from our findings that mostly it is only the single and widowed who will be involved in full time spiritual ministry. Possibly at first a rush of women might enter to prove a point, but in the long run I do not think there will be more than at present are in the legal or medical professions. In 1908, for example, 20% of the ministers of the Church of the Nazarene were women, and only 6% by 1973. I have recently heard of a husband's being minister in one church and his wife assistant minister in a neighboring area, but marriages or churches which can successfully survive such an arrangement for long are rare, I believe, unless the church is regarded merely as a job and not as a ministry.

For those who feel religion is the root cause of woman's need for liberation, we have attempted to show that, in the case of Christianity at least, this has largely been the fault of consciously or unconsciously biased translators and commentators. We found that God created woman in his image, to share dominion over the earth, and with freedom to exercise choice. It was Eve's choice which made her the fallen wife of a fallen man, with very unpleasant consequences leading often to great degradation of woman, especially among pagan societies.

Woman's position has fluctuated throughout most of history, it seems, in proportion to the general spiritual quality and closeness to God of the people of the time. When pagan influence was greatest in Israel, the general condition of woman was lowest, yet God on several such occasions used women to overcome Israel's enemies, initiate a return to a right relationship with God or preserve from extinction the whole nation.

Similarly, we saw that as it has been introduced and accepted in country after country Christianity consistently raised the position of women. This was due mainly to Christ's distinctive treatment of women, so contrary to the practice of his day, but also to the remarkable instructions for wives in the Epistles and the even more revolutionary ones for husbands—which unfortunately have not yet been fully put into practice by the majority of even Christian couples. The seeds of the present emancipation of woman were sown in the great religious revivals of the nineteenth century, largely through the work of Lord Shaftesbury and his supporters in England who introduced much legislation to improve the lot of women. In America too those who fought for the abolition of slavery on Scriptural grounds began to realize the need for the emancipation of women.

Although we found no set of roles or duties forming the blueprint of the ideal woman, we did discover one trait especially precious to God (partly because of its rarity, perhaps?), namely, a meek (or gentle) and quiet spirit. This is not only desirable in wives, to whom Peter addressed the words, but in every believer, and was characteristic of Christ himself. This obviously does not necessarily involve retiring into a corner, but is the spirit in which we should live and operate, something which does not come naturally to any of us, as has been evident in many places in this book. Christ promises that "the meek shall inherit the earth"—one of the many paradoxes he seems to delight in. Another is that, oddly, we feel most free and most fulfilled when we are submissive to Christ as he was to the Father, as exemplified in the words "I delight to do thy will."

Therefore, instead of blindly following custom or tradition, it seems best for woman to "choose that good part," like Mary, and sit at Christ's feet to hear his instructions for each situation as it arises; then attempt to follow them in the spirit he prizes so much. For many women these directions may largely concern a husband and children, and in what area do we need his help more? Fortunately, we do find some guidelines in the Scriptures for these responsibilities. But God may also have some surprises for us. So each needs to receive her personalized operational procedures and Christ's power to perform them. Only then can we qualify for that wonderful quality of relationship with himself which he promised: "Whosoever shall do the will of my Father in heaven, the same is my brother and my sister and mother."

REFERENCES

Adeney, Walter F. *Women of the New Testament.* London: James Nesbit, 1901.

Andelin, Helen B. *Fascinating Womanhood.* Santa Barbara: Pacific Press, 1963.

Babbage, Stuart Barton. *Christianity and Sex.* Downers Grove, Ill.: InterVarsity Press, 1963.

Baldwin, Ethel May, and David Benson. *Henrietta Mears and How She Did It.* Glendale, Cal.: Regal Books, 1960.

Barackman, Paul F. *Proclaiming the New Testament: The Epistles to Timothy and Titus.* Grand Rapids: Baker Book House, 1964.

Barclay, William. *Daily Study Bible: Letters to Timothy, Titus and Philemon.* Philadelphia: Westminster Press, 1956.

Baxter, J. Sidlow. *Explore the Book.* Grand Rapids: Zondervan, 1960.

Bayne, Paul, and Thomas Goodwin. *Puritan Exposition of Ephesians.* Sovereign Grace Book Club, 1958.

Birnie, W. S. *The Search for the Twelve Apostles.* Wheaton, Ill.: Tyndale House, 1973.

Blaiklock, E. M. *The Century of the New Testament.* Downers Grove, Ill.: InterVarsity Press, 1962.

Boldrey, Dick and Joyce. "Woman in Paul's Life." *Trinity Studies,* Vol. 22, 1972.

Brow, Robert. *Religion: Origins and Ideas.* Downers Grove, Ill.: InterVarsity Press, 1966.

Bruce, F. F. *The Growing Day.* London: Paternoster Press, 1951.

_____. *New International Commentary on the New Testament: Acts of the Apostles.* Grand Rapids: Eerdmans, 1951.

Calvin, John. *New Testament Commentaries: The First Epistle of Paul the Apostle to the Corinthians.* Trans. John W. Frazer. Ed. David and Thomas Torrance. Grand Rapids: Eerdmans, 1963.

_____. *Commentary: Timothy, Titus, Philemon.* Trans. T. A. Snail. Ed. David and Thomas Torrance. Grand Rapids: Eerdmans, 1964.

Christenson, Larry. *The Christian Family.* Minneapolis: Bethany Fellowship, 1970.

Cohen, A. *Everyman's Talmud.* New York: E. P. Dutton, 1949.

Daniélou, Father Jean, S. J. *The Ministry of Women in the Early Church.* Trans. Glyn Simon. London: The Faith Press, 1961.

Dayton, Donald W. and Lucille S. "Women as Preachers: Evangelical Precedents." *Christianity Today,* May 23, 1975.

Dobson, James. *Dare to Discipline.* Wheaton, Ill.: Tyndale House, 1972.

Edersheim, Alfred. *The Life and*

Times of Jesus the Messiah. Grand Rapids: Eerdmans, 1965 (orig. 1886).

Evening, Margaret. *Who Walk Alone*. Downers Grove, Ill.: InterVarsity Press, 1974.

Fitzmyer, J. V. "Features of Qumram Angelology and Angels of 1 Corinthians." *New Testament Studies*. Cambridge: The University Press, 1957.

Gangel, Kenneth. *The Family First*. Minneapolis: His International Service, 1972.

Glen, J. Stanley. *Pastoral Problems in 1 Corinthians*. Philadelphia: Westminster Press, 1964.

Guthrie, Donald. *New Testament Introduction*. Downers Grove, Ill.: InterVarsity Press, 1971.

_____. *The Pastoral Epistles*. Grand Rapids: Eerdmans, 1957.

Hague, Dyson. *Through the Prayer Book*. London: Longman, Green and Company, 1932.

Hardesty, Nancy. "Woman: Second Class Citizen." *Eternity*, January 1971.

Hastings, James, ed. *The Greater Men and Women of the Bible*. Edinburgh, 1915. Quoted by Ryrie.

Hendricks, Howard. *Say It with Love*. Wheaton, Ill.: Scripture Press, 1972.

Hendriksen, William. *New Testament Commentary, 1 and 2 Timothy and Titus*. Grand Rapids: Baker Book House, 1957.

Héring, Jean. *First Epistle of Paul to the Corinthians*. Trans. A. W. Heathcote. London: Epworth Press, 1962.

Hiebert, D. E. "The Apostle Paul: Women's Friend." *The Christian Reader*, June-July 1973.

Hunt, Gladys. *Ms. Means Myself*. Grand Rapids: Zondervan, 1972.

Hurley, James B. "Did Paul Require Veils or the Silence of Women?" *Westminster Theological Journal*, Vol. 35, No. 2, 1973.

Jeremias, Joachim. *Jerusalem in the Time of Jesus*. Trans. S. H. and C. H. Cave. London: SCM Press, 1969.

Kelly, J. N. D. *Epistles of Peter & Jude*. New York: Harper and Row, 1969.

Lambert, L. C. "Apostles." *International Standard Bible Encyclopedia*. Chicago: Howard Severance Co., 1915.

Lange, J. P. *Genesis: A Commentary on the Holy Scripture*. New York: Scribners and Son, 1868.

Leupold, H. C. *Exposition of Genesis*. Grand Rapids: Baker Book House, 1942.

Little, Paul. *How to Give Away Your Faith*. Downers Grove, Ill.: InterVarsity Press, 1966.

Lloyd-Jones, D. Martyn. *Studies in the Sermon on the Mount*. London: Inter-Varsity Fellowship, 1959.

Lock, Walter. *International Critical and Exegetical Commentary: Pastoral Epistles*. Edinburgh: T. T. Clark, 1924.

Luce, H. K. *Cambridge Greek New Testament for Schools and Colleges: St. Luke*. Cambridge: The University Press, 1949.

McLaren, Alexander. *Exposition of Holy Scripture, St. John*. New York: Hodder and Stoughton, n.d.

McNally, Jane A. "The Place of Woman in the New Testament Church." Unpublished master's thesis, Wheaton College, 1944.

McPheeters, Julian. *Proclaiming the New Testament: The Epistles to the Corinthians.* Grand Rapids: Baker Book House, 1964.

Mill, John Stuart. *The Subjection of Women.* Cambridge: MIT Press, 1970.

Moloney, J. C. *Understanding the Japanese Mind.* Tokyo: Charles Tuttle and Co., 1954.

Money, John. "Biological Imperatives." *Time*, January 8, 1973.

Monsen, Marie. *The Awakening.* London: CIM, 1961.

Moore, Katharine. *Women.* England: B. T. Batsford, Ltd., n.d.

Morgan, G. Campbell. *The Corinthian Letters of Paul.* London: Charles Higham Son, 1947.

Myers, John B. *William Carey.* London: Partridge and Co., 1887.

Narramore, Clyde. *A Woman's World.* Grand Rapids: Zondervan, 1963.

Nielson, Maria, and Paul Sheetz. *Malla Moe.* Chicago: Moody Press, 1956.

Olsen, Viggo. *Daktar/Diplomat of Bangladesh.* Chicago: Moody Press, 1973.

Phillips, J. B. *Ring of Truth: A Translator's Testimony.* London: Hodder and Stoughton, 1967.

Pollock, John C. *Hudson Taylor and Maria.* London: Hodder and Stoughton, 1962.

Poppin, Ruth. *Priscilla: Author of the Epistle to the Hebrews.* Jericho, N.Y.: Exposition Press, 1969.

Pratt, Dwight M. "Woman." *International Standard Bible Encyclopedia.* Chicago: Howard Severance Co., 1915.

Pulpit Commentary. Vols. 19 and 21. Ed. H. D. M. Spence and Joseph F. Exell. Grand Rapids: Eerdmans, 1950.

Ramm, Bernard. A critique of an article by Nancy Hardesty. *Eternity*, January 1971.

Ramsey, Sir William. *Cities of St. Paul.* New York: A. C. Armstrong and Son, 1908.

Ryrie, Charles C. *The Place of Women in the Church.* Chicago: Moody Press, 1968.

The Sacred Scriptures of the Japanese. Trans. Post Wheeler. London: George Allen and Unwin, 1952.

Sayers, Dorothy. *Are Women Human?* Downers Grove, Ill.: InterVarsity Press, 1971.

Scanzoni, Letha, and Nancy Hardesty. *All We're Meant to Be.* Waco: Word Books, 1974.

Shedd, Charles W. *Letters to Karen.* Nashville: Abingdon, 1965.

Strachan, James. *The Captivity and the Pastoral Epistles.* New York: Fleming Revell, n.d.

Thompson, W. M. *The Land and the Book.* New York: Harper and Brothers, 1882.

Tournier, Paul. *To Understand Each Other.* Richmond: John Knox Press, 1962.

Tuggy, Joy Turner. *The Missionary Wife and her Work.* Chicago: Moody Press, 1960.

Vos, Howard F., ed. *Religions in a Changing World.* Chicago: Moody Press, 1959.

Wilson, Dorothy Clarke. *Lone Woman.* Boston: Little, Brown Co., 1970.

Wright, Fred H. *Manners and Customs of Bible Lands.* Chicago: Moody Press, 1953.

BIBLICAL PASSAGES DISCUSSED